# CRAPPIE
## WISDOM

## An In-Fisherman
## Handbook of Strategies

# CRAPPIE
## WISDOM
## An In-Fisherman
## Handbook of Strategies

Doug Stange
Gary Korsgaden
Dan Sura
Steve McCadams
Rich Zaleski
Dave Csanda
Bob Ripley
Al Lindner
Ron Lindner

*Published by*
Al Lindner's Outdoors, Inc.

Book Compiled by Bob Ripley and Dan Sura
Cover Art by Larry Tople
Artwork by Dan Vickerman
Typesetting by Bang Printing
Litho Prep by Quality Graphics
Printing by Bang Printing
Copyright 1985 by Al Lindner
All rights reserved
Published by Al Lindner's Outdoors, Inc.
P.O. Box 999, Brainerd, Minnesota 56401
Printed in the United States of America

ISBN 0-9605254-4-0 (Volume 5)

ISBN 0-9605254-7-5 (5 Volume Set)

First Edition, 1985
Second Printing, 1987
Third Printing, 1987

Library of Congress Catalogue
Card Number 85-081299

ISBN 0-9605254-4-0 (Volume 5)
ISBN 0-9605254-7-5 (5 Volume Set)

# ACKNOWLEDGEMENT

Countless individuals are directly or indirectly responsible for assembling all the priceless information in a book as complete as this one. Because fishing is an ancient art which draws on experimental tradition, we are indebted to those many men and women who have fished, studied, and triumphed with the authors, thus adding to the wealth of crappie wisdom.

In particular, we want to thank people like Dan Gapen and the legendary Joe Ehrhardt for their invaluable input. A special thanks goes to the inimitable Bill Binkelman for developing the background theory which the Calendar Periods are based upon. Of course, pros like Bill Dance, Gary Roach, Doug Hannon, Horace Carter, Larry Dahlberg and Tom Neustrom all deserve a note of thanks for their contributions. We are also grateful to Professor Jeff Gunderson, Sea Grant Fisheries agent—University of Minnesota, for his fish cleaning and keeping tips. We also offer a special *IN-FISHERMAN* "hats off" to fisheries biologists Mike Colvin, Missouri, and Bill McLemore, Kentucky, for their invaluable assistance with very pertinent scientific studies. In addition, the fisheries departments of California, Nebraska, Oklahoma, Iowa, Wisconsin, Indiana, Michigan, Maryland, Arizona, Ohio, Kentucky, Missouri, Georgia, Arkansas, Montana, Minnesota, Texas and Mississippi all supplied bits and pieces of information which helped solve the crappie puzzle.

No book of this type would be complete without the numerous photos and illustrations which add to the book's enjoyment and educational value. Therefore we are especially grateful to our technicians: Jim Lindner for his striking photography and Dan Vickerman for his detailed illustrations.

This short list could certainly be expanded, but suffice to say that this book could never have been written by just the nine major authors. Each author has shared in major breakthroughs on crappie location and presentation in different waters. Their combined on-the-water experience, both individually and with crappie anglers all over North America, enables them to pass on to you their many secrets, tips and tricks in this original edition of *Crappie Wisdom: A Handbook of Strategies*.

# TABLE OF CONTENTS

# INTRODUCTION

The crappie has been called *everyone's fish*. Indeed, it is exactly that: A fish anyone can fish for—a bank fisherman with a cane pole or an angler outfitted with a $25,000, ultra-deluxe bass boat.

Yes, the rainbow trout may be more beautiful; the musky larger and more savage; and the bass surely more acrobatic. Yet, in every pond, pit, river, reservoir and lake where it swims, the crappie wins the popularity contest hands down.

From the timber-filled, sprawling impoundments of Texas to the stark, sharp, rocky banks of the northern border, crappie cultists are legion. They tie their boats to shallow brush, anchor in deep water or line banks awaiting a "school of slabs."

Why all this attention and devotion? Well, for anyone who has thrilled to the satisfaction of "getting into them," the answer is simple. They are just plain fun, and what more can any angler ask?

Yes, big crappies are fun to catch. They also are no slouch when it comes to fighting, especially on light tackle. And, of course, their reputation as table-fare is also legend. Yes, anytime you have a fish that is accommodating on the hook, fights well, and also tastes good, you have all the ingredients for wide-spread, indeed, universal popularity.

Yet, in spite of this widespread interest, popular acclaim and angling attention, the crappie is not well understood by anglers. Indeed, in some waters and during some seasons, its activities are still a mystery.

However, a number of major advancements in crappie fishing have occurred in the last few decades. The use of depth finders, graphs, and new fishing systems have all helped put together the pieces of the crappie puzzle.

Crappie fishing is more than just "minnow soaking," tiny-jig pitching or structure fishing. For example, we know that predictable crappie movements occur in lakes. We've determined that crappies may use timber as cover in some reservoirs, yet avoid such cover areas in others. We are now aware of a complex predator/prey relationship that affects not only the health of a crappie fishery, but also fish location and how fish react in a particular body of water. We have cracked their seasonal code: how crappies will most likely respond in spring, summer, fall and winter. We also definitely know how and why they react differently in lakes, rivers, pits or reservoirs.

All of these new facets and dimensions—indeed, formerly missing dimensions—are part of this fascinating book titled *CRAPPIE WISDOM*.

x

# Chapter 1

# CRAPPIE

### The Calico Scrapper

How do you spell fun? For many anglers all across North America, it's C-R-A-P-P-I-E. Catching a bunch of good eating, slab-sized crappies is a fantastic way to spend a day. Crappies bite well and put up a respectable fight. That's fun! Crappie fishing is also a great way to introduce kids to fishing. Crappies are biters, and if you can find 'em, you can generally catch a mess of 'em.

Each year, young and old alike take buckets of crappies through the ice in winter and in the shallows during spring. And even though summer crappies may be a bit of a mystery to some folks, they are still catchable once their habits are understood.

Add all this to the fact that crappies can be caught by using a wide variety of simple techniques, on everything from a cane pole to a boron rod, and you have the makings of a great time. You'll also fill the freezer. So, whether you soak minnows from the bank or cast ultralight jigs from the deck of an ultra-sophisticated bass boat, you can get in on the action. The essence of crappie fishing is understanding crappie habits. That's what this book is all about: catching crappies all season long on any body of water.

The crappie is a fairly adaptable critter, as evidenced by its widely diverse geographic distribution and the numerous aquatic environments it inhabits. Crappies provide angling thrills to folks throughout the United States and southern Canada. Lakes, rivers, reservoirs, ponds, pits and canals are all "home" to the crappie. But, as happens so many times with other species, there are first-rate and there are fourth-rate crappie waters. What factor or combination of factors makes some bodies of water prolific producers of slab crappies, while other waters only produce so-so fishing, and still others host merely paper-thin, featherweight fish? Good question, and a tough one to answer.

Let's begin our study of this fascinating fish by reviewing a few crappie facts. Like all fish, the crappie is at one time both predator and prey. Simply stated, all fish are predators. While the "predator" crappie is munching on zooplankton, insects or small minnows, the "prey" crappie may be munched on by a still larger predator like a pike or bass. Big fish eat smaller fish, and so on; it's the food chain game of who eats whom. In general, if the amount of varied prey is sufficient to support predators, the potential exists for slab crappies.

*The crappie's normal feeding method is not really an "attack." Usually, they simply "suck in" their prey from underneath, then close their mouth and swallow. Crappies aren't blessed with the strong jaws of bass or the teeth of pike, and this limits the type of prey they can successfully take.*

*The feeding apparatus of a crappie resembles a funnel. Pull a crappie's lips open sometime and note the "intake tube." This funnel-type feeding apparatus limits the size prey a crappie can consume. Food items must be small enough to be sucked in whole and not needed to be rearranged before swallowing. Also note that most of the mouth is a paper-thin membrane.*

Ron Lindner's "environmental door" concept helps explain this complex environmental relationship. In order to sustain life, crappies and all fish need certain conditions from birth to death. The entire life process is like a series of doors along the fish's path of life. First, the various doors must be present; second, the fish must be able to move through them. The first door could be spawning habitat; a second, nursery areas for young fish; and a third, living areas for adult fish. Available prey, water quality, competing species and fishing pressure (in some cases) all have a bearing on whether the doors ultimately open, how far they open, or whether they open at all.

All of these factors, plus others, affect the crappie's ability to survive and grow in any body of water. Various fisheries studies indicate that the life span and growth rates of crappies vary widely from one water to another. For example, in some waters few crappies live longer than 3 years, yet in others many typically live 8 years or more. Growth-wise, a 4-year-old crappie can be only 7 inches long in one lake and more than 12 inches long in another. Biologists are trying to solve this mystery and isolate the factors which affect longevity and growth.

Crappies will adjust to a body of water as best they can, using the available environmental options. These options vary, depending on the body of water. Lakes, rivers and reservoirs are all different and offer varying environments. Yet, by simply "reading" the water and applying a little basic information on the crappie's lifestyle, you can locate prime areas in each body of water you fish. It all boils down to understanding how a body of water functions and what predator/prey relationships exist.

# CRAPPIE CHARACTERISTICS

The crappie's body construction is an exercise in moderation. Its flat, relatively compact body allows it to make quick, responsive turns and function in and around weeds and brush. Its moderately sleek, head-to-tail construction allows successful, but limited use of open water.

Much like bass, crappies appear to be ambush predators only when at rest and in a negative or neutral feeding mood. When actively feeding, however, there is no doubt that crappies are hunters.

# SUSPENSION TENDENCIES

On many waters, suspension is a way of life for crappies. In other words, they often suspend at various depth levels in lakes and reservoirs. While it's impossible to make hard-and-fast rules about how crappies suspend, there are some general tendencies.

In many lakes, crappies suspend in order to take advantage of the drifting masses of zooplankton (microscopic animals) and minnows that are their common prey. Similarly, crappies often suspend in reservoirs and feed on zooplankton and young shad that inhabit open-water areas. Many times, the depth at which zooplankton suspend is controlled by light intensity and defensive movements. Some zooplankton like Daphnia (water fleas) often migrate vertically in response to changing light levels. Daphnia rise when it's dark and descend when it's light. Others like Copepods depend on darting, evasive ac-

*Crappie Angler of 1900's*

tion to escape predators. Crappies make major locational changes during the day in response to zooplankton movement. Thus, they follow their food on a daily as well as seasonal basis.

Generally speaking, crappies will roam until they encounter a suitable prey. If there are no zooplankton (or other prey) on a structural element, crappies will generally move through the area. However, in areas where concentrations of prey are high, crappies will remain until the food is grazed down and then they'll move on.

The "hunt" usually takes them to where zooplankton or minnows—probably their preferred forage—are. That's usually "confined open water" or cover such as brush or weeds. Resting crappies may suspend in confined open water or near obvious cover. The point is, crappies are opportunists. Their tendency to suspend, and their body construction, allow them to function in cover or confined open water.

# CONFINED OPEN WATER

What about "confined open water?" While crappies often suspend, they are not a true, open-water fish. True open water involves large expanses of water where fish relate to light penetration, water stratification, forage, and occasionally the bottom. True open-water fish are powerfully built and streamlined, can easily travel distances, and are able to quickly charge into free-roaming schools of bait. Chinook salmon and stripers are examples of true, open-water fish.

## Crappie and Confined Open Water

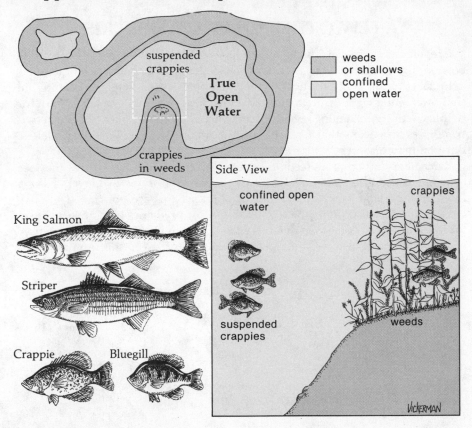

Open water is divided into two categories: "confined" and "true" open water. True open water involves large expanses of water, and fish inhabiting such areas have streamlined shapes and powerful muscles to function in this environment. Striped bass and chinook salmon are examples of true, open-water fish.

Crappies are not true, open-water fish, even though they love to suspend. The crappie's flattened body and moderately sleek, head-to-tail construction enables successful use of cover such as weeds and timber, and "confined" open water. Bluegills often suspend and use confined open water, too, but are even better shaped for using cover.

Confined open water is open water on a much smaller scale. Confined open water is open water relatively close to, or surrounded by cover such as timber, brush, weedlines, the bottom or the surface. Crappies are opportunists that function well in cover, or confined open water. Thus, they have their own particular niche.

On the other hand, "confined" open water is open water on a smaller scale. Confined open water is always *near* definite structural conditions. For example, in large bays, there's often confined open water in the center, but the bottom, surface, shoreline or weedline are still relatively nearby.

In main-lake areas, open water extends off weedlines, timberlines or points; but at some spot, all association with the weedline, timberline or point is lost. At that location, we enter true open water. But the water *relatively close to* a weedline, timberline, point or large inside turn in the drop-off is "confined" open water.

Crappies often use confined open water but rarely use true open water. Obviously, there are exceptions.

## A FEW OTHER CHARACTERISTICS

Crappies are light-sensitive fish, and in clear bodies of water they often bite best during twilight hours, after dark, or in deeper water during midday.

In lakes with a bit of water color, crappies often bite consistently in shallower water right through midday. However, even on these lakes, look for twilight activity; changing levels of light intensity often trigger crappie activity. Our experience is that night bites are not consistent on dark-water lakes. But you may disagree.

Remember that crappies feed *up* better than *down*. In other words, they see forage and baits better parallel with or, better yet, *above* eye level. Take a look at where and how the eyeballs in ol' paper lips are positioned—pretty well up and forward on the face. Actually, most predators have their eyes set topside and forward. The result is a *tendency* to feed up. However, the crappie is one of the most notorious up-feeders we know of. Keep this in mind when you're presenting baits.

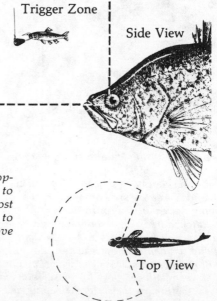

Trigger Zone

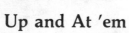

Side View

Top View

### Up and At 'em

*Most predators have their eyes set top-side and forward, resulting in a tendency to feed up. But the crappie is one of the most notorious up-feeders we know of. Try to position baits parallel to, or slightly above crappie eye level for best results.*

# MIGRATION

Crappies are the gypsies of the freshwater world. Roaming like nomads in search of food, a school of crappies will usually locate near a food source of some kind. While crappies are generally not considered long distance migrators, in some rivers and riverine (fast flow-through) impoundments they might move seasonally to locate suitable habitat or prey. A study on Wheeler Reservoir, a TVA impoundment, showed that tagged white crappies migrated 80 miles upstream and 8 miles downstream. Even though this example may be extreme, it indicates that crappies will migrate long distances in some waters. It's not their normal behavior, however.

On many slower flowing rivers and streams, crappies may move several miles upstream in spring and stage in the tailwaters below dams. Anglers in the know can easily catch a bunch of crappies in adjacent slack water areas or eddies. Further, on other rivers during low-water years in fall and winter, crappies typically migrate to locate areas of deeper water. In general, deeper pools, slower flowing side channels, flood-plain lakes and connected lakes are all potential holding areas. These spots can be tough to find, but they will hold numbers of crappies.

# SCHOOLING BEHAVIOR

A crappie is a crappie, but there are two distinct crappie species—white and black. In addition, in waters where both species are present, hybrids sometimes occur.

While the behavior of the crappie cousins may be somewhat different, a tendency to school is common. Crappies are extremely gregarious critters. In general though, white crappies do not school as tightly as black crappies. While the schooling tendency can mean super fishing for anglers, it can also spell doom for crappies.

By their basic nature, crappies are fairly aggressive fish; in fact, they are the smallmouth bass of the panfish world. Crappies are definitely *biters*, and when this is combined with their schooling behavior, the results can be a feast-*then*-famine situation on some waters. Believe it or not, the adult crappie population on some bodies of water can be quite fragile and over-harvesting can lead to a lake with few, good-sized fish. No, the lake isn't fished out, but it is *fished down* and may not produce any number of big crappies for several years. We found out the hard way.

A couple of years ago, big crappies (honest pounders) were plentiful in one of our favorite central Minnesota lakes. Lake "X" provided a quality environment for crappies. It is a 250-acre, fertile lake with fairly clear water, healthy weedgrowth on the flats (reeds and cabbage), hard bottom and plenty of confined open-water areas. Northern pike control the deep weedlines while largemouth bass rule the flats as the top predators in the lake. Crappies, meanwhile, school in the confined-open-water areas adjacent to the weedline. In summer they suspend just off the weed edge. In winter, the fish school heavily in the deeper areas.

During winter two years ago, the word leaked out that the big crappies were "on a bite" in Lake X. A dozen or so local ice fishermen hit the lake and pounded the crappies. Nearly everyone was taking a bunch of good-sized crappies every time out. Eventually the word got out and the steady fishing pressure and removal of fish took its toll. The average size decreased and the larger, older fish were scarce as hens' teeth. In two years the lake was fished down to a point where you'd be hard-pressed to catch a couple big crappies. While the lake still has a viable crappie population, it'll be several years before any number of big fish return.

Remember, fishing pressure can make a difference on some waters. So, catch a lot of fish, keep some to eat and release the rest. We're not advocating a wholesale catch and release practice for crappies, but rather a selective-harvest approach. In a nutshell: Take what you can eat and don't waste the resource.

## THE SMALL-CRAPPIE SYNDROME

The national average crappie is about 8 to 10 inches long, weighs 1/2 to 3/4 of a pound and is 3 years old. Obviously, average size varies depending on the fish's environment. While eating-sized fish comprise the daily catch of most folks, in some areas, giant slab crappies can be taken. Prime northern waters can yield 2-pound-plus fish, while 3-pound-plus crappies are caught each year in southern lakes and reservoirs. However, under marginal conditions, stunted, paper-thin crappies die of old age—the small-crappie syndrome.

While many factors affect the crappie growth rate, one of the most important is the abundance and quality of food. In order for crappies to develop and grow, they must have suitable prey at each stage of their life.

Typically, young crappies prey heavily on plankton and insects; however, adult fish feed on small baitfish, when they're available. In fact, in many waters, baitfish comprise the majority of the adult crappie's diet. Apparently, a high-protein, minnow diet is essential for growing slab crappies. Prime, northern, black-crappie waters have healthy baitfish populations for prey, while in southern waters, white crappies prey heavily on newly hatched gizzard or young threadfin shad. The result can be big crappies and lots of them.

The "small-crappie syndrome" is a challenge facing many biologists. Why are many waters teeming with pint-sized crappies? Too many fish (crowding), limited habitat, lack of quality food, and overharvesting have all been suggested as probable causes.

*Feast your eyes on these slab-sized black crappies. Veteran anglers Gary Roach and Ron Schara teamed up to catch these often overlooked Canadian crappies. Their secret: Rock piles and Fuzz-E-Grub jigs.*

Currently, some states use panfish management programs to control crappie populations, prevent stunting, and provide a better quality fishery. Introducing slot-size limits on predators like largemouth bass and transplanting or thinning out stunted panfish are typical procedures. In addition, progressive-minded fisheries people are experimenting with prey management. The small-crappie syndrome is the bane of anglers in some waters, yet the reasons for this problem are not fully understood.

Mike Colvin, a fisheries research biologist from Missouri, has compiled a large amount of data from ongoing reservoir research projects. He coupled the data with his research studies and concluded that on the reservoirs studied, most of the crappies were small because they were young, not stunted. Most of the fish were growing well but hadn't lived long enough to get big. Tagging studies on Missouri reservoirs have revealed that anglers harvest about 60% of the adult crappie population. In addition, some fish die from natural causes, and as a result, less than 10% of the crappies ever live to be 4 years old. So, few crappies over 10 inches long are harvested. No wonder there are few big fish.

Crappie overharvest was not considered possible until recently; however, it is a reality. The management plan for the study-lake was to reduce the bag limit and implement a 10-inch-minimum size limit on selected waters. As a result, the average size has increased to about 11 inches. Catch and release of small crappies will yield big fish on some reservoirs. The end result is to provide a balanced fishery with good numbers of eating-sized crappies.

On some waters, crappies often experience dramatic population fluctuations. They can be extremely abundant for several years; then their numbers suddenly drop, although the average fish may run larger than normal. What happens? No one knows for certain. There are many theories, but not much concrete evidence.

One possible theory seems logical and explains the fluctuating nature of some crappie populations. After a highly successful hatch, the surviving crappies become the dominant-year-class. During successive years, hordes of dominant-year-class crappies swallow up swarms of their own fry and seal the doom of the other year-classes for several years.

Finally, after the adult, dominant-year-class begins to thin out or die off, the population stabilizes as younger fish are recruited into the population. Eventually, a healthy population of fish with several year-classes represented is present. However, after another super successful, crappie hatch, the cycle will start over again. It makes sense, but may be too simplistic to explain all crappie population variations.

Fisheries biologists don't have the answer. However, they are investigating the phenomenon. Research studies aimed at pinpointing the factors involved in the variation of survival rates of newly hatched crappie fry are currently being conducted. The end result is to manage the crappie population and minimize boom-or-bust fisheries.

# SUMMARY

Obviously, consistent crappie fishing is more challenging than most folks realize. Spring fishing usually isn't too tough, but it can be difficult to catch big, suspended slabs in the middle of summer. Consistently successful fishing takes a combined knowledge of crappies and their habits, plus a definite ability to work them effectively. Above all, it takes patience. Yet patience is aptly compensated for when you locate fish and are able to pull them up as fast as you drop in a line.

You are especially rewarded when you find crappies in a unique area or situation that few anglers know about but which you figured out and experimented with yourself. The information contained in this book will put you into the elite class of successful anglers who are able to do just that.

Chapter 2

# THE CRAPPIE'S PROFILE

Even though the crappie is one of, if not the *most* popular panfish in this country, the crappie's life style in some waters is still a bit of a mystery. To date, only a handful of biologists have conducted any extensive, ongoing crappie research. However, by combining the data from scientific studies with practical, on-the-water experience and observation, we know enough to be able to sketch the crappie's life story in many waters. Before you can catch white or black crappies consistently, it is essential to have a fundamental understanding of what makes them tick.

White and black crappies are members of the sunfish family (Centrarchidae) which also includes largemouth and smallmouth bass, bluegills, pumpkinseeds, rock bass, and others. These fish characteristically have wide, laterally flattened bodies that resemble the shape of a spade. Centrarchids have spines in their dorsal and anal fins. The pelvic fins in crappies are located beneath the pectoral fins and the anal fin is about the size of the dorsal fin. Large eyes are another characteristic of the sunfish family, and this trademark is particularly obvious in crappies.

White and black crappies are the only members of the genus Pomoxis. While there are many physical similarities between them, there are also noticeable differences. Interestingly, in waters where their range overlaps, the two species intermingle and hybridization occurs. These hybrids can confuse the issue, because they typically display traits from both parents.

## WHO'S WHO CRAPPIE IDENTIFICATION

What's the difference between black and white crappies, and why is it important to anglers? Well, knowing which crappie species is present or dominant in a body of water can give a clue to understanding the overall water environment. Changes in the distribution and abundance of both species may serve as "biological indicators" of lake productivity and water quality. In addition, fish location and presentation options may be affected.

### WHITE CRAPPIE

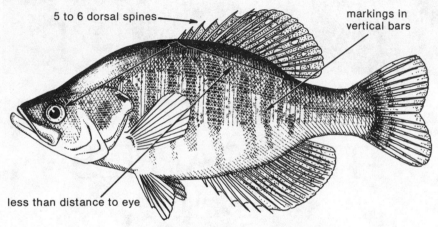

5 to 6 dorsal spines

markings in vertical bars

less than distance to eye

Scientific Name: Pomoxis annularis
World Record - 5 lbs. 3 oz.
Alias: silver crappie, white perch, pole crappie, white, and many others

While both species resemble each other in body shape and overall appearance, there are some fairly significant, visible differences. Generally, both fish have a golden to olive-green or brownish-green back with many bluish-green and silvery reflections, irregular dark mottling on their silvery sides and a white belly.

Here are some clues to help you tell them apart. Usually, the white crappie has a lighter overall appearance and seems to be slightly more elongated than the black. The white is normally paler in color, and the bluish-black blotches on its sides tend to be arranged in 5 to 10, dark, vertical bars. In contrast, the black crappie has a darker, heavily speckled, more mottled appearance.

A word of warning: The characteristic markings are not a foolproof guide to black and white crappie identification, because the markings of both species intensify during spawning. During the Spawn Period, the male, black crappie normally appears heavily mottled, with dark, purplish-black blotches over most of its body. Meanwhile, the male white crappie's markings visibly darken around the head, breast and back. These colorations are produced by hormones and are lost soon after spawning occurs. In waters that contain both white and black crappies, identification can be difficult.

So who's who? At times it is difficult to tell. Further, there is a tendency for crappies from clear waters to have more prominent markings than fish from dark, murky waters. Remember, depending on the Calendar Period and the body of water a fish lives in, identification by color can often be tricky. So, don't rely on color alone to distinguish between black and white crappies.

A glance at the accompanying crappie illustrations shows that the mouths of both species of crappies are large and moderately inclined. A line drawn at a right angle to the corner of the mouth will intersect the dorsal fin of the black

## BLACK CRAPPIE

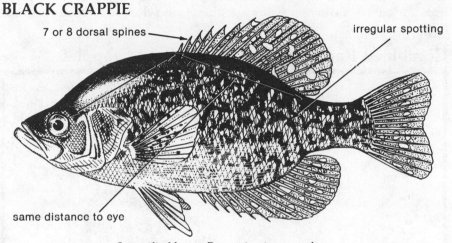

7 or 8 dorsal spines

irregular spotting

same distance to eye

Scientific Name: Pomoxis nigromaculatus
World Record - 6 lbs.
Alias: calico or strawberry bass, speckled crappie, crappie, and numerous others

crappie but will fall in front of the dorsal fin of the white crappie. This difference can be used as a secondary identifying characteristic. The crappie's mouth is made up of soft tissue and, as many anglers have discovered, it tears easily. Among the crappie's numerous aliases is "papermouth," and it sure fits.

Here are a few additional clues to help you draw the line between black and white crappies. The dorsal fin is shorter in the white than in the black crappie and is a reliable distinguishing characteristic. Usually, the white crappie has only 5 or 6 spines in the dorsal fin, while the black crappie has 7 or 8.

Another peculiarity is the distance from the dorsal fin to the eye. In the white crappie, the distance from the front of the dorsal fin to the eye is distinctly longer than the length of the dorsal fin. In contrast, this distance and the length of the dorsal fin are about equal in the black crappie.

# DISTRIBUTION

Originally, crappies were native only to the area from southern Canada and the Great Lakes to Florida, and from Nebraska to the Gulf coast. However, since the turn of the century man has introduced both species into suitable waters throughout North America. Apparently, they are quite adaptable. Crappies have found a niche in numerous waters and have often flourished. Through stocking programs, both state and federal agencies have greatly expanded the crappie's range. Additionally, fish rescue operations and reservoir construction have extended the crappie's distribution. Today, their range includes the lower 48 states, southern Canada and northern Mexico.

The black crappie was originally found from the Canadian border, through the Mississippi River watersheds and along the Atlantic coast to Florida. The white crappie was native to the mid-states and south to the Gulf coast. When you look at the crappie distribution map, you'll understand why crappies are such popular fish. Except for lakes and rivers in the high elevations of the Rocky Mountains where crappies are absent, the crappie is an all-American fish.

## Combined Range of Black and White Crappies

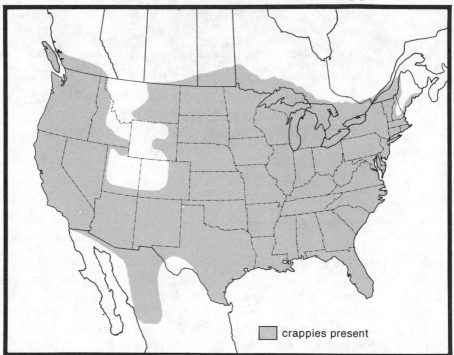

crappies present

White and black crappies thrive in many ponds, pits, lakes, rivers, bayous and reservoirs. Yet, even though their ranges overlap considerably, the white crappie is usually more abundant in the turbid, warmer waters of southern reservoirs, while the black crappie is normally more common in the natural lakes of Florida and the North.

Obviously, a host of factors affect how a particular fish adapts to its environment, and certainly there is no simple answer as to how they accomplish it. In a nutshell, environmental conditions that favor one species may limit another.

For example, black crappies inhabit the cooler, clear-water, natural lakes of the northern United States and southern Canada. You'd be hard pressed to find any number of white crappies in these waters. Apparently, the environmental conditions that the lakes in this area provide are suitable for black crappie survival and growth. However, this same environment is inhospitable to white crappies, and they are seldom present. On the other hand, the black crappie plays second fiddle to the white crappie in many, murky, warm-water reservoirs of the South. Here the white crappie is king and the black crappie scratches out an existence.

The accompanying map shows the combined range of the black and white crappie without detailing their individual distribution. Here are a couple of interesting facts concerning the occurrence of white and black crappies:

(1) The white crappie isn't present in Florida. The white crappie is normally considered to have the more southern range of the two species and is more tolerant of turbid waters. However, the black crappie dominates in Florida's natural lakes and rivers.

(2) The reservoirs of the central United States are primarily the "white crappie's domain." In fact, studies show that on some large reservoirs, white crappies comprise 90% or more of the crappie population.

(3) Black crappies are far more common in tidal rivers and brackish waters along the East and Gulf coasts. Apparently, the black crappie can tolerate brackish water better than the white crappie. Many times, these brackish-water fish are overlooked by anglers. For instance, crappies inhabit virtually all the fresh and brackish, headwaters of Chesapeake Bay's tributary systems. Yet, even though it's within reach of millions, few anglers utilize this fishery.

(4) Rivers, pits and ponds are scattered throughout the country from Maine to Montana, and all of these waters can provide crappie fisheries. For reasons no one can explain, black crappies inhabit some waters, white crappies, others, and they reside together in many more. Which of these waters develop a quality fishery is dependent on many factors like crappie abundance, available prey, competing species, water quality and others. In rivers, the older, more fertile ones with an extended flood plain are best. For example, the Mississippi, Missouri, Columbia, and Ohio rivers all provide excellent crappie fishing opportunities in waters adjacent to the mainstream and in backwater areas.

(5) Pits and ponds are common in many areas of the country and can offer topnotch, largemouth bass and crappie fishing. Depending on the environment that each provides, these smaller waters can be a feast or famine affair. Overcrowding and a limited food supply in some will yield only small, thin crappies, while others with a balanced fish population and plenty of food can produce some real tackle busters. In fact, several state record crappies have been taken from ponds.

Contrary to common belief, crappies and other fish don't appear to prefer any particular set of environmental conditions. They simply *adapt* to whatever conditions a lake, river or reservoir provides. Some species of fish are more adaptable than others to various environments and can tolerate marginal conditions better. Normally, these fish will prosper. Many factors are involved, like habitat, predator/prey relationships, water clarity, competition, feeding efficiency, and others. Therefore, depending on the environment in any given body of water, it could contain black crappies, white crappies or both, plus hybrids.

In general then, black crappies are more abundant in cool, clear, deep, natural lakes and reservoirs. But, they may also be found in Florida waters with temperatures as high as 80°F. Typically, these natural lakes contain marl, sand or gravel bottoms with some vegetation present.

On the other hand, white crappies are far more common in the warm, murky, shallow lakes and impoundments of the South. Depending on location, these waters can provide a variety of aquatic environmental conditions. Standing timber, brush, areas of both hard and soft bottom, vegetation and stained-to-dark water are common features.

Regardless of which crappie species inhabits the waters you fish, an understanding of crappie behavior plus a few presentation options will put plenty of fish on your stringer.

# REPRODUCTION

Male and female crappies are sexually mature and begin spawning when they're 2 to 3 years old and 6 to 9 inches in length. But, in waters where crappie growth rates are fast, fish may mature in one year. Age is more important than size, because a stunted fish may spawn when it's only 4 inches long, but 3 years old. One researcher reports that larger fish appear to spawn deeper and earlier in the year than smaller fish. By spawning early, these larger fish face less competition for prime spawning sites from other crappies and largemouth bass.

Crappies are spring spawners through most of their range. The bulk of their spawning activity usually occurs from March through May. However, studies indicate that in some areas in the South, spawning activities may begin as early as mid-February, and in the North as late as mid-July.

Under normal weather conditions, the bulk of the crappie spawning activity will occur when the water temperature ranges from about 60°F to 68°F. However, some spawning activities have been observed at temperatures as low as 50°F and as high as 80°F. These varying spawning temperatures depend on seasonal weather trends which affect how rapidly the water warms. Water clarity also plays a part, because shallow, turbid waters typically warm faster than deep, clear waters. For example, when most fish in a shallow, dark-water reservoir may have finished spawning, in a nearby, deep, clear-water reservoir or lake, the bulk of the crappies may be just beginning to spawn. Interestingly, the angle of the sun's rays and length of daylight also seem to have an influence on triggering crappie spawning activities.

Studies note that crappies often spawn deeper than other panfish. This habit enables them to survive in carp- and gar-infested waters because most of their nests are outside the activity areas of rough fish. While crappies typically spawn in water from 2 to 10 feet deep, fish nests have been spotted in water less than 12 inches deep to more than 20 feet deep.

Biologists have linked crappie spawning depth in reservoirs to water clarity and have come up with this rule of thumb: The clearer the water, the deeper they spawn. This fact is important because water clarity varies from one body of water to another and even within the same waters. For example, a dark-water reservoir may have crappies spawning at 1 to 3 feet deep, while in a clear-water reservoir, crappies may spawn 10 feet deep or more. Obviously, water clarity will affect crappie location and is one of the most important pieces of the crappie puzzle.

Observations indicate that during the early Pre-spawn Period, crappies will congregate in areas adjacent to actual spawning grounds. As the water warms to the mid-50°F's, the males move into shallow water and scout the area for the best nesting sites. At this time, males will assume their darker spawning colors. After establishing a territory, each male sweeps out a shallow, bowl-shaped nest about 6 to 10 inches in diameter. Nest building takes about 2 days to complete. Meanwhile, the females are located nearby, awaiting the onset of spawning.

## Crappie Spawning Depth

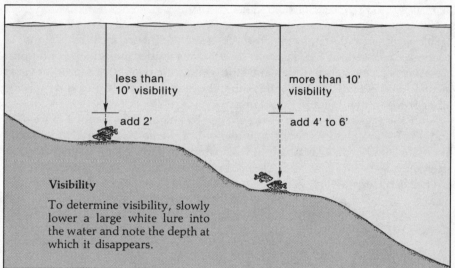

less than
10' visibility

more than 10'
visibility

add 2'

add 4' to 6'

**Visibility**

To determine visibility, slowly lower a large white lure into the water and note the depth at which it disappears.

*While reservoir crappies have been observed spawning in water ranging in depth from 1 to 24 feet, water clarity controls the depth at which crappies spawn. If visibility is less than 10 feet, add 2 feet to the maximum depth you can see in order to estimate the spawning depth. If visibility is over 10 feet, add 4 to 6 feet to approximate the spawning depth.*

*Knowing this likely depth can help you find potential, crappie spawning areas on reservoirs. This method may not work in natural lakes where crappies often spawn in shallow, weed or reed cover. Still, it's a good tip to keep in mind.*

*Missouri Department of Conservation research data*

Depending on the available habitat, nests can be found on a wide variety of bottom materials, such as gravel, sand, rubble, marl, muck, clay, or a combination of these materials. Usually, nests are located in the backs of protected bays and coves, near submerged vegetation, brush or stumps. In waters where prime spawning habitat is at a premium or where competition for spawning sites is high, crappies may spawn on rocks or fallen trees along steep banks.

Yearly fluctuations in water levels are common on some rivers and reservoirs, and as water levels change, crappies will seek out the best available habitat. What's best this year may be high and dry next year. In addition, unstable weather and receding water levels can cause crappies to abandon their nests.

After the nest is completed and the water temperature remains suitable, the female moves into the spawning area and is recruited by a male. The female deposits her eggs which are fertilized by the male, and then she leaves. Crappies usually spawn in colonies which contain 3 to 50 nests and females may spawn with more than one male. Hybrids are fairly common since white and black crappies often intermingle.

The number of eggs that a female produces varies with the size of the fish. Females weighing around 8 ounces may contain 20,000 to 60,000 eggs, while larger fish may produce 150,000 or more eggs. Even though crappies are believed to be very prolific, a Missouri study points out that females may only deposit 20 to 30 percent of their eggs.

Under suitable conditions, incubation of the eggs usually lasts 3 to 5 days. Stable weather and water temperatures in the 70°F's are ideal conditions. In contrast, incubation can last up to 15 days under marginal conditions. However, egg mortality is high and studies indicate over 50% mortality when incubation is extended. During this time, the male guards the nest and prevents other fish from entering the nest area.

After the eggs hatch, the fry are guarded by the male for several more days until the fry are mature enough to move out of the nesting area. There is only limited scientific data available on distribution patterns of young crappies after they leave the nest and scatter. Evidence suggests that young crappies often inhabit open-water areas.

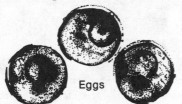
Eggs

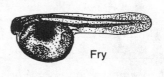
Fry

Biologists believe that fluctuations in year-class strength are a result of poor survival of the young crappies (less than 1/2-inch long) shortly after they desert the nest. Unfortunately, the cause(s) of this poor survival rate is not known at this time. But, the result can be a feast or famine crappie fishery that is common in some waters.

Biologists are studying this phenomenon and have come up with several theories. Predation by bass or dominant-year-class crappies is one explanation. Another theory is that the overcrowding of crappies may prevent egg formation. Still others suggest predator/prey relationships, water quality or temperature as causes.

# AGE

Crappies are generally considered to be short-lived fish; however, their longevity (life span) is similar to other members of the sunfish family. On many waters, crappies typically live 3 to 6 years, with individuals in some waters reaching 8 years or more. The oldest reported crappie was an ancient, 13-year-old fish. In comparison, other sunfish like bluegills and pumpkinseeds normally live from 4 to 8 years. Largemouth bass, another relative, typically live from 6 to 10 years in many waters, with some fish reaching 12 to 15 years of age. Thus, even though they don't appear to live a long time, crappies have a "normal" life span on many waters when compared with other family members.

## Age vs. Growth Rates of Crappies from Selected Waters

| Species | Water | Length (Inches) At End of Each Year | | | | | | | | |
| | | 1 | 2 | 3 | 4 | 5 | 6 | 7 | 8 | 9 |
|---|---|---|---|---|---|---|---|---|---|---|
| White | Lake Moultrie, South Carolina | 2.2 | 8.2 | 11.3 | 13.4 | 14.6 | 15.0 | 14.9 | | |
| White | Kentucky Lake, Kentucky | 4.6 | 7.9 | 10.4 | 11.9 | 12.8 | | | | |
| White | Missouri, (State Average) | 2.7 | 5.7 | 8.1 | 9.6 | 11.0 | 11.5 | | | |
| White | Lake Decatur, Illinois | | | 7.3 | 9.1 | 10.5 | 10.6 | 12.2 | 12.3 | |
| White | Oklahoma, (State Average) | 2.9 | 5.9 | 7.8 | 9.8 | 11.9 | 13.2 | 14.2 | 15.0 | |
| White | Mississippi River, Minnesota | 2.6 | 6.0 | 9.1 | 10.8 | 11.7 | | | | |
| Black | Norris Reservoir, Tennessee | 5.0 | 10.9 | 12.2 | | | | | | |
| Black | Clear Lake, Iowa | 2.3 | 5.1 | 7.2 | 8.6 | 10.5 | 11.6 | 11.9 | | |
| Black | Lake Moultrie, South Carolina | 2.3 | 6.3 | 10.6 | 12.4 | 13.2 | 14.0 | 15.0 | 15.0 | |
| Black | Lake George, Florida | 4.4 | 8.1 | 9.9 | 11.5 | 12.5 | 12.1 | | | |
| Black | Lake Havasu, California | 2.9 | 6.7 | 8.6 | 9.9 | 10.7 | | | | |
| Black | Lake Harris, Florida | 1.9 | 4.2 | 6.6 | 8.5 | 9.8 | 11.2 | 12.2 | 13.0 | 13.8 |
| Black | Wisconsin (Southern) | 4.3 | 7.0 | 8.3 | 9.8 | 10.1 | 10.1 | 11.0 | 11.2 | 12.3 |

*The accompanying chart shows the yearly growth (in inches) of white and black crappies in selected lakes, rivers and reservoirs. Note that crappies in southern waters generally grow faster than those in northern waters. In addition, black crappies in northern, natural lakes normally live longer than white crappies in southern reservoirs. Typically, 6-plus-year-old white crappies and 8-plus-year-old black crappies are considered ancient. While some fish live longer, they're relatively rare in most waters.*

Overall, the black crappie is generally considered to have a longer life span than the white crappie. However, the longevity of both species is highly variable and is regulated by many factors. In the end, the environment a crappie lives in determines how long it lives.

For example, a study in Lake of the Ozarks Reservoir, MO, found few white crappies more than 3 years old. Additionally, an Oklahoma study concluded that over 95% of the crappie population was less than 5 years old. These findings seem to indicate a short life span. Yet by comparison, in Minnesota and Florida some black crappies live from 8 to 10 years. Apparently, a short life span may be characteristic of crappie populations in some waters, while crappies may live twice as long in others. While biologists don't have absolute, concrete answers to this puzzle, some believe that high adult mortality may be due to stress (physiological burnout) during hot summer months, disease or overharvesting. Current research studies are aimed toward answering the interesting question of why relatively few crappies live longer than 3 or 4 years in some waters.

# GROWTH

The small-crappie syndrome has plagued anglers for years. Why do some waters produce only small, stunted fish while others grow 2-pound slabs? Once again, there is no single, clear-cut answer.

The rate at which crappies grow is directly linked to several environmental factors. Habitat, turbidity and temperature of the water, amount and type of available food, geographical location, competition for food and living space, plus other factors, all play a role. Growth rates for crappies can vary greatly in different waters and can even vary from year to year in the same body of water.

Crappie growth may be fast or slow in all parts of the range but, in general, growth is faster in the South than in the North. For example, a 3-year-old white crappie in a southern reservoir might be 10 inches long; whereas a 3-year-old black crappie in a northern, natural lake would be about 7 inches long. In addition, in waters where both exist, one species will usually dominate. Depending on the environment, the odds could tip in favor of either the white or black.

It's a balancing-act game, with each fish situated at opposite ends of an environmental see-saw. Water clarity, prey, competition, temperature, habitat, plus a host of other factors, all determine which direction the environment shifts and, ultimately, which species of crappie will dominate. These same conditions also determine the abundance, growth rate, and size of the fish.

# DIET

Crappies are predators and are neither general nor specific in their feeding habits. They are mainly sight feeders as their large eyes might suggest. At times, crappies are opportunistic feeders and may take advantage of an aquatic insect hatch. At other times, they may feed almost entirely on small fish. Actually, crappies are intermediate, semi-selective feeders. They may consume a wide range of food items in some waters or be selective and feed on only a few items in others. It all depends on what's available.

The amounts and types of food items eaten also vary with the time of the year, crappie size, and the availability of prey. Both white and black crappies eat zooplankton, crustaceans, aquatic insects and fish. Zooplankton is the major food of most young crappies. As they grow, small larvae and adult, aquatic insects become very important foods. Ultimately, small fish become the most important food item of adult crappies in most waters.

Seasonally, the adult crappie's diet may vary to take advantage of the most abundant food items. A typical pattern for adult crappies features plankton and aquatic insects as the dietary mainstay during spring and early summer.

## Typical Aquatic Food Chain

*"The Game of Who Eats Whom"*

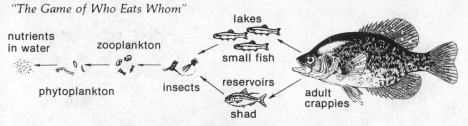

### What Crappies Eat

| | |
|---|---|
| Shad | Zooplankton |
| Aquatic Insects | Minnows |
| Sunfish | Carp |
| Catfish | Black Bass |
| Striped Bass | Drum |
| Bluegills | Crappies |
| Crustaceans | |

*Size is of the essence, and small is best. Normally, adult crappies eat young-of-the-year fish, if available. However, their diet can vary from one body of water to another, and even seasonally on the same body of water.*

As summer progresses, young-of-the-year fish become available and are used as forage. In fall, fish are the primary food in most waters. During winter, food items vary depending on location of the water. While fish and insects may be important items in the South, zooplankton, miscellaneous aquatic insects and minnows (if available) are common forage in the North.

In waters containing both black and white crappies, their diet, growth rate and survival may vary dramatically. A recent study indicates that adult black crappies are less adapted than white crappies to capturing preyfish in turbid waters. Blacks apparently don't feed efficiently in warmer, turbid waters, and simply expend too much energy in search of prey. Thus, adult black crappies may be forced to continue feeding on plankton and insects, while their cousins—white crappies—are able to switch forage types and dine on small fish. Thus, in dark waters containing mixed populations, whites usually have the edge, because they're able to utilize the forage base more efficiently.

Once crappies reach about 6 inches in length, they're not highly adapted to feeding on small plankton because the larger spaces between their gill rakers prevent the retention of tiny food items. Consequently, blacks can get caught in an "energy trap" if they cannot effectively switch to a fish diet. In some turbid waters, blacks remain plankton feeders and literally "burn out" trying to feed. Therefore, white crappies dominate. Here, 3-year-old white crappies might be 9 inches long while black crappies might be only 6 inches long. It's simply survival of the fittest.

*Here are several zooplankton that panfish commonly feed on. Copepods sense predators and make darting, evasive maneuvers to avoid panfish. Daphnia exhibit a constant bobbing or fluttering movement, but offer no evasive actions. However, they have the ability to migrate vertically in the water to coincide with the low-light levels which makes them difficult to see.*

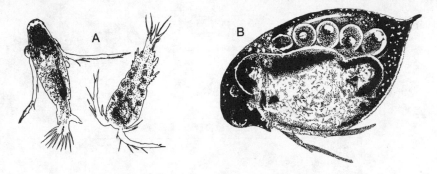

*(A) Here are two types of copepods. The one on the left is a calanoid copepod; on the right is a cyclopoid copepod. They reach sizes of about 1/10 of an inch.*

*(B) The common water flea or Daphnia is about the size of a pinhead.*

On the other hand, given a cooler, clearer-water environment, blacks often prosper. Here, they can compete for available food and space on an equal (or better than equal) basis with white crappies. There are also numerous "in between" waters with both species present, and when the environment favors one species or the other, that species will generally dominate.

## AVAILABILITY OF PREY

Apparently, for a lake or reservoir to support a healthy, stable, crappie population, it must provide a suitable prey during the critical transition period when crappies switch to a fish diet. Basically, crappies are flesh eaters (carnivores), and small fish are important food items. In fact, in some reservoirs, studies show that, seasonally, young gizzard and threadfin shad comprise a majority of the crappie's diet. Crappies will gorge themselves on plentiful, high-protein shad, if available.

Prey size also seems to be very important. Crappies generally utilize smaller, young-of-the-year shad in the 1- to 3-inch range. Once shad grow over 4 inches in length, crappies are unable to use them as a food source; they simply too large to eat. But, by dining on younger shad, crappies are able to grow rapidly to world-class size.

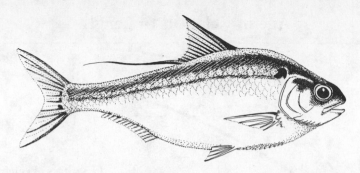

Young threadfin and newly hatched gizzard shad are the keys to good crappie growth in many impoundments. The presence (or lack) of young shad in some reservoirs seems to be related to the growth and overall condition of the crappie population. In some cases, the white crappie's diet is composed of 45 to 90 percent shad.

Threadfin shad have multiple spawns—spring and fall—on some waters. This yields an abundance of high-protein forage for the crappies and can result in numbers of slab-sized fish.

In reservoirs where shad aren't a primary prey, crappies will feed upon the fry of largemouth bass, white bass, perch or sunfish. They also eat insects, crustaceans, mollusks, and various minnows. However, while crappies can "hack" this diet, they generally don't flourish on it.

A similar transition to a fish diet takes place in natural lakes. However, since shad may not be available, largemouth bass fry, perch, bluegills and miscellaneous minnows take the place of shad in the crappie's diet.

Jim and Al Lindner combined to catch a bunch of early-spring, pre-spawn crappies. These fish were caught from a shallow bay of a natural lake on ultralight tackle, 4-pound-test line and 1/16-oz. jigs.

# Age in Relation to Length

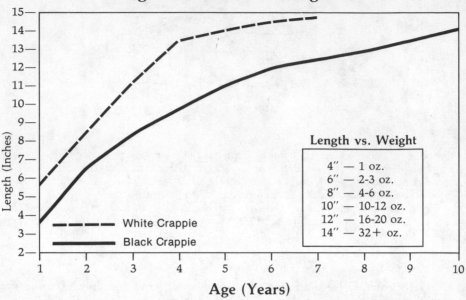

Length (Inches)

Age (Years)

Length vs. Weight

4" — 1 oz.
6" — 2-3 oz.
8" — 4-6 oz.
10" — 10-12 oz.
12" — 16-20 oz.
14" — 32+ oz.

White Crappie
Black Crappie

This graph illustrates the approximate length for different year classes of white and black crappies. Growth rates vary considerably between waters, yet the values reflect typical growth in some better lakes and reservoirs. In general, male and female crappies grow at similar rates, although hybrids are fast growing and predominantly males.

Weight-wise, the black crappie is heavier for its length than the white crappie. Yet, the white crappie grows faster in many waters. Depending on diet and many other factors, the weight of crappies can also vary from the approximate values. All in all, crappie longevity and weight is tied to the local environment. With optimum conditions, a crappie will double its weight as it grows from 8 to 10 inches and nearly double again when it reaches 12 inches. Slab, 2-pound crappies are usually 14 to 16 inches long and 5 to 8 years old—honest-to-goodness trophies.

In small lakes and reservoirs, pits and ponds, the crappie's growth rate depends on the amount of available prey and other factors. In many waters, crappies are stunted because too many fish must compete for a limited prey resource. With limited prey, growth is slow and the maximum size of adult fish may be only 4 to 6 inches. On the other hand, small waters with a balanced fishery can grow slab-sized crappies. Competition for food and living space is less, and the fish may grow and thrive if conditions permit.

## Chapter 3

# INTRODUCTION TO THE CALENDAR PERIODS

To catch crappies 365 days a year requires an indepth knowledge of crappie behavior on a yearly, seasonal and daily basis. This may sound difficult, but it's easier than you might think. The foundation of successful crappie fishing is built upon understanding the crappies' way of life and how they adapt all season long to their changing aquatic environment.

Our normal system of measuring time is the Gregorian calendar, which contains 365 days and 12 months. It's the calendar hanging on your wall and built into the LCD watch on your wrist. Actually, it's a good, accurate system for recording daily, monthly and yearly periods; however, the calendar is *fixed* and doesn't take into account the whims of nature that affect the biological community.

The *IN-FISHERMAN* Calendar, on the other hand, divides the year into 10 periods of fish response. These seasonal periods replace the standard days, weeks and months of the normal calendar. Because the *IN-FISHERMAN* Calendar Periods are at the mercy of Mother Nature, they do not last a certain number of days, nor do they occur on specific dates each year. Since the Calendar Periods depend on climate and water conditions, they will vary in length from year to year depending on weather trends. And, if you want crappies tugging on your line, you must recognize the Calendar Periods and predict the crappies' response.

Calendar Periods which might last a few days one year could last a month the next year. For example, last year in "Secret Lake" the crappies may have completed spawning during the first week of May, while this year, due to a late spring, the crappie spawning period in Secret Lake might run from Memorial Day until mid-June. Obviously, the timing of the Calendar Periods fluctuates.

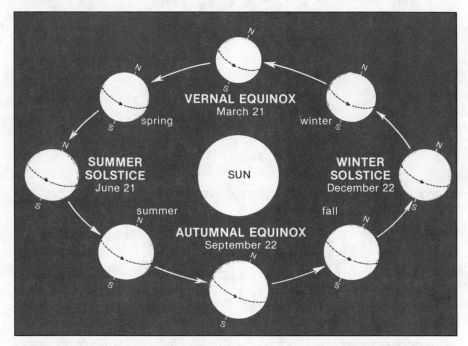

*Spring, summer, fall and winter are common events in the temperate zones. During these separate and distinct seasons the pendulum swings noticeably between periods of lightness and darkness. We can easily recognize seasonal patterns in nature.*

*On land, seasonal changes are quite evident, but under the water it's difficult to see nature's forces at work. Consequently, aquatic seasonal cycles are a confusing mystery to some people. However, it is in this mysterious and constantly changing environment that fish live, so to catch crappies with consistency, you must be in touch with their aquatic environment.*

*Crappie behavior is not haphazard. A host of factors affect fish, and there are sound reasons for each and every activity. In order to survive, fish simply adapt to conditions. Studies show that the photoperiod (length of daylight) regulates the tempo of the environment, from microorganisms to top-of-the-line predators. Seasonally, these light levels change as the earth rotates around the sun. The intensity and duration of light in its yearly cycle can regulate migrations, spawning, and feeding, and may trigger other activities.*

Additionally, a Calendar Period might occur months earlier in one region of North America than in another. For instance, in areas of Canada, the Summer Calendar Period might arrive in July and only last a few weeks. Meanwhile, in Florida, the Summer Period may arrive in May and last for 5 months or more. This difference in timing is caused by the change in the angle of the sun to the earth's surface as you proceed from the equator northward. The more direct angle of the sun in the South provides an overall warmer environment.

There is a south-to-north progression (Florida to Tennessee to Minnesota) in the onset of the Calendar Periods since southern states begin warming earlier in the year than northern ones. In fact, spring usually arrives about one week later for every 100 miles you proceed north. Conversely, fall arrives earlier in the northern states and progresses southward.

Some of the *IN-FISHERMAN* Calendar Periods relate primarily to the crappie's biological demands, such as reproduction. These include the Pre-spawn, Spawn and Post-spawn Periods. Other periods like the various Summer, Fall (Cold Water), and Winter (Coldest Water) Periods relate more to water temperature and seasonal environmental conditions.

Thus, Calendar Periods are not simply the seasonal conditions of a body of water. A lake, river or reservoir may be in a seasonal time frame (spring, summer, fall or winter), but the *crappies' response* to that environment determines their Calendar Period. In any given body of water, different species of fish, as well as different groups of the same species, can be in different Calendar Periods at the same time. Since not all crappies spawn simultaneously, groups of Pre-spawn, Spawn and Post-spawn fish can be present at the same time, and the location and attitude of each group will be different. There are subtle, but significant, changes in behavior that affect the "catchability" of crappies during each Calendar Period.

You might assume that the best time to fish would be during a Calendar Period when the water temperature is at an optimum for crappie metabolism, causing them to feed the most. But, it doesn't always work that way. The available food supply, timing of feeding movements, and overall population levels and competition, all play an important role in angling success. We considered these factors when we developed the *IN-FISHERMAN* Calendar Periods.

Once you learn to "read the signs," you'll have little difficulty identifying one period from another and determining when various species are in different Calendar Periods. The difference between the unsuccessful angler and the truly successful one often boils down to the ability to recognize seasonal movements and the crappies' response patterns. If you know the Calendar Periods from A to Z, you'll be several boat lengths ahead of the crowd and on your way to more and bigger crappies.

In the final analysis, the only way to understand how different Calendar Periods function in a particular body of water is to spend enough time on the water identifying these patterns. Comparing notes with other anglers will help you get a grasp on crappie behavior during the Calendar Periods. Keeping a daily log of weather and water conditions, as well as fish feeding patterns, will also help. A review of last year's fishing log often provides an insight into seasonal fishing patterns you may not have noticed before. In this way, you can learn both the seasonal circumstances that trigger fish response, and the locational patterns that result from them.

As we examine the Calendar Periods in depth, we'll include clues on crappie location and behavior that'll help you understand the ins and outs of crappie activity on any body of water.

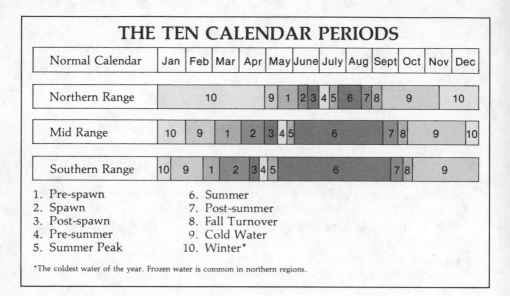

## THE TEN CALENDAR PERIODS

| Normal Calendar | Jan | Feb | Mar | Apr | May | June | July | Aug | Sept | Oct | Nov | Dec |
|---|---|---|---|---|---|---|---|---|---|---|---|---|
| Northern Range | 10 | | | | 9 | 1 | 2 3 4 5 | 6 | 7 8 | 9 | | 10 |
| Mid Range | 10 | 9 | 1 | | 2 | 3 4 5 | 6 | | 7 8 | 9 | | 10 |
| Southern Range | 10 | 9 | 1 | 2 | 3 4 5 | | 6 | | 7 8 | 9 | | |

1. Pre-spawn
2. Spawn
3. Post-spawn
4. Pre-summer
5. Summer Peak
6. Summer
7. Post-summer
8. Fall Turnover
9. Cold Water
10. Winter*

*The coldest water of the year. Frozen water is common in northern regions.

*The key to understanding the 10 Calendar Periods of fish response is to realize that the periods can (and do) vary in length from year to year, and in some waters they may overlap from time to time. Obviously, unusually warm or cool weather will affect the length of the periods. They can vary as much as 4 weeks from one year to the next. Remember, the periods are not based on the Gregorian calendar, so they do not occur on specific dates each year. Instead, the Calendar Periods are based on nature's clock.*

*In addition, the Calendar Periods vary by regions of the country. Being in a warm climate, the rivers, lakes and reservoirs of the South experience an extended Summer Period and brief Cold Water and Winter Periods. In contrast, the lakes along the U.S./Canadian border normally have extended Cold Water and Winter Periods and a brief Summer Period. So, crappies in Florida or Texas could be in the Spawning Period while those in northern Minnesota are still "iced up" in the Winter Period.*

*Bodies of water located between these two extremes experience Calendar Periods that lie somewhere in between these examples, with the overall length of the periods adjusted accordingly. For example, fish in the TVA reservoirs of Kentucky/Tennessee experience intermediate Calendar Period lengths when compared with fish in northern and southern waters.*

*The IN-FISHERMAN Calendar Period guide can be used to determine what crappies will be doing on a season-long basis. The normal calendar is included as an approximate reference point. Using this information, you can create a "Crappie Calendar" for your locality.*

# CALENDAR PERIOD REGIONAL TIMETABLE

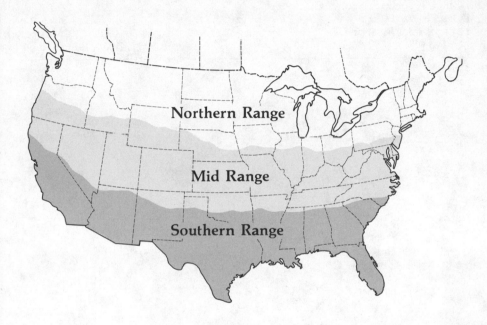

The timing of the crappie's Spawn Period illustrates the region-by-region progression of the Calendar Periods. Region (latitude), water temperature, weather trends, length of daylight, and inter- and intra-species competition for habitat are just a few of the factors which influence the exact timing of the spawn. Remember, not all crappies spawn at the same time even in the same body of water. While the bulk of the adult fish on a given lake may spawn during a few days of ideal conditions, there will still be some early- and some late-spawning fish.

Regionally, the onset of crappie spawning may begin in early March in the South or as late as mid-July in southern Canada. The following chart lists typical spawning months for crappies in representative areas:

# TYPICAL SPAWNING MONTHS

| AREA | MONTH(S) |
|---|---|
| Florida | March-April |
| Alabama | March-April |
| Texas/Oklahoma | March-May |
| Kentucky/Tennessee | April-May |
| Missouri/Illinois/Iowa | April-June |
| Ohio | April-July |
| Oregon | March-June |
| Minnesota/Wisconsin | May-July |
| Ontario | June-August |

## Chapter 4

# THE CALENDAR PERIODS

## Crappies Throughout The Seasons

To catch crappies consistently, you must understand their fascinating lifestyle throughout the changing seasons. Crappies follow the rhythm of nature with their own distinct patterns of behavior. As the water warms from spring into summer, crappies respond to the increasing pace of life with more movement and aggressiveness. Then, as the water cools from fall into winter, the tempo of life gradually slows and crappies become more sedentary and selective. Good crappie anglers understand these seasonal tendencies and adjust their tactics to keep in step with nature's changing tune.

This chapter describes the fundamental principles of crappie location and behavior during each of the *IN-FISHERMAN* Calendar Periods. Once we lay the foundation, we'll take a more detailed look in the following chapters, at each Calendar Period. Let's begin our adventure as winter gives way to early spring.

# THE SPRING SEASON
Which includes: Spring Cold Water, Pre-spawn,
Spawn, and Post-spawn Periods

## THE COLD WATER PERIOD (SPRING)

A Time of Preparation
*Surface Water Temperature Range: Mid 30°F to 50°F*
*General Fish Mood: Neutral*

The Spring Cold Water Period is a time of preparation—a prelude to the crappie's annual spawning ritual. It is also a period of transition from the lethargy of winter to the cool-water environment of spring.

In northern lakes, the Spring Cold Water Period begins just after ice-out with water temperatures in the low 30°F. In more southerly waters, it may commence with water temperatures in the low 40°F, depending on how low the water temperature dropped over the winter. In either case, it arrives as winter grudgingly releases its icy grip and the water begins to warm.

In northern natural lakes, crappies generally suspend along or somewhere adjacent to the deep weedline/first drop-off area at ice-out. In small lakes and ponds, it's not uncommon for them to be smack-dab in the center of the deepest hole in the lake from 5 to 20 feet below the surface. Reservoir fish display a similar tendency, although the fish usually tend to be more object-oriented, relating to deep treelines, channel edges, etc., rather than suspending away from cover.

Stable, warm weather—particularly calm, sunny days—will start drawing some crappies into the shallows almost immediately, if sheltered areas exist. These occur in the form of channels, bays, cuts, harbors, backwaters, etc. In essence, they are areas of shallow water that are exposed to the sun and protected from the wind. The best ones generally lie on the northern shores of lakes or impoundments since these areas receive the best sun exposure and have the most shelter from harsh north winds.

Many anglers think these initial, shallow-water forays are pre-spawn movements. They're not. Actually, they're associated with food. Crappies follow minnows into the warming shallows as the tiny baitfish seek the microscopic plankton that are beginning to bloom there.

The best shallow crappie areas usually have some form of cover to attract and hold fish in the general area. In natural lakes, cover generally occurs in the form of reeds, dock pilings, brush, and remnant shallow weeds from the previous year. In rivers and reservoirs, flooded brush, stumps, fallen trees and fish attractors do the trick.

Early, shallow crappie movements occur at the mercy of Mother Nature. Stable weather draws the fish in, and cold-front conditions drive them back out again. Thus, depending on the conditions, you may find the bulk of the crappies in a bay or cove area to be: (1) shallow (ideal conditions); (2) along the first drop-off outside a shallow, protected cut (intermediate conditions); (3) suspended outside the drop-off (frontal conditions). However, just knowing that they'll be somewhere in the vicinity of shallow bays, backwaters or cuts gives you a starting place to begin your search.

In general, lakes or reservoirs with shallow bays or cuts will see shallow crappie movements just after ice-out or just as the water begins to warm. However, when bodies of water lack such protected areas, it may take several additional weeks for the wind-exposed shallows to warm sufficiently to attract fish. In such lakes, the bulk of the fish usually remain suspended along the first drop-off/channel edge until the shallows warm up enough to attract them.

As the water continues to warm up toward 50°F, the environment grows more stable. The bulk of the crappies will generally be somewhere in the area from the extreme shallows out to the first drop-off, although they will begin shifting their activity toward areas where they will eventually spawn. These may or may not be the same areas they used earlier, depending on the available bottom content and cover. It all depends on what options the body of water offers.

# THE PRE-SPAWN PERIOD
## A Time of Anticipation
*Surface Water Temperature Range: 50°F to 63°F*
*General Fish Mood: Neutral to Positive*

At this stage, crappie activity begins centering around spawning areas. In reservoirs and rivers, these generally occur (1) where the bottom is sufficiently soft—generally sand/marl, but not mucky—for crappies to sweep out a nest; (2) near some form of cover; (3) at the appropriate depth. This combination of factors varies from lake to lake, but there are several guidelines you can use to locate fish.

In general, bay, backwater or cove areas with cover (timber, stumps, brush piles, etc.) will attract most of the fish, rather than main-lake shorelines. However, the fish will really key in on the sections of these general areas with cover at the proper depth. This depth varies with water clarity, but is generally *slightly below* the depth of maximum sunlight penetration. Crappies may even forego areas with decent bottom and cover if they're too shallow, and may elect to spawn around deeper fish attractors or on horizontal branches of flooded timber if it lies in their favored depth range. This is particularly true if the fish face severe competition for spawning areas with largemouth bass.

In any case, pre-spawn crappies will congregate around these areas as the water rises above 50°F. Males are the first fish to enter the spawning areas and remain there. Females may mill in and out, or stay a bit deeper, right up until the actual time of spawning. This is particularly true in natural lakes where crappies spawn around reed or weed cover in the shallows. This form of natural cover tends to draw pre-spawn fish shallower than they might move on reservoirs with the same water clarity.

Early pre-spawn males will move directly into generalized areas of cover. When they first move in, they'll mill about and display an overall spooky attitude. However, the longer they remain in the shallows, the more aggressive and territorial they become. Hormonal changes begin to trigger a darker color change in the males. In clear-water natural lakes, you can often spot them as dark spots inside the tangled masses of reed clumps.

The more the water warms, the more fearless the fish become. They are quite easy to catch with a variety of bobber presentations—particularly once they select their spawning site and begin sweeping out a nest. Eventually, a male will seek out or attract a female and spawning will occur.

The actual spawning act may only take a couple of hours. However, spawning usually requires several days and is resumed as more eggs and milt ripen in the fish. Most females deposit their eggs within a day or two unless the process is interrupted by unstable weather.

In general, all the crappies in a body of water do not spawn at exactly the same time, since all areas of a lake do not warm up at the same pace. Thus, you can expect the shallowest, most protected areas to see spawning use first, while it takes a bit longer for deeper or more exposed areas to warm enough for spawning to commence.

# THE SPAWN PERIOD

## A Time of Tension
### Surface Water Temperature Range: 64°F to 72+ °F
### General Fish Mood: Negative

This is a brief and variable period usually lasting from one to three days for female crappies and a little longer for males. Fish may spawn earlier or later, but most of the eggs will usually be deposited somewhere within this temperature range. Fish which spawn extremely deep (20 feet in clear reservoirs) may appear to spawn later, but when you consider how long it takes the water temperature at the spawning depth to warm to the proper level, the general rule applies.

While a fish that has not spawned yet is still technically in its Pre-spawn Period, in reality, the closer it comes to spawning, the less likely it is to strike a bait or exhibit other pre-spawn traits. While feeding activity is practically non-existent during spawning, some fish may make reflex strikes at intruders into the nest area. Since crappies tend to spawn in loose groups, some fish in an area may be spawning while others are in a pre-spawn or post-spawn attitude.

In smaller bodies of water, most crappie spawning will occur over a span of a couple weeks. In larger reservoirs, however, all areas do not warm up simultaneously. Therefore, in some areas, the fish may have finished spawning, while in others they are in the process or are preparing to do so. In the event that spawning areas are limited, the fish may make use of them in "waves," with fish staging outside the spawning areas until nesting sites are available.

Eventually, the bulk of the spawning activity in an area will occur, and the females will begin filtering out of the shallows. The males remain behind, fanning the nest to oxygenate the eggs and guarding the nests from hungry predators.

# THE POST-SPAWN PERIOD

## A Time of Recuperation
### Surface Water Temperature Range: Mid-70°F
### General Fish Mood: Negative to Neutral

Post-spawn is a somewhat mysterious period, largely because of the lack of concentrated female crappies. We can generalize and assume that the water temperature will usually be in the 70°F, but water temperature is not the only factor influencing fish behavior. Since it is a recuperation period, time is also of the essence. Depending on the body of water and local weather conditions, it may take a couple weeks for the crappies to recuperate from the rigors of spawning.

The location and behavior of male and female crappies is quite different during this period. After spawning, the male protects the nest against predators and fans the nest to provide oxygen, remove waste and prevent siltation. The eggs generally take about a week to hatch, although the male usually remains and guards the fry until they disperse from the nest.

During this time, male crappies are extremely vulnerable to fishing pressure. It can be like "shooting fish in a barrel" once you locate them. However, we suggest that you do not remove the fish, or better yet, do not fish for males on the nest. Removing the male crappie from the nest simply allows the eggs to be eaten by predators like bluegills. We suggest fishing for other species, or searching for female crappies outside the spawning area.

After leaving the nest, females will filter out across the adjacent area. Small groups of fish may linger around shallow cover like fish attractors or weed clumps; in general, however, they'll slowly move toward the nearest drop-off or developing weedline area.

Drop-off fish do not school tightly at this time, although there may be a large aggregation of fish in general areas. These deeper fish may suspend anywhere from 5 to 15 feet beneath the surface and slowly roam about in search of food. While they may be adjacent to a channel edge or weedline area, they are more likely to be scattered across a wide band from just inside to just outside it.

These loose groups of crappies typically roam slowly back and forth along channel edges and drop-offs, perhaps stopping occasionally at a distinct feature like a weed clump, underwater point, or channel bend.

Eventually the male fish will leave the nest and join the females, forming larger and more distinct schools. Depending on conditions, Post-spawn slowly blends into the Pre-summer Period.

In general, once you no longer see fish on the nest, the Post-spawn Period has ended.

# THE SUMMER SEASON
## Which includes: Pre-summer, Summer Peak, Summer, and Post-summer Periods

## THE PRE-SUMMER PERIOD
### A Time of Transition
*Surface Water Temperature Range: Mid-70°F*
*General Fish Mood: Neutral to Positive*

While Post-spawn is considered a resting stage when crappies scatter and feed sporadically, a change in behavior is imminent. The crappies require nourishment, and the resumption of more regular feeding patterns indicates the beginning of Pre-summer. This usually happens once the water temperature reaches the mid-70°F.

Pre-summer is a time of emerging weedgrowth and developing food chain. The environment begins springing to life with insect hatches, clouds of newly hatched fry, and activity of all kinds. Feeding opportunities and patterns develop at a variety of depths, and some crappies may be caught on flats, along drop-offs, or suspended.

In general, however, crappies will continually shift deeper during this stage. They'll filter out across shallow flats, and perhaps use timber or weed clumps on the deeper edges. They'll roam channel edges in reservoirs or weedlines in natural lakes, and leave the backwaters in rivers for areas with a bit more current flow. Still, the variety of feeding opportunities (insects, larvae, minnows, fry) lends itself to fish feeding fairly actively all day long in a variety of areas.

Slowly, and perhaps imperceptibly, crappies begin zeroing in on the habitat they'll occupy during the upcoming Summer Period. In natural lakes and ponds, points and turns in the deep weed edge draw more and more fish. In reservoirs, deeper, timbered channel edges toward the mouths of the coves collect schools of crappies. The extreme shallows may become nearly devoid of crappies, while the drop-offs and confined open water outside them begin to host most of the fish.

Pre-summer is a time of transition when a body of water transforms from the cooler-water environment of spring to the warmer-water environment of summer. Crappies begin to regroup, and classic patterns begin to emerge.

# THE SUMMER PEAK PERIOD
## A Time of Fulfillment
*Surface Water Temperature Range: Mid to Upper 70°F*
*General Fish Mood: Neutral to Positive*

As early summer progresses, the Pre-summer Period develops into the Summer Peak. Basically, it's the time when summer patterns kick into high gear and schools of fish set up on classic summer spots. At this time, it is impossible to not feel nature's increased rhythm; nature is alive, conscious and moving.

Most of a lake's ecosystem reaches its maximum development during this cycle. All of the cool- and warm-water species will have spawned. The transformation from a cool to a warm environment is complete. Insect hatches explode, and rooted weedgrowth matures. In natural lakes, distinct weedlines develop, and crappies roam their edges like race cars circling a track. In reservoirs, crappies gorge themselves on shad along the edges of creek and river channels. Crappies congregate in heavy schools, and the action can be fast and furious. It's a great time to be on the water.

Basically, then, a combination of environmental factors stimulates Summer Peak activity: (1) The fish are hungry, aggressive and catchable; (2) Heavy schooling creates competitive group activity and fast-action fishing; and (3) The lake is alive and brimming with food. It is truly a time of fulfillment.

# THE SUMMER PERIOD
## A Time of Plenty
*Surface Water Temperature Range: Maximum Temperature of the Year*
*General Fish Mood: Neutral to Positive*

Summer arrives and with it come hordes of mosquitos and water skiers. But to anglers, summer brings the "dog days"—scorching sun and high humidity. "Dog days" is a misnomer that implies lethargy, but this is an illusion. More than at any time of year, nature is in full gear converting the sun's energy to living matter.

Abundant prey is available in the form of fry, fingerlings and insects. Lakes blossom with food, and fish often become more selective in their choice of meals. Controlling factors like thermoclines, sunlight, increased metabolism and competing species all demand order. Nature responds by regulating feeding times.

Crappies become a mystery to many folks at this time, largely because people are still seeking to catch them in the shallows. But the fish have moved. Their love of deeper cover and confined open water takes them far out of the realm of shallow-water anglers.

Summer crappies roam the edges of cover, generally somewhere in the 12- to 22-foot range; the clearer the water, the deeper they'll usually be. Active fish may be right on the edges of cover or penetrate slightly into it, while inactive or resting fish often suspend a distance outside.

This general rule applies equally well to natural lakes, strip pits, ponds and impoundments; only the types of cover vary. In natural lakes, the best summer areas are deep cabbage or coontail weed edges—particularly the points and turns in those edges—and rock piles that rise slightly above the level of deepest sunlight penetration. Here, the underwater weed forest or moss-covered rocks attract and hold the baitfish that crappies thrive on.

In most reservoirs, flooded timber, deep stumps, and manmade fish attractors take the place of natural weed cover. But the same principles apply. Crappies use the best "wood" along the edges of creek and river channels, and select a prime depth range based on water clarity. Active fish are in and around the cover, while fish suspended outside are usually either moving or not aggressively feeding.

Suspension is common—particularly during the daylight hours. During summer, crappies often shift the majority of their feeding activity on clear-water lakes toward the twilight and night hours. Fishing the edges of cover during the hours before and after dawn and dusk often brings the best summertime catches. However, some dark-water lakes and reservoirs may have crappies feeding during the bright light of midday.

In general then, summer crappie activity occurs deeper than in spring, although the fish still remain above the thermocline if one exists. They roam the confined open water zone near cover and relate to it at a suitable depth based on water clarity, although prime conditions like twilight or cloudy weather may draw them a bit shallower. Where cover is abundant, crappies have many options and you must search for them. Where cover is scarce, as in many highland reservoirs, even a single flooded tree can attract and hold fish.

Basically, summer is a time of plenty—plenty of food, plenty of cover, and plenty of distractions in terms of boat traffic, sunlight penetration, cold fronts and the like. This completes the warming trend for the year.

## THE POST-SUMMER PERIOD
### A Time of Impending Change
*Water Temperature Range: The Water Begins Cooling*
*Rapidly From its Highest Temperature Range*
*General Fish Mood: Neutral to Positive*

Post-summer, in effect, is a reversal of the Pre-summer process. It occurs at the tail end of summer when a body of water begins changing back from a warmer to a cooler environment. Hot days with dead-calm periods, followed by cool nights, are typical. The days grow shorter, sending a signal to the eco-system that things are slowing down.

Most of the food in any lake, river or reservoir has already been produced for the year, and the time of plenty slowly gives way to diminished food supplies. Weeds thin out, insect hatches dwindle, and river-water levels are generally low, often forcing the fish into deep holes or river bends.

Crappies generally respond to the changing environment by holding tighter to cover and showing less of a tendency to suspend. You might fish your way along a weedline or timberline and never spot a suspended fish with your depth finder, and yet catch a nice bunch of crappies by casting a jig up into the flooded trees or weeds. Thus, you must "fish 'em" to find 'em, rather than being able to locate them visually with your depth finder.

This tendency can work in your favor, however, by concentrating on the crappies on the deep edges of cover. This places them in easy-to-locate areas and makes them easier to catch all day long. Once you find them, you can usually catch a bunch of fish from a small area, and not have to worry about following a suspended, moving school.

Post-summer is a time of impending change when the aquatic environment begins winding down from the hectic pace and warm water of summer.

# THE FALL SEASON
## Which includes: Turnover and Fall Cold Water Periods

### THE TURNOVER PERIOD
#### A Time of Turmoil
*Water Temperature Range: Variable*
*General Fish Mood: Very Negative*

As a time of turmoil, the Turnover Period is relative. First, all bodies of water do not thermocline during summer, so they do not "turn over" as such. Most rivers are a case in point. Lakes and reservoirs, too, may or may not stratify. Usually, shallow bodies of water—which the wind periodically stirs

up—or ones with a lot of current flowing through them, are fairly immune to the stratifying process. Consequently, the fish in these waters are not subjected to as much stress as fish in waters where the transition from a warm- to a cold-water environment is an explosive event. Nonetheless, the change from a warmer- to a cooler- to a colder-water environment demands some adjustment.

The most classic (drastic) turnover situation occurs in bodies of water which set up (stratify) in distinct temperature layers during the summer. Since cold water is heavier than warm water, the warmer water stays on top and the colder water sinks and builds up on the bottom; in between lies the narrow band of rapid temperature change from warm to cold called the thermocline.

In these waters, a thermocline condition usually remains in effect throughout the tail end of the Post-summer Period. As the sun grows less direct, seasonal, hard driving, cold winds and rain begin chilling the surface temperature of the water very quickly. As the heavier (colder) water begins sinking, it comes in contact with the warmer water below. This action forces the lighter, yet warmer, deeper water back to the surface. Eventually, the narrow thermocline layer ruptures, and a mixing or "turning over" process takes place. As the wind beats the water, the mixing action continues until it thoroughly homogenizes the water to a point where the whole body of water is the same temperature. This process also reoxygenates the deep water.

Turnover usually occurs after several days to a week of the first late-summer cold snap characterized by a succession of dark, cold, wind-driven, rainy days. This is a signal that the Cold Water Period is about to arrive. At times, you can actually smell the stagnant bottom water as it rises to the surface. You might even see dead weeds, decomposed fish and other bottom debris floating on the surface or washed ashore.

The actual turnover process itself takes place once the thermocline layer ruptures. But the turmoil that takes place usually adversely affects the fish for a period of time before and after this event actually occurs. In general, once the water temperature drops to about 55°F and the water clears perceptibly, cold water fishing patterns emerge.

Fishing during the Turnover Period on bodies of water that actually thermocline is tough, to say the least. However, since all bodies of water do not turn over at the same time, it is usually best to switch to waters which have already turned over--or bodies of water which have not yet begun to—or to waters which don't thermocline.

Exactly what happens to fish, and crappies in particular, during turnover, has yet to be documented. In fact, anglers are some of the best sources of information about this turbulent time. Fish are stressed during unstable conditions, so the best fishing usually occurs in areas where the turnover effect is minimized. Shallow waters are usually best, or perhaps, the shallowest areas of a lake which are least affected by the main-lake turnover.

If you're forced to fish a lake under these conditions, seek out the best available shallow-water cover. While you probably won't get into numbers of fish, a few stragglers could save the day from being a complete waste. Areas with weeds or wood are good choices.

The Turnover Period is a time of turmoil when fish activity grinds to a halt, although action will pick up as conditions gradually stabilize.

# THE COLD WATER PERIOD (FALL)

### A Time of Stability
*Surface Water Temperature Range: 55°F and Below,*
*Down Near the Lowest Temperature of the Year*
*General Fish Mood: Neutral*

This period spans the entire time frame from the end of Turnover to freeze-up, or down to almost the coldest water of the year on bodies of water that don't freeze. It is a gradual slowing down and stabilization of the entire eco-system. The water temperature descends to nearly its lowest level of the year, and the crappie's metabolism slows in response to the cooling water.

The combination of falling water temperature and diminishing light levels appears to stimulate crappies to shift into deeper water. In many cases, the turnover has literally opened the door to deeper, formerly unusable areas which were below the thermocline during summer. Now, some of this deep, reoxygenated water becomes usable.

Early on, fall crappies may still relate to the deep edges of healthy weed beds in natural lakes. In fact, they remain in such areas if the weeds remain healthy or if there is a lack of suitable structural elements in deeper water. However, once the weeds begin to die or competition for space with other larger predators becomes too tough, the crappies will leave. In some cases, they begin suspending in confined open water again on a regular basis.

If deeper, rocky points or sunken islands are available, however, these become extremely attractive to crappies. On meso lakes, humps in the 20- to 30-foot range may draw schools of fish as fall progresses.

Reservoir crappies begin schooling very heavily in deep (15- to 30-foot) creek channel bends with cover (wood). In flatland impoundments, the best areas generally lie at the mouth of coves as fish shift away from the current of the main lake. In highland impoundments which generally lack cover, even a single tree on a steep point may attract fish.

On large rivers, crappies leave the current areas in favor of deep (5- to 15-foot) backwaters or connected natural lakes. Apparently, the fish don't want to fight current in the cold water, so they stack up in slack-water areas. Huge schools of fish are possible by late fall. In small rivers without deep back-waters, however, the fish may be forced into deeper, main-river holes, pools and channel bends as the water level drops.

In all cases, crappies usually show less tendency to suspend near the surface. They may suspend, but it'll usually be within 5 or 10 feet of the bottom. Crap-pies often lie right on the bottom, in fact, and are very hard to distinguish on your depth finder, unless they become active and start swimming around, slightly above the bottom.

The Cold Water Period is a time of stability. While everything may move at a slower pace, it is nevertheless prime time for crappie angling. Heavy school-ing concentrates fish in distinct areas, and once you locate them, you can have a field day. Slow, careful, bottom-oriented presentations are generally best to tempt the fish into biting.

# THE WINTER SEASON
## Which includes: The Winter Period

### THE WINTER PERIOD
#### A Time of Tranquility
*Surface Water Temperature Range: When a Body of Water is at its*
*Coldest for an Extended Period of Time*
*General Fish Mood: Neutral*

This time frame spans the longest period of the coldest water of the year. Ice is common in the crappie's northern range; in fact, ice may cover the waters for up to 5 months or more in some areas. In more southerly waters, ice cover may occur only briefly in coves or wind-protected bays, while the main lake doesn't freeze. In other waters, the temperature may not even drop below 40°F, depending on geological location. In any case, the Winter Period encom-

*In the North, winter offers both cold weather and hot crappie action. Here, Don Pursch, Camp Fish Senior Instructor, hefts a real braggin'-sized crappie. The magic lure? A tiny ice-fishing lure fished about 4 inches below a small Kastmaster spoon.*

passes the longest period of the coldest water of the year.

Crappies continue to feed regularly all through the Winter Period, and in the North they can provide some of the best opportunities for ice fishing. In the South, open-water angling can be equally as good, although far fewer anglers pursue them at this time of year. Apparently, trying to fish a 1/16-ounce jig, 20 feet deep, from a boat, in the face of winter wind/rain/snow/sleet is too much of a challenge (grief!) for most folks. However, fishing from a toasty-warm fish house lying on top of a stable ice platform opens up numerous possibilities for crappie success.

In general, crappies relate to the same types of areas they used during the· Fall Cold Water Period. The deep edges of cover (weeds or timber), channel edges, rocky humps, etc., all produce fish. The best areas usually lie in less than 30 feet of water and seldom as much as 40. In very small lakes, ponds, or small bays, the fish may actually move out right over the basin in the center of the deepest hole.

Similar to the Cold Water Period (Fall), most early and midwinter crappie activity will occur near the bottom. The fish may suspend within the first 5, 10 or 15 feet from the bottom, but are still somewhat bottom-related. Later in the period, as the ice cover thins or the water begins to warm, the crappies may show a tendency to suspend nearer the surface.

In all but lakes, rivers and reservoirs with the darkest water, the best winter crappie activity seems to occur around the low-light periods of dawn and dusk, or at night. Anglers night fishing from fish houses note that fish are attracted to the lighted area beneath their holes, just as night reservoir anglers see crappies drawn to the glow of the lanterns they lower below bridges. All in all, night fishing can be surprisingly productive during the winter months.

Crappies are extremely concentrated and catchable at this time *if* you fish very slowly with small lures and/or live baits, presented at their precise depth level. It may take a bit of experimentation, but it can pay dividends of big crappies and lots of 'em, when you hit the right combination.

Now let's take an indepth look at the various bodies of water that crappies live in. The following chapters on crappie waters will familiarize you with the details of lakes, rivers and reservoirs. Then, in later chapters you'll learn how to catch crappies all season long.

## Chapter 5

# INTRODUCTION TO CRAPPIE WATERS

In order to fully understand crappie behavior and location in any body of water, you must first determine the type of lake, river or reservoir you are fishing. The *IN-FISHERMAN* has classified each. The following chapters describe the classification procedure and identify those waters which can support viable crappie populations. We'll examine, in depth, the prime types of lakes, rivers and reservoirs that house crappies, and we'll explain how to identify each of them. The classification system is easy to understand and is an efficient method for analyzing waters. It's a building block in our educational process.

To begin with, it is important to understand how to categorize various bodies of water. We do this because different types of waters provide different kinds of fish habitat. Since fish location and behavior can vary between different kinds of bodies of water, you must have some idea of what options the fish have, in order to catch them consistently.

Natural lakes, for example, can be broken into "age stages" that begin at the

48

youngest stage (primarily cold-water environments), advance to the middle-aged stage (primarily cool-water environments), and finally proceed to the oldest stage (primarily warm-water environments). In between these major categories lie numerous waters in transitional stages as well. These environmental shifts affect the entire fish community, and understanding them is vital to your fishing success.

## Forces That Cause Lakes To Age

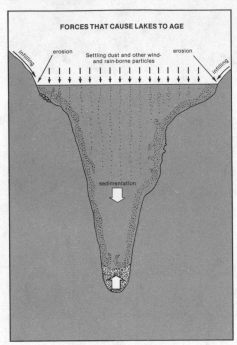

*A number of natural forces combine to "age" a lake. Two are gravity and the weathering process. As a result, you have the following: 1. INFILLING—higher surrounding terrain tends to fill in lower terrain; 2. EROSION—large material is broken down into smaller material; 3. SETTLING—rain and wind-borne particles settle to fill in areas; and 4. SEDIMENTATION—material accumulates at the bottom of bodies of water.*

Yes, there are many different lake types, and each category often has a distinct bearing on crappie population, location and behavior. This aging process is also true for rivers and reservoirs since they take on the characteristics of the surrounding terrain. In short, all waters are not alike, and you must approach them in the proper fashion in order to score consistently.

## UNDERSTANDING WATER CLARITY

Water is the common ingredient in all lakes, rivers and reservoirs. Yet, even water characteristics can vary. Think of it: Some waters are visibly clearer than others. Water clarity is a very important factor in understanding any aquatic environment. Many times it is a key to fish location and influences your choice of presentation.

Let's take a closer look at water clarity, how to determine it, and how it affects fish behavior. As a matter of fact, water clarity has several major effects on crappie location, behavior and feeding strategies.

Take your generic lake—a hole filled with water. Now add fish, weeds, plankton, siltation, and run-off from the surrounding land. You no longer have clean, clear water, but some stained, off-colored variations. Even the clearest lakes, rivers and reservoirs aren't completely clear. Add even a few impurities, and the water is bound to pick up some color which affects the clarity.

How clear is clear? Well, you have very clear, clear, medium-clear, sort-of-clear—it's pretty tough to come up with an exact way to break it down. But you really don't have to. For all intent and purposes, fish response will be basically the same in any of these conditions providing the water is clear enough for the fish to see fairly well. How clear is that? Well, if you want a yardstick to work by, lower a white lure, like a jig, into the water on a sunny day, and if you can still see it at a depth of 6 feet or more, figure the lake to be clear.

When a white lure disappears between about 2 and 6 feet, consider that to be stained; by stained water, we mean discolored. The fish can still see fairly well, and weeds can still grow, but not like in clear water. Even though fish do not have clear vision, they make up for it through their sense of hearing.

See the difference? Clear-water fish can do one heck of a job on sight alone, but when they inhabit stained water, vision begins to lose its primary importance. Stained-water fish rely more on a mixture of sight and hearing (sound/vibration) to locate their prey.

## The Three Basic Degrees of Water Color

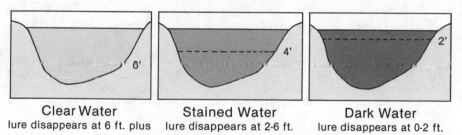

| Clear Water | Stained Water | Dark Water |
| lure disappears at 6 ft. plus | lure disappears at 2-6 ft. | lure disappears at 0-2 ft. |

*Lower a white lure into the water. Note the depth at which it disappears. This gives you a general idea as to fish behavior and the relative importance of sight vs. sound/vibration.*

Let's carry it a step further. Put your white lure into the water, and if it vanishes in less than 2 feet, it's dark water. How'd you like to be down there trying to find your way around? It's pretty tough to see anything.

In dark water, vibration becomes extremely important. Fish can't see what's out there, but they can sense vibration and sound through their lateral line and inner ear. You can't count on fish to see much unless they are really close. But if you put some kind of noisemaker down there, chances are they can find it easier.

To help you visualize clear, stained and dark water designations, simply think of each in terms of weather conditions. Consider this analogy: Clear water would be similar to a bright, sunny day when visibility for you may be miles. A hazy or light-to-medium fog condition would approximate stained water, where your visibility may vary from a few hundred yards to a couple hundred feet. Dense fog would be comparable to dark water where visibility can be limited to several yards. Since visibility is restricted, sight becomes of secondary importance. For example, fog horns warn mariners of unseen dangers.

It's much the same for fish that inhabit the diverse waters of lakes, rivers and reservoirs. In essence, visibility is limited by decreasing water clarity, and fish must use other senses to locate food as the water becomes darker.

## FISH BEHAVIOR

Most clear-water fish tend to feed at low-light hours like dawn and dusk, or during darker, overcast days. They can often be at a variety of depths, and can see your offering. Dark-water fish, conversely, often feed during the brightest hours. In fact, many dark waters experience "hot," midday bites under sunny skies. These fish are often restricted to shallow locations, and a little sound/vibration in your lure will help them find it.

Now, if clear-water fish are generally sight oriented and dark-water fish are vibration conscious, what about stained-water fish? Well, since that's an in between condition, you get in between reactions. The feeding times tend to be more spread out, fish can be on several patterns in different locations, and both sight and sound/vibration play an important part in lure selection. Slightly stained water makes "sight" lures like tiny jigs the higher percentage baits, whereas a darker stain reduces visibility and means you should use an action lure of some kind. It's an environmental balancing act, and water color is a key ingredient.

Besides affecting crappie behavior, water clarity will influence your presentation options. In clear-water conditions, you may have to use 2- or 4-pound test line for crappies; in dark water, you can often move to 12- or 20-pound

| Clear Water | Dark Water |
| --- | --- |
| Fish can see well | Fish can't see much at all |
| Fish rely heavily on sight | Fish rely heavily on sound/vibration |
| Good light penetration | Poor light penetration |
| Oxygen is deeper | Low oxygen in depths |
| Weeds grow deeper | Weeds restricted to shallows |
| Fish can be found deeper | Fish often restricted to shallows |
| Fish feed more toward morning and evening, or at night | Fish feed more toward midday |
| Fish are more active on cloudy days | Fish are more active on sunny days |
| Heavy schooling | Fish tend to be scattered |
| Fish roam | Fish are object-oriented |
| Fish chase lures | Fish don't chase lures |
| Fish are spooky | Fish are less spooky |
| Water warms or cools slowly | Water warms or cools quickly |

**STAINED-WATER FISH FALL
SOMEWHERE IN BETWEEN**

test line. By making these adjustments your catch rate will be greatly increased. Water clarity dictates these differences.

Clear-water fish rely heavily on sight and are generally less restricted in behavior due to their more varied environment. Dark-water fish rely heavily on sound and often live in a far more restricted environment, with fewer options. Stained-water fish are nearest the balancing point. Depending on the degree of water color, their behavior can swing either way.

*Clear-water fish rely heavily on sight and can see well. The rule-of-thumb when fishing it is light line and small lures. Even if you look closely you'll barely see the 2-pound test line, split shot and tiny jig.*

## PERMANENT VS. TEMPORARY WATER CLARITY

So far, we've discussed clear-, stained- and dark-water conditions. They're more or less "permanent" or "typical" conditions caused by the local environment (surrounding soil, run-off, wind erosion, etc.). But what happens when it rains unusually long or hard, or when a heavy wind tears up a shoreline and washes all sorts of foreign material into a lake? Or how about when an algae bloom temporarily fills the water with suspended particles? Shouldn't that have a categorization all its own?

Normally clear water becomes dirty or turbid when rain or wind introduces outside substances into the lake. This is especially common in rivers and reservoirs. It might be a temporary condition, which changes the environment or a portion of the environment for a period of time. In this instance, normally clear water *temporarily* behaves like stained water, and the fish must respond by relying more on their ability to detect sound/vibration. Similarly, normally stained water temporarily takes on the characteristics of dark water under these conditions. Sight is reduced, and fish must rely more heavily on sound than they normally would. In order to catch fish, you'd use the same tactics that you'd normally rely on when fishing lakes with characteristically dark or turbid waters.

| Permanent Conditions | Temporary Conditions |
|:---:|:---:|
| Clear | Normal |
| Stained | Dirty |
| Dark | Muddy |

## SUMMARY

As you can probably begin to see, many factors come into play when you evaluate the different environments that fish live in. The better you understand the options that fish have, the more effective you'll be at catching them. Water clarity is one such critical factor affecting these options. Be sure to keep it in mind as the following chapters describe the different classifications of lakes, rivers and reservoirs. Once you get a "feel" for them, you'll be able to predict crappie location and behavior wherever you travel.

## Chapter 6

# NATURAL LAKES

Every body of water has its own unique personality, a personality characterized primarily by its overall physical make-up. No two lakes are exactly alike. The lake's predator/prey relationships, amounts and types of aquatic vegetation, and numerous other structural considerations determine its classification. Very broadly, lakes are classified into three geological age groups: oligotrophic (young), mesotrophic (middle-aged), and eutrophic (old).

No matter where your favorite lake is situated, that body of water is constantly *changing*. In some remote areas, the change can be so slight that it passes unnoticed and might take a century or more to show a visible change. In other waters, this change might occur in 10, 5, or even fewer years.

This is the natural aging process (eutrophication) that all lakes pass through. In essence, according to water quality standards, a lake is getting older not so much in time as in *condition*. The initial stages of change may take thousands of years, but the final ones may happen quickly—especially with the addition of manmade causes. Throughout this process, the total environment of a lake—its structural condition, food chains, vegetation levels and dominant fish species—changes considerably. Man-caused eutrophication (aging) is due to expanding human population and, consequently, waste product disposal.

These changes in lakes have occurred so quickly that man has accomplished in a generation what nature would have taken hundreds or even thousands of years to do.

So, we classify natural lakes according to their environmental condition, not their chronological age. A lake is basically either young, middle-aged or old. Since some lakes are in between these broad types and almost defy classification, our classifications should not be taken as absolute. Instead, each category is meant to be a convenient point of reference—a definition we can start to learn from.

As lakes "age," their character changes. Generally speaking, geologically "young" lakes are deep and clear; older lakes are shallow and murky.

The natural order is such that on one end of the aging scale we find young lakes (oxygen-rich, deep water) which can support fish like lake trout and whitefish. At the other end, we find old lakes (weed-choked, oxygen-poor water) which can only support fish such as carp and bullheads.

A lake trout cannot live in a shallow, murky, weedy, low-oxygen, warmwater lake of the midwestern prairies; and carp have a tough time making it in the rocky, cold-water, weedless environment of a Canadian shield lake. Between these two extremes fall lakes of all types—each more or less hospitable to certain species of fish. We categorize natural lakes in the following nine phases.

# THE AGING PROCESS

THE STABLE, YOUNG, INFERTILE,
COLD-WATER ENVIRONMENT PHASES
    1. Early stage oligotrophic
    2. Mid-stage oligotrophic

THE TRANSITION FROM COLD- TO
COOL-WATER ENVIRONMENT PHASES
    3. Late stage oligotrophic
    4. Early stage mesotrophic

THE STABLE, MIDDLE-AGED, MODERATELY FERTILE,
COOL-WATER ENVIRONMENT PHASE
    5. Mid-stage mesotrophic

THE TRANSITION FROM COOL- TO
WARM-WATER ENVIRONMENT PHASES
    6. Late stage mesotrophic
    7. Early stage eutrophic

THE STABLE, OLD, FERTILE,
WARM-WATER ENVIRONMENT PHASE
    8. Mid-stage eutrophic

THE TRANSITION FROM WARM- TO
VERY WARM-WATER ENVIRONMENT PHASE
    9. Late stage eutrophic

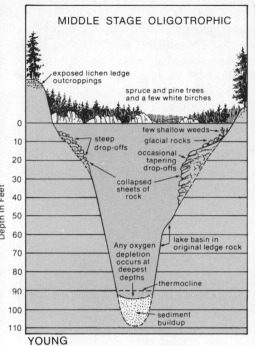

### MIDDLE STAGE OLIGOTROPHIC

exposed lichen ledge outcroppings

spruce and pine trees and a few white birches

few shallow weeds
glacial rocks

steep drop-offs

occasional tapering drop-offs

collapsed sheets of rock

Any oxygen depletion occurs at deepest depths

lake basin in original ledge rock

thermocline

sediment buildup

Depth In Feet

YOUNG

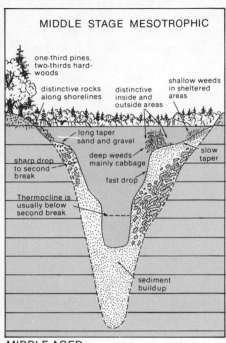

### MIDDLE STAGE MESOTROPHIC

one-third pines, two-thirds hardwoods

distinctive rocks along shorelines

distinctive inside and outside areas

shallow weeds in sheltered areas

long taper sand and gravel

deep weeds mainly cabbage

slow taper

sharp drop to second break

fast drop

Thermocline is usually below second break.

sediment buildup

MIDDLE-AGED

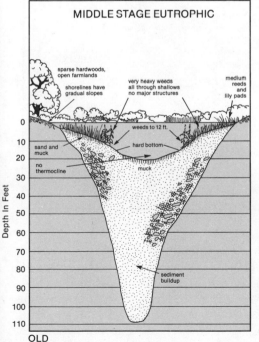

### MIDDLE STAGE EUTROPHIC

sparse hardwoods, open farmlands

very heavy weeds all through shallows no major structures

medium reeds and lily pads

shorelines have gradual slopes

weeds to 12 ft.

hard bottom

sand and muck

no thermocline

muck

sediment buildup

Depth In Feet

OLD

The aging process depicted in the accompanying illustrations shows the basic changes of the lake basin, depths and weedgrowth.

When you analyze a particular lake, remember that these categories are simply points of reference to work from. However, as you become familiar with the system, you will be able to more easily recognize a lake as being early stage eutrophic—instead of late stage mesotrophic, etc.

The youngest type of lakes—oligotrophic—typically have rock basins and are found almost exclusively in the upper portions of the North American continent. They usually have steep, sharp drop-offs, few weeds, pine-studded shorelines and a fish population composed chiefly of cold-water fish like lake trout and members of the whitefish family. The nutrient level of the water is usually low and oxygen is available in deep water at all times. Thus, the lake is termed infertile. Normally, "oli" lakes support low gamefish populations; a few pounds of gamefish per acre is common.

As this type of lake ages, the shorelines become less gorge-like and the drop-offs less abrupt and steep. Big boulders turn to smaller rock, and more sand and gravel becomes apparent. Weedgrowth develops. The trees that bound the lake also tend to change. Since the surrounding terrain changes, the water quality takes on a new character (more nutrients). These are the first signs of the transitory process between the oligotrophic and mesotrophic categories.

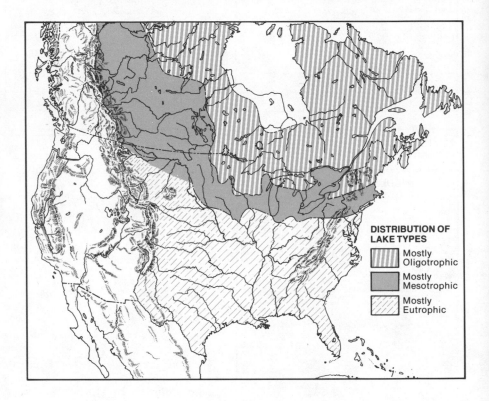

**DISTRIBUTION OF LAKE TYPES**

Mostly Oligotrophic

Mostly Mesotrophic

Mostly Eutrophic

Little by little, the lake changes and eventually develops characteristics typical of a middle-aged (mesotrophic) lake. When a lake reaches its mid-mesotrophic stage, much of the exposed rock, except right along the shoreline, is gone. Sand and some gravel now prevail in the lake's basin. The shoreline tapers become more gradual, more weeds appear in the shallows, and the trees that surround the lake begin changing from evergreens to hardwoods. A distinct thermocline and oxycline usually form. The lake is moderately fertile and is capable of producing many pounds of gamefish per acre.

By the time the next transition (mesotrophic to eutrophic) stage occurs, a lake, by geological aging standards, is getting old. First, it is becoming shallower. Sand begins turning to muck or clay in certain sections, and the erosion process results in less extensive shoreline tapers than in the mid-meso classification. Secondary drop-offs in deep water are obliterated or less defined.

Marshy areas usually dot certain adjacent sections. Hardwood trees and flat shorelines, rather than steep cliffs or high hills, rim the lakeshore. The lake is changing from a cool- to a warm-water environment.

When a lake shifts into its mid-eutrophic stage, it becomes a true warm-water environment. In its oligotrophic stage this body of water was a cold-water environment; in its "meso" stage, a cool-water environment; and now in its eutrophic stage, a warm-water environment.

By geological standards, this lake is now quite old. It has become very shallow, and the erosion process is near completion. Farmlands usually surround these waters. Thermoclines generally don't develop or last a long time. Shallow weedgrowth is thick, and sandy areas become quite soft. Water color becomes darker, so weeds only grow in shallow water, and the shoreline just sort of blends into the basin of the lake. Such lakes are often called "dishpan lakes" due to their overall depth and shape. Typically, these old lakes are very fertile and have high fish populations, although a significant percentage may be rough fish.

In a nutshell, this is the aging process all natural lakes go through. Study the accompanying drawings carefully, so you understand the different types of natural lakes. Most importantly, as you learn to recognize lake types, you'll learn what to expect in terms of crappie size and probable population density.

## NATURAL LAKE TYPES

| OLIGOTROPHIC | | | MESOTROPHIC | | | EUTROPHIC | | |
|---|---|---|---|---|---|---|---|---|
| EARLY | MIDDLE | LATE | EARLY | MIDDLE | LATE | EARLY | MIDDLE | LATE |
| CONDITIONS OF ENVIRONMENT | | | | | | | | |
| COLD WATER | | TRANSITION STAGES | | COOL WATER | | TRANSITION STAGES | | WARM WATER |

LAKE TROUT

GAR
BOWFIN
BULLHEAD

WALLEYE

LARGEMOUTH BASS

CRAPPIE

*The accompanying chart shows which species of fish will probably be present as a natural lake ages. Oligotrophic lakes are the youngest and eutrophic lakes the oldest, geologically. In between these two extremes lie mesotrophic lakes.*

*Crappies appear in late "oli" lakes. In fact, there are many lakes in southern Ontario that have viable populations of good-sized crappies. However, the prime, crappie waters for slab-sized fish are mid- to late-"meso" lakes which offer "confined open-water" environments.*

*By the time a lake reaches the mid-eutrophic stage, crappie populations may be high, but the average size fish is usually small. Apparently, inter- and intra-species competition for food and habitat takes its toll.*

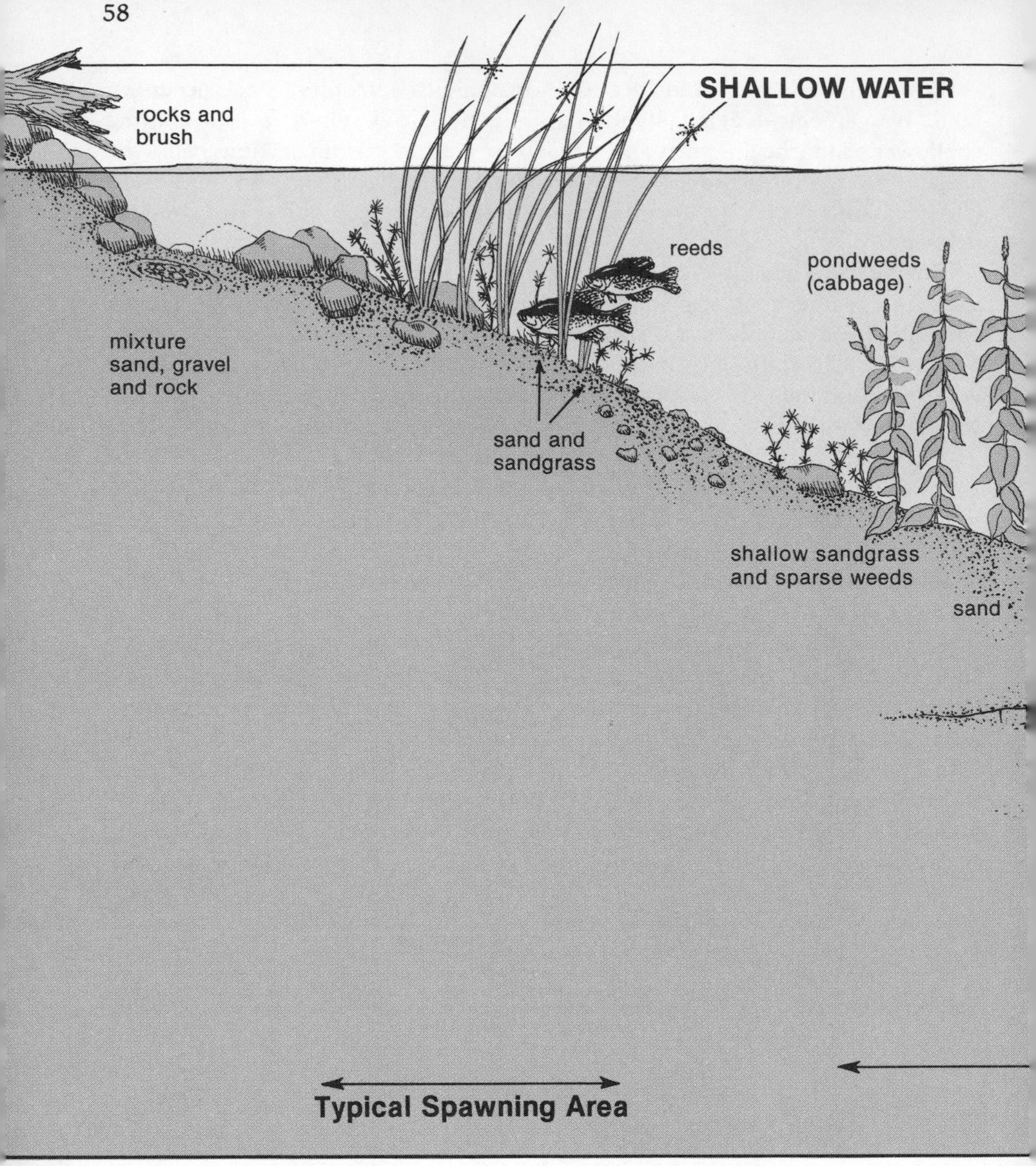

rocks and
brush

**SHALLOW WATER**

reeds

pondweeds
(cabbage)

mixture
sand, gravel
and rock

sand and
sandgrass

shallow sandgrass
and sparse weeds

sand

**Typical Spawning Area**

The cross-section on these two pages shows the various structural elements that could be found in many—but not all—natural lakes. The depths are relative. The edge of the weedline, for example, could occur at 8 feet or 18 feet, depending on water clarity. Some lakes might have extensive weedgrowth on the flats, and others very little. Reeds might be present or not. Some lakes have only one breakline or drop-off; others may have two. The shallow water, food shelf might be extensive or very short. There might be exposed rock or a limestone ridge, or there might be none. It all depends on the LAKE CLASSIFICATION TYPE.

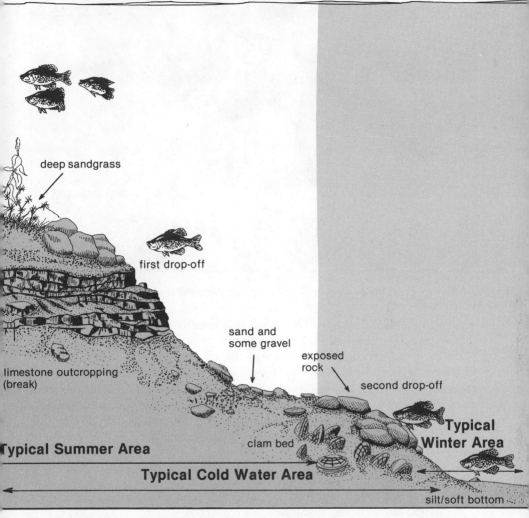

CONFINED
OPEN-WATER ZONE

DROP-OFF AREA

BASIN

deep sandgrass

first drop-off

sand and
some gravel

exposed
rock

second drop-off

limestone outcropping
(break)

clam bed

Typical Summer Area

Typical
Winter Area

Typical Cold Water Area

silt/soft bottom

Nevertheless, the terminology holds. The shoreline is always the shoreline. The edge of the weeds is always a point of reference. Familiarize yourself with these terms. They will be used constantly.

Crappies use various portions of a natural lake on a seasonal basis. Note that during summer the crappies make heavy use of the confined, open-water area and often suspend within this zone at various depths. The key to catching summer crappies is usually finding schools of suspended crappies just outside structural elements and presenting a lure at the proper depth to entice a strike.

*Many natural lakes produce jumbo crappies. This young fella caught this 1-3/4-pound fish from a deep reed bed in spring. Note the dark spawning color pattern of this male fish.*

In the final analysis, this will help you fish smarter—not harder!

As a lake ages, the distribution of the various gamefish species also changes. "Oli" lakes chiefly support cold-water fish species like trout and whitefish. However, as the lake becomes more fertile and moves toward the mesotrophic stage, the cold-water fish begin to disappear. Walleyes often become the dominant species while crappies and bass begin to establish populations. The combination of weedgrowth, prey species and structural elements in these middle-aged lakes make them very conducive to supporting a variety of cool- and warm-water fish.

In fertile lakes, plants will root and form shallow weedbeds. Most oligotrophic lakes, however, do not have the proper conditions for such weedbeds. Instead, the plant life is free-floating and suspends at levels where species such as whitefish can graze on them and still remain within range of the trout. In these lakes, plant life is more abundant in deeper water than in the shallows.

In eutrophic (very fertile) lakes, shallow, rooted plant life provides both food and cover for all fish. Walleyes, crappies and other "semi open-water" fish begin to disappear, and the species associated with weeds, such as bluegills and largemouths, become dominant. The plant and animal life that sustained an open-water fishery in a mesotrophic lake diminishes sharply. This change continues until the lake ultimately degenerates to a point where only rough fish can survive.

Besides a lake's classification (which may not always fit into a neat little pigeonhole), another key element to understanding crappies is the available structural conditions. Some of the key items are: bottom configuration, bottom content, vegetation and water characteristics. In other words, what's the shape of the lake and how deep is it? What's the bottom composition—sand, gravel, rock or muck? What types of weeds are present and how deep is the weedline? What is the water clarity? Does the lake thermocline? All these features are important and play a significant role in determining where the crappies can be.

*Youngsters and crappies go together like peanut butter and jelly. Several kids caught this nice mess of fish from shore. They used a simple cane pole, small bobber and minnow to get'em.*

Obviously, no two lakes are the same; however, the structural conditions on many are similar. This similarity allows the *comparison* of lakes and aids in generalizing crappie location within a lake. Review the elements of structure and familiarize yourself with the terminology, because a thorough understanding of the principles will help you visualize what's beneath the surface of a lake.

Our information on crappie behavior, coupled with an understanding of a lake's structural conditions, are two of the key ingredients for success.

# SUMMARY

Many lakes contain crappies, yet very few of them have the capacity to produce honest, 2-pound-plus fish. So, if you're after big slabs, be certain to select a lake that contains the size fish you're looking for.

Large, deep, clear lakes with plenty of open water generally grow the largest crappies. Crappies, by their basic nature, are a fish that often suspends in open water adjacent to some form of cover, and these lakes usually give the fish plenty of prime habitat. Therefore, when you're looking for crappies, figure on the best trophy lakes to be at least 500 acres or more in size.

Based on our *IN-FISHERMAN lake classification system, such lakes are* termed mesotrophic, or middle-aged. They're not only large, but are generally quite fertile as well. These lakes support an abundance of baitfish, insects and other aquatic life that crappies feed on. And, their varied structural make-up—scattered rock piles, sunken islands, weed-rimmed drop-offs, etc.—provides prime environments for both predator and prey. All in all, middle-aged lakes offer the best combination of elements for producing trophy crappies.

If you examine smaller, shallower (older) bodies of water, trophy crappies become noticeably rare. After all, such lakes generally have a restricted, open-water environment. Weeds are more prevalent, often choking the shallows. The entire life cycle of the crappies might, therefore, take place *within* the weedgrowth. Since crappies are not particularly suited to that type of environment, their growth predictably suffers. Such lakes are generally more conducive to largemouth bass or bluegills, and the crappies in these waters seldom approach trophy size.

In summary, this information, coupled with a few simple questions to the proper individuals (fisheries personnel, other anglers or bait shop owners), is the basis for evaluating a lake's potential. Of course, there's no better way to check out a lake than to fish it; however, this is a good procedure for narrowing down several possible lakes to a couple logical choices.

## Chapter 7

# RIVERS

Rivers come in many shapes, lengths and widths, and provide habitat for numerous species of fish. There are clear mountain rivers, silt-laden agricultural rivers, brackish tidal rivers, stained swamp rivers and many more. All are different in character and, therefore, provide varying aquatic environments for fish. While many rivers can support crappies, some rivers provide a better environment than others. In fact, different stretches of the same river can have contrasting personalities and, consequently, different fish species.

Similar to lakes and reservoirs, rivers age geologically. *Young, middle-aged* and *old* are terms used to describe a river's age. For example, a young, clear, cold-water river plunges downhill, flowing over and cutting through solid rock; here, trout and grayling could thrive. As a river matures, it becomes increasingly fertile, flows more slowly and begins to meander. In this mature section, the cool-water environment favors species of fish like walleyes and smallmouth bass. Finally, in old age, a river winds through a flood plain where the warm-water environment supports largemouth bass, catfish and rough fish. Each aging stage tends to favor specific species of cold-, cool- or warm-water fish.

Where do crappies fit in? Actually, crappies could exist in isolated stretches of most rivers that provide minimal environmental requirements. Yet, while they could "hack it" in a marginal situation, they'll rarely flourish. Oddswise, middle-aged and old rivers (or stretches) provide large areas of suitable crappie habitat with abundant prey. Depending on location, such rivers can be either slightly cool- or warm-water environments. Typically, these rivers offer a diversity of habitat that supports healthy fish populations.

Middle-aged and old rivers are slow-flowing, shallow rivers with broadened flood plains. The wide flood plains can create huge, complex, backwater areas with abundant crappie habitat. Flooded backwaters, oxbow lakes, and connecting lakes can be excellent crappie areas. Flooded brush, stumps and timber are common crappie attractors in river backwaters.

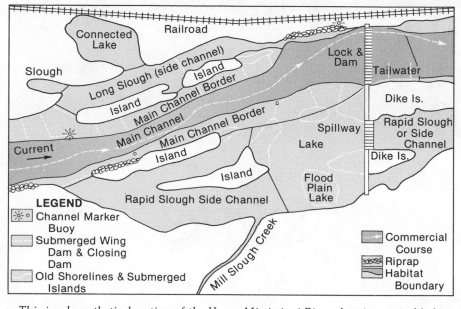

*This is a hypothetical section of the Upper Mississippi River showing typical habitat areas. High and low water dictates the movement of fish from backwaters to the main channel. Side channels have reduced current while attached lakes provide very little current.*

In addition, a maze of channels often provides a connection to other prime spots. Since backwaters can be a mile or more from the main channel, they don't function like a river. Current flow is usually negligible, and flooding is often controlled by a dam. Actually, these backwaters function more like a reservoir than a river. In fact, many are reservoirs and should be approached as such.

In summary, the combination of moderately high fertility, reduced current, abundant prey and ideal habitat create a crappie paradise. Backwaters of the Mississippi, Ohio, Tennessee and St. Lawrence Rivers are all prime examples of river areas that offer hot, crappie action—both in numbers and size.

## Oxbow and Flood Plain Lakes

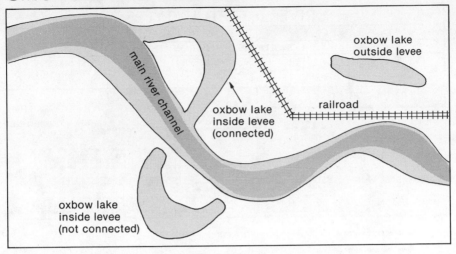

*In the lower sections of the Mississippi River, oxbow lakes are very important crappie waters. Some oxbows are connected to the main river; some are not. A few lie outside the levee system while others lie inside the levees included in the flood plain. Oxbows connected to the river channel and lying within the levee systems normally provide the best crappie fishing.*

# RIVER CLASSIFICATION

Since there are variations in the aging progression along the sections of a stream, as well as some overlap between the abundance and presence of the cold-, cool- and warm-water fish species, the only way to view a stream is by stretches. In this sense, a particular stretch can be young, old, or somewhere in between in terms of geological makeup.

For instance, a stream might be quite shallow, have a slow taper for several miles, and possess a number of backwater areas with soft bottom and aquatic weedgrowth. Here, crappies and largemouth bass might find adequate habitat. But all of a sudden, this same stream might break into a sharp gradient as it shoots through a rocky, cliff-like area, creating a rapids and finally pouring into a boulder-based pool. This younger stretch, although further downstream, could house smallmouth bass and possibly stocked rainbow trout.

Different stretches of the same stream can have different personalities and different fish species. Rarely is a stream the same from beginning to end, because few regions are geographically consistent.

Because of these limitless variations, we devised the following method of classifying streams. With these categories, we can identify and recognize most river stretches found in North America. Of course, there will be exceptions; those parts in transition between types are much like a natural lake that has eutrophic bays while the main body of the lake is mesotrophic in character.

These classes are best viewed as guidelines to better understanding the rivers you fish and the quantity and types of predominant fish you can expect to find in them.

# Distribution of Species by River Age Category

| RIVER (STRETCH) TYPES | | | | | | |
|---|---|---|---|---|---|---|
| VERY YOUNG | YOUNG | ADULT | MATURE | MIDDLE-AGED | OLD | VERY OLD |
| CONDITIONS OF ENVIRONMENT | | | | | | |
| BEST SUITED FOR COLD-WATER SPECIES | TRANSITION STAGES | BEST SUITED FOR COOL WATER SPECIES | | TRANSITION STAGES | BEST SUITED FOR WARM-WATER SPECIES | |

VARIOUS TROUT
WALLEYE
SAUGER
CRAPPIES
SMALLMOUTH BASS
LARGEMOUTH BASS

Key: ▬▬▬▬ strongest populations
▬ ▬ ▬ ▬ weaker populations

This chart shows the species present in each river category. Notice how a particular fish's numbers peak and then gradually fade out as the river evolves. Note that each aging stage tends to favor certain varieties of cold-, cool-, or warm-water species.

Young, picturesque trout streams found in the mountains are usually unpolluted and unaffected by the hands of man. Despite their beauty, these streams are quite infertile since they run over rock beds and gain few nutrients from the land. For this reason, very young and young streams cannot support large fish populations. This relatively sterile environment limits them to a few types of fish.

Cold-water species such as trout disappear in the adult stage. In these sections with less gradient and a warm climate, the water flows slower and warms to a higher temperature where trout cannot survive. The environment now favors cool-water fish like smallmouth bass. In the mature stage, other cool-water fish like walleyes, saugers, northern pike and muskies enter the picture. Then, as a river gets older, the cool-water species begin to fade. Warm-water fish like largemouth bass and catfish become dominant, and rough fish like carp become common.

| | | |
|---|---|---|
| 1. | VERY YOUNG | —Brook trout and/or grayling |
| 2. | YOUNG | —Stocked trout and pike |
| 3. | ADULT | —Appearance of cool-water fish |
| 4. | MATURE | —Good populations of smallmouths and some crappies |
| 5. | MIDDLE-AGED | —Crappies, walleyes and saugers |
| 6. | OLD | —Crappies and largemouth bass |
| 7. | VERY OLD | —Mostly rough fish and a few crappies |
| 8. | TIDAL | —Backwaters of the ocean. Sometimes crappies. |

Within this context, we can isolate stretches which best support crappies. These conditions usually occur in river stretches we term Mature, Middle-Aged, and to some degree, Old.

The accompanying charts describe the generalized makeup of the key river types.

| | MATURE | MIDDLE-AGED | OLD |
|---|---|---|---|
| **SHAPE OF CROSS-SECTION** | Flood Plain | Broadened Flood Plain — Channel Bottom is Completely Smooth — Sand and Gravel Deposits | Bluffs may Form — Natural Levees — Sand and Mud Deposits |
| **SOURCE AND GEOGRAPHICAL DRAINAGE AREA** | This stretch may either emerge from or cut through a pastoral landscape, usually composed of sandstone and other soil types.<br><br>The drainage area can include farmland as well as major urban and industrial areas, which can have a major impact on pollution levels.<br><br>The number of tributaries start to decrease at this stage. | This stage often has a farmland origin.<br><br>The drainage area is very large and fertile due to adjacent agricultural areas.<br><br>Tributaries consist mainly of adult rivers. | Of pastoral origin and with a very large drainage area, siltation is common and considerable and must be controlled by dredging. A very broad, expansive flood plain has developed along with natural levees. This bottomland is highly prized farm acreage.<br><br>There are a very few tributaries. |
| **WATER CLARITY** | The water will be semi-clear to semi-murky. During high water periods, it will be very turbid, especially around agricultural areas, usually taking four to five days to clear up after a rain. Slower-running water will make the temperature higher.<br><br>Aging will accelerate because of agricultural and industrial pollutants. | The water is murky to quite turbid most of the time due to the suspended mineral and soil particles and increased organic nutrients.<br><br>Turbidity is a constant factor because of the large size of the watershed, a situation that makes angling difficult.<br><br>Where this river broadens into a large lake, settling will occur and water quality will temporarily improve. | There is constant turbidity. Quality improves slightly where tributaries enter. |
| **PROBABLE SPECIES PRESENT** | Walleyes, sauger, some smallmouths, northern pike, muskies, catfish, white bass, sturgeon, a few largemouths, perch, crappies, carp, suckers, buffalo, and rock bass. | Northerns, saugers, walleyes, some smallmouths, crappies, a few muskies, silver bass, good largemouths and catfish. | Largemouths, catfish, crappies, some northern pike if the temperature remains low.<br><br>The water temperature will determine available species. |

| | MATURE | MIDDLE-AGED | OLD |
|---|---|---|---|
| **TYPICAL ILLUSTRATIONS** | These stretches can be found in major drainage areas in any part of the country.<br><br>For example, large stretches of the Mississippi and the lower Allegheny River in Pennsylvania. | The St. Lawrence River bordering the U.S. and Canada has middle-aged stretches, as does the Detroit River, and, of course, a good part of the Mississippi and Ohio Rivers. | Large rivers like the lower stretches of the Mississippi, the Ohio, and the Arkansas Rivers are examples. |
| **KEY I.D. FEATURE** | The ability to produce quantities of preferred game species such as walleyes, smallmouths, sauger, crappies, and northern pike.<br><br>Deep pools provide refuge, and backwaters with cover (hooded brush) provide crappie spawning grounds.<br><br>A mature stream can produce good populations of several kinds of gamefish; sandy, rock sections with fast water will hold smallmouths while the deeper, slower sections or pools will contain walleyes. | The presence of naturally reproducing walleyes and saugers mixed with fair levels of largemouth bass, plus some crappies, smallmouths, and northern pike.<br><br>There is a diversity of habitat for just about any kind of fish.<br><br>This is the last stage for quantities of naturally reproducing cool-water fish like smallmouths. Crappies become more abundant. | The absence of cool-water fish, especially the disappearance of natural walleyes.<br><br>Oxbows are present. |
| **GRADIENT AND DEPTH** | Gradient: 1.5- to 2-foot drop per mile.<br><br>Depth: Depth will vary. Some stretches will be four to five feet deep, while deeper holes can be fifteen to twenty feet. There is a lot of eight- to ten-foot water. | Gradient: One- to 1.5-foot drop per mile.<br><br>Depth: Depth will vary from shallow, one foot deep, weedy backwater pockets to forty-foot pools. Runs to twelve feet are common. Under dams, gouges of fifty feet can occur. | Gradient: very slow, one to .5 foot drop per mile.<br><br>Depth: depths can be quite substantial, running to twenty feet or more. Sixty-foot holes are not uncommon.<br><br>Depth is a function of the amount of siltation and dredging activity. Most of these rivers are dredged.<br><br>Gamefish location is often limited to banks and backwater areas. |

| | MATURE | MIDDLE-AGED | OLD |
|---|---|---|---|
| **GEOGRAPHICAL MAKE-UP AND BOTTOM CONTENT** | The main channel is composed mostly of sand. Siltation is now a significant factor; wing dams are sometimes constructed to control this.<br><br>There are some rock outcroppings.<br><br>Aquatic growth is common, along with a higher nutrient level. | Flows mostly through soft sedimentary rock and sandy subsoils.<br><br>Sand is the dominant riverbed material.<br><br>Time and erosion have pulverized the rocks and gravel.<br><br>There will be a few rock outcrops along the banks of the river.<br><br>This stage will exhibit well developed flood plains; flooding is common. | The stream bed flows over gravel and sandy areas (its own deposits). A hardwood forest occupies the flood plain. Sand mixed with mud forms the bottom. Rock and gravel are rare. |
| **COMMON TRAITS** | Rapids nonexistent; at best, a few shallow "riffles" will occur.<br><br>Mature rivers can and do overflow their banks. They will begin to meander and develop flood plains.<br><br>On this river stage, dams actually create miniature impoundments. Although they are called "pools," they function much like reservoirs.<br><br>At certain times of the year, usually spring or fall, several species could be stacked up against the dam!<br><br>The stream is an *IN-FISHERMAN* paradise and is the first stage that produces multiple quantities of preferred gamefish. | This stretch usually flows by river towns and metropolitan areas where pollution can be a severe problem. It is at this stage that a river really starts to show the buildup of nutrients, erosion, and pollution.<br><br>Except for trout and salmon, just about any type of fish can survive. This stream will offer the most pounds of gamefish per acre, if it is unpolluted.<br><br>Flood plains can create backwater sloughs or flat, high, fertile fields.<br><br>A dredged, midship channel is usually maintained for barges, and dams with locks are common. | This stretch has often been straightened, leaving oxbow lakes connected or not connected to the main channel. Some oxbows are located within levees, while others lie outside. Flood plains create backwater sloughs and side channels. |

*Do rivers contain crappies? You betcha, and here's the proof. Flooded backwater areas provide prime crappie habitat in many rivers.*

## Chapter 8

# RESERVOIRS

What are some of the best crappie waters for both size and numbers of fish? Reservoirs! Yes, many impoundments provide world-class, crappie fishing action on a year-'round basis. The crappie is the undisputed king of many reservoirs.

Most anglers have heard of the fantastic crappie fishery on some southern impoundments. Many reservoirs offer mind-boggling fishing action for eatin'-sized and trophy crappies, all season long. In fact, their reputation for producing crappies is almost legendary. Each year, folks catch millions of tasty, 1/2- to 1-pound fish from reservoirs in many diverse areas of North America. Some impoundments also turn out a fair share of 2-, 3-, and occasionally even 4-pound-plus fish! And, the current world record white crappie which weighed 5 lbs. 3 oz. was caught from Enid Dam Reservoir, Mississippi, in 1957.

Obviously, the reservoir environment provides that special combination of ingredients which produces crappies, and lots of them. Let's take a closer look at reservoirs and pinpoint common denominators that may affect the growth and survival of crappies in impoundments.

A reservoir is an impounded body of water that is held back by a dam. The artificially impounded water floods the natural landscape such as marshes, plains, hills, mountains, plateaus or canyons. This provides a clue to reservoir classification.

The geographic area a reservoir is situated in has a direct bearing on the resulting fishery. In general, reservoirs in the North provide a cooler-water environment than those in the South. Yet, crappies exist in each area. For instance, a Wisconsin, lowland reservoir (flowage) can offer some good walleye fishing plus overlooked crappie angling. Similarly, a lowland impoundment in Florida may provide fishing for both lunker bass and slab crappies.

Taking a cross-section of North America, you'd see that some areas might be low and sort of swampy or marshy, or rather flat like an old flood-plain region. In other places, the terrain is hilly. Still others have mountains and highland ridges rising up to form foothills. These are usually low mountain ranges like the Boston or Ouachita ranges in Arkansas, the Appalachian chain in the East, the Cumberland highlands of Kentucky and Tennessee, or the low coastal ranges of the West Coast.

These changes in terrain provide a clear-cut basis to classify waters, since reservoirs lying within each of these landforms all have the same basic configuration. In other words, they have a similar cross-section and shape. For example, all canyon reservoirs are long and snake-like with towering, sharp, nearly vertical walls. On the other hand, waters impounded in flood plains tend to be wide with expanses of shallow flats.

## KEYS TO IMPOUNDMENT CLASSIFICATION

The *IN-FISHERMAN*, impoundment classification system identifies six

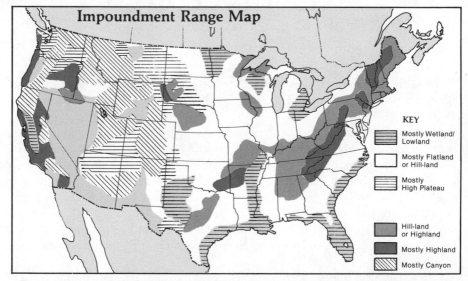

*Reservoirs constructed in similar landforms—even if they're in different parts of the country—are enough alike that we can fit them, for identification purposes, into six basic groups. These groups are: canyon, highland, plateau, hill-land, flatland, and wetland/lowland.*

broad categories: canyon, plateau, highland, hill-land, flatland, and low-land/wetland. These classes are based on regional and geological aspects of North America's various landforms. Very simply, natural and manmade characteristics place an impoundment into one class or another. We'll discuss mainly reservoirs of more than 1000 acres, because many smaller ones defy orderly classification.

The basic shape of an impoundment is the major factor in determining its overall classification. By simply studying a topographical map of an impoundment, you'll be able to fit it into its broad classification slot. While there are some discrepancies, most times the classification is correct.

The broad classification of a reservoir's individual personality is also important. This personality is unique and depends on local factors such as bottom content, water characteristics, vegetation types, availability of prey, and fish species present. All of these may vary with the location of the impoundment.

A few of the most important facets of a reservoir's personality are: (1) annual water level fluctuation, (2) water clarity, (3) fertility, (4) temperature, and (5) effects of wind. All of these affect the personality of a reservoir which directly affects the resulting crappie fishery. By understanding both the reservoir's classification *and* its personality, you'll gain insight into the location and behavior of crappies.

## PRIME RESERVOIRS

Prime crappie reservoirs usually fall into the flatland or hill-land classification. Barkley Lake, KY/TN; and Santee-Cooper, SC; are classic flatland examples and display the following features: stained water; shad forage; minimal water level fluctuations; shallow cuts and coves containing weeds, brush or timber; and a large, moderately shallow, main-lake area. In other words, they have lots of good, crappie habitat. Obviously, there are many other features to consider, and many other reservoirs have crappies in both size and numbers. However, flatland impoundments seem to be ideal and often provide the magic combination of ingredients to grow big crappies.

Hill-land reservoirs can also provide an excellent crappie environment—especially the upstream sections which are similar to a flatland reservoir. Toledo Bend on the Texas/Louisiana border is a prime example. Highland or plateau reservoirs can also offer a quality fishery in sections of the impoundment that contain hill-land/flatland characteristics. However, the greater depth and scarcity of cover in these reservoirs often preclude their being prime crappie waters.

Canyon reservoirs are normally a tough environment for panfish; however, a limited fishery may exist in some. Lowland/wetland impoundments, meanwhile, can offer good fishing, depending on the region and available habitat. In general, the crappies run small if the reservoir is weed-choked. If there are open-water areas and a modest amount of cover, the fish can grow to decent size.

# TYPICAL IMPOUNDMENT FEATURES

The accompanying illustrations show various impoundment features. There are so many regional variations, that we were forced to adopt or coin words or phrases to describe them. For example, we dropped the word "bay" and became more specific by using the terms "cove" or "cut." The accompanying example is not meant to depict any specific type of impoundment. It is simply a composite. Note that it is divided into three sections.

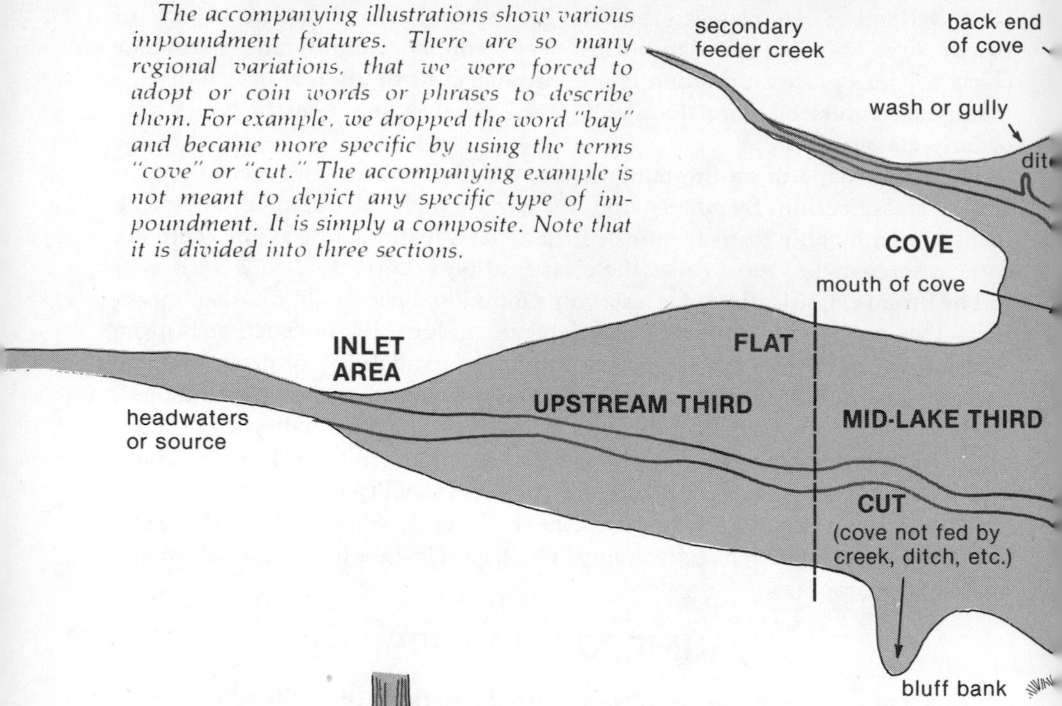

secondary feeder creek

back end of cove

wash or gully

dit

**COVE**

mouth of cove

**FLAT**

**INLET AREA**

**UPSTREAM THIRD**

**MID-LAKE THIRD**

headwaters or source

**CUT**
(cove not fed by creek, ditch, etc.)

bluff bank

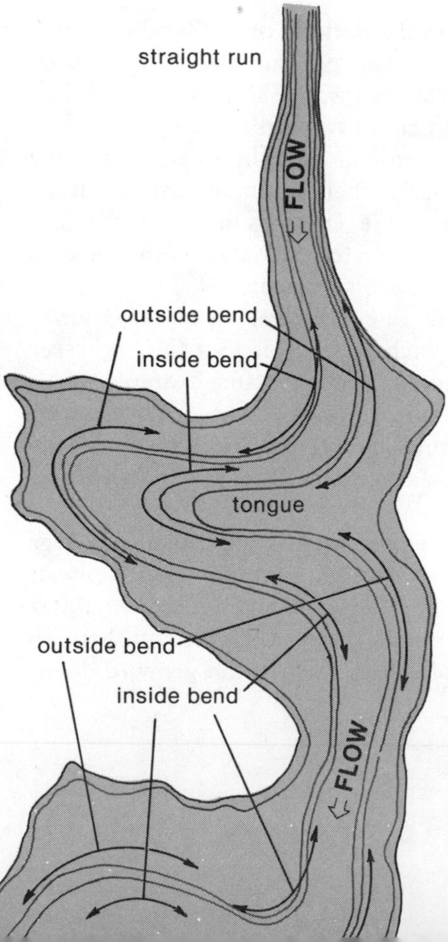

straight run

FLOW

outside bend

inside bend

tongue

outside bend

inside bend

FLOW

## RIVER OR CREEK CHANNEL BED

This illustration shows the difference between an inside and outside bend. The outside bend of a river or creek is "washed" the hardest by the water flow. Tongue areas are especially attractive. Remember, obstructions such as a fallen tree can slow the flow and provide cover.

primary
feeder
creek

## RIVER ARM

large tributary

— creek channel

— creek
   point

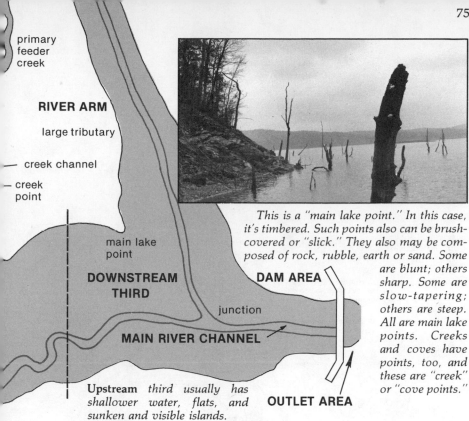

main lake
point

**DOWNSTREAM
THIRD**

**DAM AREA**

junction

**MAIN RIVER CHANNEL**

**OUTLET AREA**

*This is a "main lake point." In this case, it's timbered. Such points also can be brush-covered or "slick." They also may be composed of rock, rubble, earth or sand. Some are blunt; others sharp. Some are slow-tapering; others are steep. All are main lake points. Creeks and coves have points, too, and these are "creek" or "cove points."*

**Upstream** *third usually has shallower water, flats, and sunken and visible islands.*

**Mid-lake third** *is the most varied in structure and usually the widest portion of lake.*

**The downstream** *third has the deepest water and the steepest slopes.*

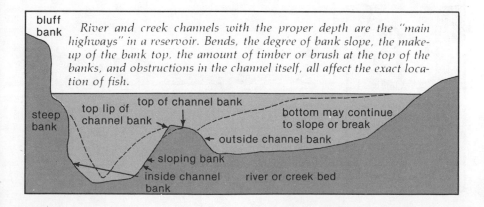

bluff
bank

*River and creek channels with the proper depth are the "main highways" in a reservoir. Bends, the degree of bank slope, the make-up of the bank top, the amount of timber or brush at the top of the banks, and obstructions in the channel itself, all affect the exact location of fish.*

steep
bank

top lip of
channel bank

top of channel bank

bottom may continue
to slope or break

← outside channel bank

← sloping bank

← inside channel
bank

river or creek bed

# CANYON IMPOUNDMENT

*Examples: Lake Powell, UT; Lake Havasu, AZ/CA; Lake Mead, NV/AZ; Flaming Gorge, WY/UT.*

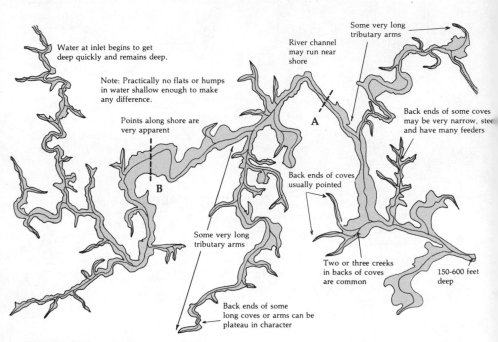

Water at inlet begins to get deep quickly and remains deep.

Note: Practically no flats or humps in water shallow enough to make any difference.

Points along shore are very apparent

River channel may run near shore

Some very long tributary arms

Back ends of some coves may be very narrow, stee and have many feeders

Back ends of coves usually pointed

B

A

Some very long tributary arms

Two or three creeks in backs of coves are common

150-600 feet deep

Back ends of some long coves or arms can be plateau in character

## TOP VIEW

## CROSS-SECTIONS

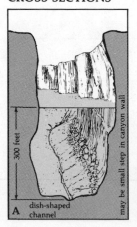

300 feet

dish-shaped channel

may be small step in canyon wall

A

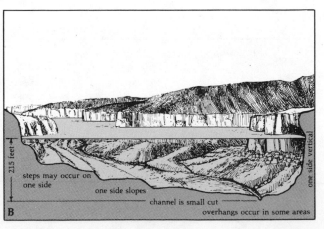

215 feet

steps may occur on one side

one side slopes

channel is small cut

one side vertical

overhangs occur in some areas

B

# PLATEAU IMPOUNDMENT

*Examples: Lake Meredith, TX; Roosevelt, AZ; Clear, CA; Ft. Peck, MT; Garrison, ND; Banks, WA.*

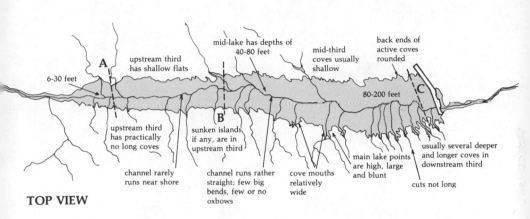

mid-lake has depths of 40-80 feet

back ends of active coves rounded

upstream third has shallow flats

mid-third coves usually shallow

6-30 feet

80-200 feet

**A**

**B**

**C**

upstream third has practically no long coves

sunken islands, if any, are in upstream third

usually several deeper and longer coves in downstream third

channel rarely runs near shore

channel runs rather straight; few big bends, few or no oxbows

cove mouths relatively wide

main lake points are high, large and blunt

cuts not long

**TOP VIEW**

## CROSS-SECTIONS

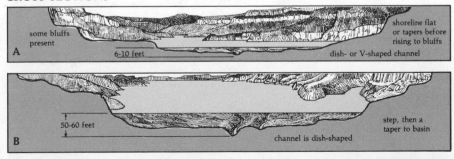

some bluffs present

shoreline flat or tapers before rising to bluffs

A

6-10 feet

dish- or V-shaped channel

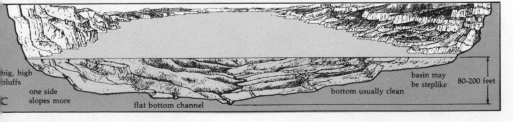

50-60 feet

step, then a taper to basin

B

channel is dish-shaped

big, high bluffs

basin may be steplike

80-200 feet

one side slopes more

bottom usually clean

C

flat bottom channel

# HIGHLAND IMPOUNDMENT

*Examples: Bull Shoals, AR/MO; Dale Hollow, TN; Broken Bow, OK; Sidley Lanier, GA; Don Pedro, CA; Hopatcong, NJ; Amistad, TX.*

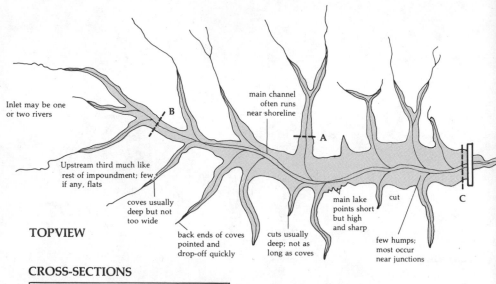

Inlet may be one or two rivers

main channel often runs near shoreline

Upstream third much like rest of impoundment; few if any, flats

coves usually deep but not too wide

**TOPVIEW**

back ends of coves pointed and drop-off quickly

cuts usually deep; not as long as coves

main lake points short but high and sharp

cut

few humps; most occur near junctions

## CROSS-SECTIONS

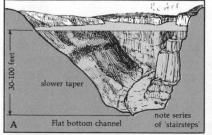

30-100 feet

slower taper

note series of 'stairsteps'

A    Flat bottom channel

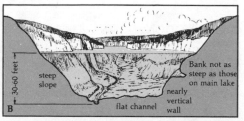

30-60 feet

steep slope

Bank not as steep as those on main lake

nearly vertical wall

B    flat channel

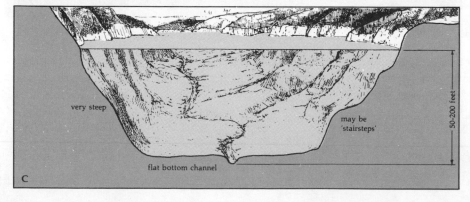

very steep

flat bottom channel

may be 'stairsteps'

50-200 feet

C

# HILL-LAND IMPOUNDMENT

*Examples: Lake Shelbyville, IL; Toledo Bend, TX; Felsenthal, AR; D'Arbonne, LA; Kinzua Reservoir, PA; Council Grove Reservoir, KS.*

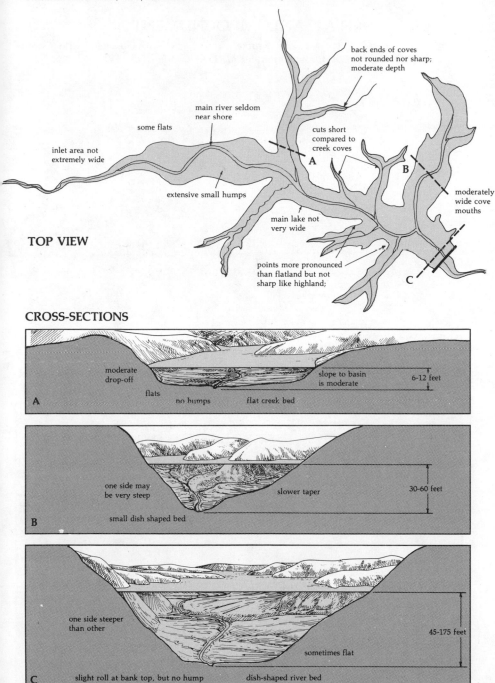

**TOP VIEW**

back ends of coves
not rounded nor sharp;
moderate depth

main river seldom
near shore

some flats

cuts short
compared to
creek coves

A

B

inlet area not
extremely wide

moderately
wide cove
mouths

extensive small humps

main lake not
very wide

C

points more pronounced
than flatland but not
sharp like highland;

**CROSS-SECTIONS**

moderate
drop-off

slope to basin
is moderate

6-12 feet

flats

no humps

flat creek bed

A

one side may
be very steep

slower taper

30-60 feet

small dish shaped bed

B

one side steeper
than other

45-175 feet

sometimes flat

slight roll at bank top, but no hump

dish-shaped river bed

C

# FLATLAND IMPOUNDMENT

*Examples: Kentucky Lake, KY/TN; Santee Cooper, SC; Ross Barnett, MS; Green-wood, NJ/NY; Carlyle, IL; Lake Seminole, FL/GA; Castle Rock, WI.*

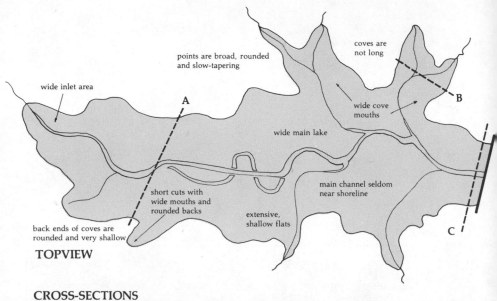

points are broad, rounded
and slow-tapering

coves are
not long

wide inlet area

A

B

wide cove
mouths

wide main lake

main channel seldom
near shoreline

short cuts with
wide mouths and
rounded backs

extensive,
shallow flats

C

back ends of coves are
rounded and very shallow

**TOPVIEW**

## CROSS-SECTIONS

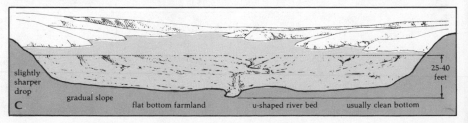

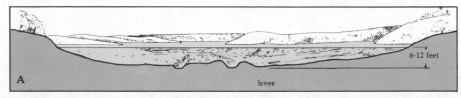

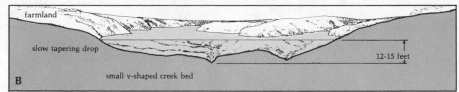

A          levee          6-12 feet

farmland

slow tapering drop          12-15 feet

small v-shaped creek bed

B

slightly
sharper
drop          gradual slope          flat bottom farmland          u-shaped river bed          usually clean bottom          25-40 feet

C

# LOWLAND/WETLAND IMPOUNDMENT

*Examples: Chippewa Flowage, WI; Bond Falls, MI; Black Bayou, LA; Taylor Creek, FL.*

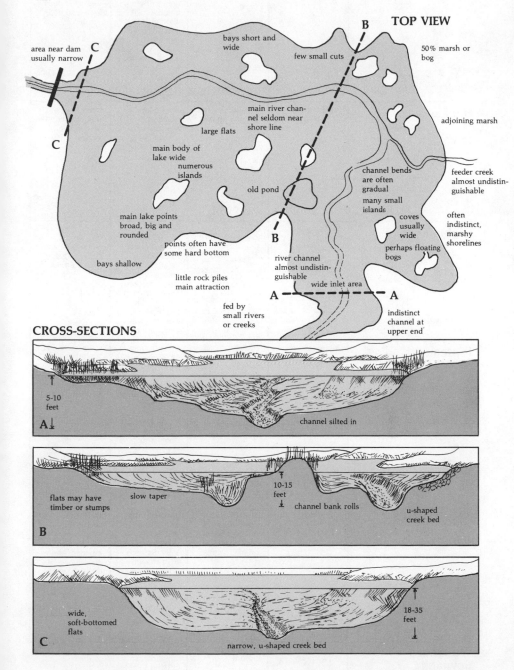

**TOP VIEW**

area near dam usually narrow

bays short and wide

few small cuts

50% marsh or bog

main river channel seldom near shore line

large flats

adjoining marsh

main body of lake wide numerous islands

old pond

channel bends are often gradual

many small islands

feeder creek almost undistinguishable

main lake points broad, big and rounded

points often have some hard bottom

coves usually wide

perhaps floating bogs

often indistinct, marshy shorelines

bays shallow

river channel almost undistinguishable

little rock piles main attraction

wide inlet area

fed by small rivers or creeks

indistinct channel at upper end

**CROSS-SECTIONS**

5-10 feet

A

channel silted in

flats may have timber or stumps

slow taper

10-15 feet

channel bank rolls

u-shaped creek bed

B

wide, soft-bottomed flats

18-35 feet

C

narrow, u-shaped creek bed

# COMPARATIVE IMPOUNDMENT CHARACTERISTICS

| Impoundment Classification | Crappie Forage | Depth | Main River Channel Characteristics | Feeders |
|---|---|---|---|---|
| **Flatland** | Shad, minnows | 20-40' at dam 6-12' upstream | Seldom near shoreline, meanders, grealy altered, straightened with levees, dikes. Trees and brush along banks. Oxbows where channel has been straightened. | Creeks or ditches usually less than 20' wide. 1-6' deep, V-shaped bed. |
| **Hill-Land** | Shad, minnows | 45-175' or more depending on region | Near center of reservoir. Natural state, usually quite straight. River bed is usually rounded. | Most have a distinct channel with sloping banks, brush and/or tree-lined. |
| **Highland** | Shad, minnows | 60-200' or more depending on size. | Often runs near shoreline. Natural state has many junctions of creeks and river channels that are mostly too deep for bass use. Flat channel with steep walls. | Some are "dry-wet" (carry water only after heavy rains), rock bottoms |
| **Plateau** | Shad, minnows | 50-200' depending on location | Runs through center of reservoir, quite straight, usually not deep with flat beds. Banks are generally clean, some brush may be found. Downstream ⅓ is generally too deep for bass use. | Little gullies or washouts from flash floods. Main feeders have high walls. Feeders most prevalent on downstream third. Short and wide at mouth. |
| **Canyon** | Shad, minnows | 500-600' downstream; a few feet to 40 or 50 ft. at the inlet | May run near shore. Less distinct downstream. Very distinct, dish-shaped gorge upstream. Usually is too deep to be used by bass. | Very long creeks and small rivers. Can be 40-60 mi. long, and are shaped like main channel. |
| **Wetland/ Lowland** | Wide variety; depends on region. | Depends on region | The diversity of lowland impoundments makes them difficult to categorize. | |

| Cuts and Coves | Points | Shoreline | Bottom Content | Brush, Timber or Vegetation | Common Man-made Features |
|---|---|---|---|---|---|
| Coves are short, shallow with a small feeder creek running through, and have wide mouths. Short cuts with wide mouths and rounded backs. May contain weeds, brush & timber. | Broad, rounded, slow tapering. Some with brush; usually lack timber. | Mainly long, slow tapers. Steeper bluff banks on rare occasions. | Black soil, mud flats, some hard clay. | Standing timber in main lake is common—mainly cypress and willow. Brush in backs of coves. "Moss" is main vegetation. | Dam, roadbeds, causeways, ponds, levees, building foundations, rip-rap, cemeteries. |
| Coves are deep downstream, and may have large timber stands. Upstream much like flatland coves. Short cuts. | Rounded, usually with standing or cut timber. Some rare cases have boulders. | Slopes quickly to 7-12 ft. of water, then gradually to main river channel. | Sand, clay, loam, some mud flats, extensive small humps. | Brush and timber in coves, "moss" on shallow flats in main lakes. Has most weed growth of any reservoir type in the South. | Dam, rip-rap, high lines and pipe lines, fence rows, rock piles, road beds, cemeteries, drainage ditches, railroad beds, building foundations, marinas. |
| Coves are deep but not wide, and can be very long. Brush and timber common, sharp rocky points, some steep walls, some flatter, shallower. Deep cuts, not as long as coves. | Short, but very sharp and steep. Some slick; some with trees or brush. Mostly rocky. | Varies from heavily-timbered, moderate slope to cliffs. "Stair-step" ledges in some cases. | Sand, clay, rock, shale, limestone. | Timber is mainly hardwoods or pines and cedar. Brush varies regionally. Moss or weeds not common. | Same as hillland except causeways, bridges, and rip-rap are not as common. |
| Coves have flat basins, short, usually wide in relation to length. Some brush may be present. Shorelines are steep in deep coves, flat in shallow coves. Short cuts with high sloping walls in downstream ⅓. Not as prevalent upstream. | Vary depending on region from very sharp to rounded. | Steep bluffs downstream; gradual slope upstream. | Varies from rocky to sandy, to silt depending on region. Usually clean. Upstream ⅓ has shallow flats. | Quite limited. Some in backs of coves. Some vegetation in upstream third. | Dam, roadbeds, marinas, spillways, others as mentioned above not common because of low populations. |
| Almost all coves are creek or river-fed. Some "dry-wet" with wide mouths can be very long. Some with 2 or 3 creeks. | Very distinct along sheer walls of reservoir and downstream portions of cove. Most composed of jagged rock. Can rise 1200 feet above water and drop 300 feet below water. | Sheer cliffs with mainly, some broken rock, slightly sloping solid rock faces or "mesas." | Mainly rock, some sand and gravel in backs of coves. | Some sage brush or other scrub vegetation found occasionally. Cottonwood trees and some highland cedar at extreme backs of coves. | Very few, some marinas, dams. |

# TVA'S FISH ATTRACTOR PROGRAM

*Natural vegetation is sparse or almost totally lacking in many TVA reservoirs. This lack of vegetative "cover" for fish, together with other factors, results in the dispersion of fish populations. Recent experimentation with manmade "cover" in the form of artificial fish attractors has proven effective in concentrating fish in the area for food and shelter, and as a location for increased angling success.*

A population study conducted on Barkley Lake indicated that brush, fish attractors harbored 19 times the weight of crappies found in open-water areas without attractors, as well as 13 times more largemouth bass.

In joint effort, TVA and Mississippi, Alabama, and Tennessee State Fisheries biologists began attractor installation in Tennessee Valley reservoirs in 1977, and to date have put over 12,000 individual structures in 18 reservoirs.

Fish attractors are especially helpful to anglers unfamiliar with reservoir topography and conditions, and to those who don't have sophisticated gear for locating natural concentrations of fish. Fish attractors can increase catch rate and angler satisfaction, and achieve a better balance of sport fish harvest with the individual reservoir's ability to produce fish.

## FISHING ON ATTRACTOR SITES

Fish attractors are piles of brush anchored to the bottom of the lake. Anglers can locate them by using a weighted line or a depth recorder. The following suggestions should help you catch fish that take cover in attractors:

1. To avoid getting hung, use wire hooks which will bend and pop free with a strong tug.
2. When fishing directly over attractors, put your anchors on either side of the brush pile to avoid scaring the fish. Slowly lower your bait or lure until you feel resistance, and then stop. (Count the turns of the reel so you can return to the same depth.) Hold a live bait steady in one place, or move a lure up and down. Both can be fished above attractors with a float.
3. If you are casting, stay to one side of the attractors and work your lure over the top or through the brush pile.
4. Trollers do well around attractors in coves, and around elongated deep-water sites. Troll parallel to strung-out brush piles, around the end, and down the other side.

Deep-water attractors are of two types and are marked by white buoys with a design depicting a fish. A single buoy indicates the center of a one-half-acre brush pile. Two buoys indicate either end of a long brush pile.

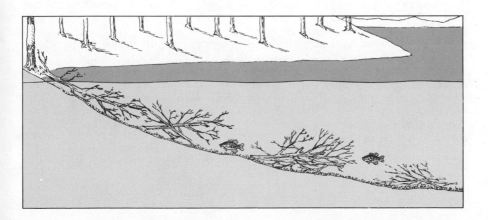

Cove attractors start in shallow water and generally extend in a straight line into deep water. Each site contains about ten brush piles. At the heads of coves, a white, 6-foot pole or a tree painted white to a height of 6 feet marks where attractors are located.

## RESERVOIR TYPES

| CANYON | PLATEAU | HIGHLAND | HILL-LAND | FLATLAND | WETLAND |
|---|---|---|---|---|---|
| CONDITIONS OF ENVIRONMENT | | | | | |
| COLD | COOL | | | COOL AND WARM | |
| TROUT | | | | | |
| | | WALLEYE—(NORTH) | | | |
| | | LARGEMOUTH BASS—(SOUTH) | | | |
| | | | | CRAPPIE | |
| | SMALLMOUTH BASS | | | | |

Key:
——————— strongest populations
— — — — — — weaker populations

Due to the wide geographic distribution of reservoirs, it is difficult to generalize about which species of fish may be present. For example, a shallow, wetland impoundment in the northern U.S. may contain walleyes and only a few largemouth bass. Yet a similarly shaped reservoir in the deep South may contain big bass and no walleyes! Obviously, geographic area plays a big part in determining the resulting fishery. In general, northern reservoirs provide a cooler environment than those located in the South, and the local environment may favor one species over another despite similar structural shape.

As far as crappies go, black crappies are typically more prevalent in northern impoundments, and whites tend to dominate in southern waters. Central-latitude lakes (Kentucky, Ohio, etc.) often have mixed populations, with the edge going to whichever species is most suited to the local environment.

Crappies tend to do best in a reservoir that provides a confined, open-water environment. There is both adequate cover (flooded trees, brush, etc.) present, and enough open water for suspended- or deep-water use. Thus, the best crappie impoundments tend to be moderately deep with a healthy amount of cover; hill-land and flatland reservoirs are classic examples.

Good crappie impoundments are seldom extremely shallow and choked with cover, as is the case with some wetland impoundments, nor are they deep or nearly devoid of cover, like most plateau and canyon waters. Some highland reservoirs, however, may host good crappie fisheries if they provide an adequate amount of submerged cover and suitable spawning areas. If not, crappies may be present, but not in significant numbers. It all depends on what's available.

## Chapter 9

# SPRING

### Cool-Water Crappies

When spring approaches, a lake comes to life. In northern natural lakes, for example, as the ice thins, the water warms and increased sunlight penetration sets off a new cycle of weedgrowth. This new weedgrowth produces more oxygen, raising the oxygen level in the water.

Other forms of life too small to be seen by the naked eye also begin to flourish. As various forms of plankton bloom, minnows feast on the newly found food, and crappies eventually follow suit. Even as the ice is retreating from the shorelines, crappies can be in the midst of a feeding binge that continues until long after the ice has left the lake.

This late-winter/early-spring feeding spree generally occurs first in small, shallow eutrophic lakes, because these lakes warm up very quickly. It's not unusual to find crappies in the shallow bays and channels of these lakes just several days after ice-out. Thus, these smaller lakes normally furnish the first open-water crappie fishing of the year, although you will seldom catch many trophies. The average fish size tends to be small since the crappies in smaller eutrophic lakes seldom achieve the large average size of their counterparts in larger, deeper mesotrophic waters.

About the time you're catching crappies in smaller lakes, larger natural lakes in the area will start becoming ice-free. After another week or so, the big lakes will finally have open water, and you can start thinking about slab crappies from these waters. Crappie location at ice-out in larger mesotrophic lakes, however, can be quite different from their location in small eutrophic lakes, depending on the available habitat. You'll have to make locational adjustments in order to contact fish.

Many mesotrophic lakes are so large and deep that they warm much slower than smaller eutrophic ones. It may take several additional weeks for a big lake to warm enough to draw baitfish and crappies into the shallows—particularly if there are no shallow bays or channels that warm up quickly. Until

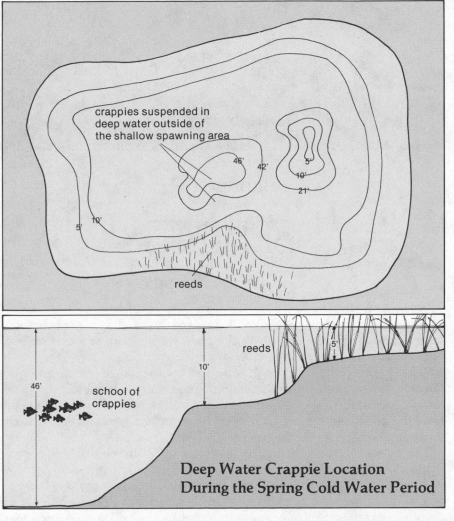

*It's common to find schools of crappies suspended outside their spawning grounds in early spring. Later, as the water warms, they make a full-fledged pre-spawn movement into the shallows. You can get in on the action early, though, by locating them even before they move into the spawning areas.*

then, the crappies remain suspended over deep water. Look for them outside of weedy flats, above sunken islands or near creek mouths.

A depth sounder or graph is an invaluable tool for locating these suspended fish. Slowly crisscross deeper areas adjacent to the shallows. Once you've located fish, it'll take actual fishing to determine whether the fish you see are crappies or baitfish.

When the ice goes out, crappie feeding periods may occur only during morning and late evening. But, as the days grow longer and the water warms, crappies will feed for longer periods of time until they seem to be feeding almost constantly. Remember, a fish's metabolism is regulated in part by the water temperature; as the water warms, the fish become more aggressive.

Eventually the water warms enough so both the baitfish and crappies enter the shallow water. The first places you'll find them are the same types of areas they use in smaller lakes—shallow weeds, back bays, channels, etc.—wherever the water is warmer than in the surrounding area.

There's one important point to remember about these ice-out, shallow-water movements. They are *not* spawning movements. Spawning usually occurs much later—at least a month after the ice goes out. Instead, these early spring cold-water movements are associated strictly with food. Crappies merely follow their food as it enters the shallow, warmer water. They will feed heavily in order to build up reserve energy for the rigors of the upcoming spawn.

Shallow, cold-water movements occur at the mercy of the weather. A stretch of warm, sunny days will draw fish into the shallows. A prolonged cold snap, however, will drive them out completely, and you'll find them suspended, once again, over deep water. Be aware that fish location can shift as the weather changes.

## PRE-SPAWN LOCATIONAL ELEMENTS ON NATURAL LAKES

As the water continues to warm, crappies shift into a pre-spawn attitude. This generally occurs when the water temperature in shallow, protected areas of the lake reaches the mid 50°Fs. The key to locating crappies at this time is to find areas of shallow water that have the proper bottom content for spawning and are warmer than the rest of the lake.

Crappies generally spawn on a bottom that consists of either soft sand, sandy loam, or marl. This semi-soft bottom allows them to fan out a circular nest in which to lay their eggs. Hard sand or gravel may be too firm for nest construction, whereas soft muck is too loose to retain the nest's shape and is very difficult for the fish to keep clean. Given a choice, crappies will choose the bottom type that best suits their needs.

On mesotrophic lakes, the areas crappies use for spawning generally have a sandy bottom. These lakes, however, usually have large expanses of sand in the shallows, so sand by itself is not the only drawing point. Cover also becomes an important factor.

In mesotrophic lakes, spawning crappies often choose reeds as a favorite form of shallow-water cover. Reeds provide a network of obstructions that hide crappies from larger predators and protect the nest from egg-stealing in-

# Typical Shallow Spawning Bay

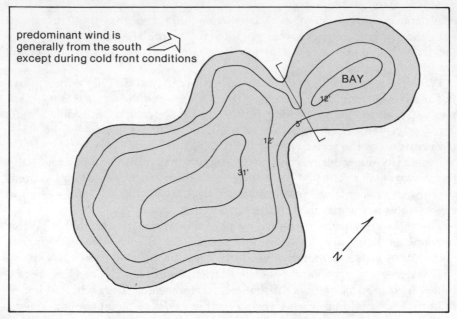

predominant wind is
generally from the south
except during cold front conditions

BAY

12'

5'

12'

31'

N

*Shallow bays located at the north end of a lake are typically the first areas to warm in early spring. They receive the most sun exposure, and also collect warm surface waters blown in by southerly winds. Then, too, they are shielded from harsh northerly winds during frontal conditions. Such bays generally draw the first, shallow-spawning movements of spring crappies.*

truders. Since meso lakes typically produce the largest crappies, you'll find that reed beds generally offer the best chance for catching trophy crappies during the spring season.

Reeds draw pre-spawn/spawn crappies in meso lakes, but where do the crappies spawn in eutrophic lakes? After all, eutrophic lakes generally have a softer bottom content and reeds are noticeably absent. In this case, crappies generally spawn around stumps or weed clumps in areas where the bottom content is conducive to spawning—the best available combination of cover and suitable bottom condition.

In eutrophic lakes, crappies often spawn in the same areas as largemouth bass. Bass are generally the predominant gamefish in eutrophic lakes and the crappies play "second fiddle" to the more aggressive largemouth. With an increase in panfish numbers and a decrease in open-water areas on these smaller lakes, the crappies are forced to "make do" in an environment they're not particularly suited to. They can hack this environment, but their numbers and size usually suffer.

The spawning areas for both crappies and bass in eutrophic lakes are typically back bays and channels where the bottom is sandy loam. Here, a thin build-up of decayed organic matter usually covers the bottom. The fish are able to sweep this away, down to a sandy base, forming a shallow, bowl-shaped nest.

When largemouths and crappies compete for the same spawning areas, largemouths generally spawn before crappies at a water temperature in the low to mid 60°Fs. About the time that largemouths have finished spawning, crappies move into the same areas to spawn. In fact, it's not unusual to see crappies and late-spawning bass in the same general area. This staggered use of limited habitat is nature's way of making the best use of available spawning habitat.

## SPECIFIC CRAPPIE LOCATION DURING THE PRE-SPAWN PERIOD

We've established that crappies prefer to spawn on a sandy type soil in the vicinity of some form of shallow cover. The final locational aspect we need to consider is water temperature. Once this is determined, pre-spawn crappies are easily located.

Crappies have an innate ability to locate and eventually spawn in shallow areas that are warmer than the surrounding water. Whether they seek the warmer water or just accidentally find it and remain there is open to debate. Nevertheless, once you locate warmer areas having the proper cover and bottom content, you'll find fish.

Typical warmer areas are small bays and channels that are located along the north shore of the lake. These areas receive the full warming effect of the sun; those along the southern shore are usually shaded since the sun is low in the southern sky at this time of year.

Furthermore, predominantly warm, southerly winds blow the warmer surface waters toward the northern shore, warming the water further still. And in the event of a cold front, the northern shoreline protects the shallows from cold, harsh, northerly winds. Thus, shallow, protected areas at the north end of the lake are generally your best bet for the earliest pre-spawn movement of crappies.

Sunlight plays an even larger part in the spawning cycle than simply warming the water. The sunlit areas support an abundance of small minnows and plankton, providing newly-hatched crappies with the food source they require. By comparison, shaded areas are cold and sterile and contain far fewer fish—adults as well as young.

Wind is another factor to contend with. The better spring crappie areas are usually fairly calm and are protected from excessive wind or wave action. High winds can force crappies out of their spawning areas and out to the deeper adjacent drop-offs. Once the weather stabilizes, the fish usually move back into the shallows. However, a long period of high winds with cool temperatures will delay and sometimes even prevent spawning. That's one reason why shallow, protected bays are good at this time of the year. They not only warm fast and hold their temperature, but the lack of high winds striking the bay allows the warm water to remain in the bay instead of being washed out and replaced by the cooler water of the main lake.

Another favorable aspect of bay areas is that the water is usually slightly darker than in the main part of the lake. Why? Many bays are heavily choked with weeds during the summer months. During winter these weeds die and fall to the bottom and decay. Small floating particles from these weeds can color or stain the water. These particles absorb the sun's energy, warming the water more rapidly than clearer, main-lake water. Cloudy water also holds its temperature longer when the weather begins to cool.

Main-lake, shoreline weed areas can also attract fish, but it's usually only during ideal spawning times—a hot sun with warm, calm days or merely a slight breeze. Play the percentages by fishing areas that are protected from wind, because you're much more likely to find crappies here than in wind-swept areas.

Creek outlets are also excellent crappie areas in spring, especially if there's cover nearby. Creek outlets act as funnels (somewhat like the drain in your bathtub) to draw off the warmer surface water. As the warm surface water is pulled toward the creek, the area adjacent to the creek mouth becomes much warmer than the main lake, creating an ideal spring spot for crappies. Such areas remain good until the temperature of both the run-off water and the lake equalizes.

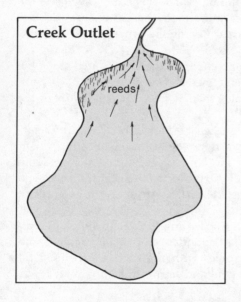

*The pulling action of a creek outlet draws warm surface waters to the area as it drains the lake. It's another good place to look for crappies in the spring.*

If cover is nearby creek inlets are also very good areas. Since creeks pour warm, spring, run-off water into the main lake, it always pays to check them out. These areas, however, only remain good as long as the run-off water temperature exceeds that of the main lake.

One last valuable point to remember about both inlets and outlets is the huge buildup of small insects, zooplankton and young baitfish for crappies to feed on. These always attract fish early in the year.

# CRAPPIE PRESENTATION

Let's begin our look at crappie presentation with crappies that are still suspended in deep water—prior to their shallow pre-spawn movement. Although suspended crappies are often difficult to locate during most of the year, they're usually fairly easy to find prior to spawning time. Why? Because you know the general vicinity of the lake they'll be in. Even if they're still suspended, they're usually close to the shallow areas where they'll spawn. This narrows down your locational options to a relatively small portion of the lake.

As soon as the ice leaves the lake, scan the shallows with polarized sunglasses to determine potential crappie-spawning areas. While you're doing this you should be able to spot any crappies that have penetrated the shallows. If you fail to spot a concentration of crappies, proceed to the first deep-water area adjacent to shallow bays or potential spawning sites and look for any crappies suspended nearby.

As we said before, the depth finder or graph is a valuable tool for spotting these fish. A systematic scan of the area will tell you the location of fish. You'll spot a wide band of fish signals up well off the bottom, which indicates suspended fish.

Begin fishing by drifting or slowly trolling across the area where you've spotted fish. Turn the power up on your depth finder; this helps you spot fish easier. Crappies appear as flashes on the dial, and stray fish may range out as far as fifty feet from the main school. You want to fish the main concentration of crappies, so try to position yourself near the biggest concentration of flashes.

Perhaps the best way to catch suspended crappies is with a tiny jig/minnow combination. Hook a small fathead minnow on the back of a 1/16-ounce crappie jig and cast it out across the crappie school. Light spinning tackle and

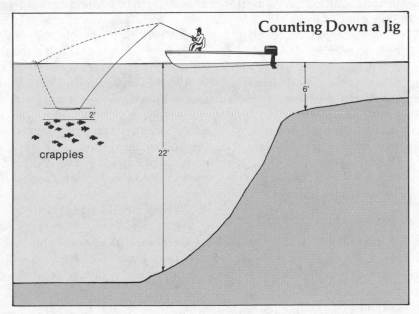

**Counting Down a Jig**

One of the best ways to catch deep-water crappies is to count a jig down to their level and then retrieve it through or slightly above the school. If they're active, they'll keep coming up to a jig cast above them. By doing this, you catch a lot of fish without spooking the school below.

If the crappies are relatively inactive, though, you've got to put the jig right in the midst of them. Then you risk spooking them. But the trick of keeping the jig above them should be kept in mind for prime conditions.

4-pound-test line enable you to do this with ease. Allow the jig to sink until it reaches a depth at, or slightly above, the level of the crappies. Then gradually swim the jig through this depth level by slowly reeling it in.

The best jigs to use in this deeper, cold water are usually tiny marabou jigs. A very slow drop rate and minimum action is perfect for crappies.

Each jig has a drop speed that is characteristic of its design. By counting "one thousand, two thousand, three thousand, etc." you'll know how far the jig has sunk. When it reaches the level where your depth finder indicates the crappies are, begin your retrieve.

It's generally best to keep the jig just above the level of the crappies, rather than below them. Crappies show a definite tendency to move up for food instead of down for it. By keeping the jig above them, you're making it an easy meal.

If you start catching crappies directly beneath the boat, you don't need to cast for them. Simply lower the jig to their level and hold it there. This is easily achieved by placing a rubber band around the spool of your spinning reel once the jig has reached the proper depth. This prevents excess line from running out. Each time you lower the jig it returns to the proper depth and stays there.

You can experiment with a slow pumping action but, in general, you don't want to add extra action to the jig by moving the rod tip. Keep the jig's movement slow and steady.

Crappies prefer this type of lure movement, particularly in cold water. They're not about to chase a meal, but they will strike a lure that is presented directly in front of them.

Suspended crappies are generally most active during the low-light periods of morning and evening. That's not to say you can't catch them during the day, however. It's just a little harder to trigger them. When you do hook a fish, let it fight momentarily in the vicinity of the school. This generally triggers their competitive urge and you may trick a number of fish into becoming active and hitting your jig.

As the weather and water grow steadily warmer, crappies progressively shift more toward the shallows. You can follow them on a daily basis and catch them long before shallow-water anglers make contact. You'll also know approximately when they're ready to move up into the shallows, so you'll be able to take advantage of it.

Just prior to their movement into the shallows, crappies remain directly outside the spawning areas, generally along a deep weedline or drop-off. They'll use this "pivot point" area for several days, and then finally move up into the shallows. Cold weather, however, often chases them right back out again. This is sort of a balancing act, with fish location and behavior depending on the weather. The weedline drop-off (pivot point) will almost always attract and hold some fish as they move in or out of the shallows. It's especially good to know these holding areas if bad weather strikes and the fish are forced out of the shallows.

The jig presentation discussed earlier is excellent for catching crappies in this holding area. You can simplify it even further by placing a bobber on the line. This keeps the jig at exactly the proper depth. The bobber is only effective, however, if the fish are within 8 feet of the surface. In deeper water, a bobber

*Spring and fast crappie action go hand in hand. Dave Csanda hoists an honest 2-pound black crappie taken from a deep reed clump.*

# Pattern Progression In Spring

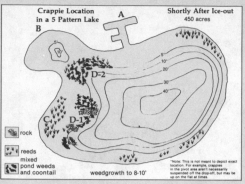

Crappie Location in a 5 Pattern Lake — Shortly After Ice-out — 450 acres — weedgrowth to 8-10'

*Note: This is not meant to depict exact location. For example, crappies in the pivot area aren't necessarily suspended off the drop-off, but may be up on the flat at times.

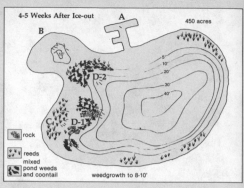

4-5 Weeks After Ice-out — 450 acres — weedgrowth to 8-10'

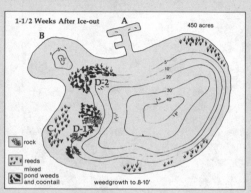

1-1/2 Weeks After Ice-out — 450 acres — weedgrowth to 8-10'

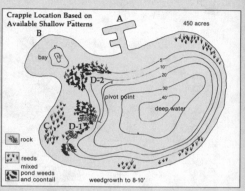

Crappie Location Based on Available Shallow Patterns — 450 acres — weedgrowth to 8-10'

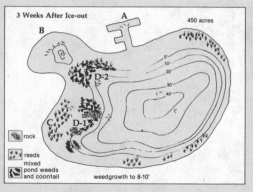

3 Weeks After Ice-out — 450 acres — weedgrowth to 8-10'

## 5 Pattern Lake

| | Shallow Patterns | | | Deep Patterns | |
| | Canals | Bays | Reeds | Pivot Point (drop-off) | Open Water |
|---|---|---|---|---|---|
| Week 1 | yes | no | no | yes | yes |
| Week 2 | yes | yes/no | no | yes | yes |
| Week 3 | yes | yes | yes/no | yes | yes/no |
| Week 4 | yes/no | yes | yes | yes/no | no |
| Week 5 | yes/no | yes | yes | yes/no | no |

At ice-out, expect crappies schooled mainly along drop-offs or in open water. If canals are available (AREA A), expect some pivot-point (drop-off) crappies to move to canals, and some open-water fish to move to the pivot point. Later, if bays (AREA B) are also available, expect more pivot-point crappies to move to them, and still more open-water crappies to move to the pivot-point. Still later, if reed beds are available (C), expect most of the remaining pivot-point and open-water crappies to move into them. Finally, deep reed humps (D-1, D-2) will draw fish. This progression may take 3 to 5 weeks, as shown in the 5 PATTERN LAKE example.

If shallow-water options aren't available, crappies hold longer in the two deep-water patterns. For example, note that the 4 PATTERN LAKE has no canals and sees little or no shallow-water crappie activity the first two weeks after ice-out. The 3 PATTERN

LAKE *has even fewer options; with no canals or shallow bays to warm up early, the crappies remain in deep-water areas for a much longer time. It may take three weeks for the shallow, reed areas to warm up enough to attract fish.*

*In short, fish relate to the available habitat. However, once you understand their options, you can catch them consistently.*

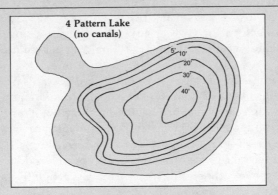

## 4 Pattern Lake
### (no canals)

|  | Shallow Patterns | | | Deep Patterns | |
|  |  |  |  | Pivot Point | |
|  | Canals | Bays | Reeds | (drop-off) | Open Water |
| Week 1 | no | no | no | yes | yes |
| Week 2 | no | yes/no | no | yes | yes |
| Week 3 | no | yes | yes/no | yes | yes |
| Week 4 | no | yes | yes | yes | no |
| Week 5 | no | yes | yes | yes/no | no |

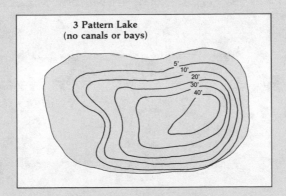

## 3 Pattern Lake
### (no canals or bays)

|  | Shallow Patterns | | | Deep Patterns | |
|  |  |  |  | Pivot Point | |
|  | Canals | Bays | Reeds | (drop-off) | Open Water |
| Week 1 | no | no | no | yes | yes |
| Week 2 | no | no | no | yes | yes |
| Week 3 | no | no | yes/no | yes | yes |
| Week 4 | no | no | yes | yes | yes/no |
| Week 5 | no | no | yes | yes | no |

Fewer shallow water patterns mean crappies spend more time in deep water.

arrangement becomes unwieldy and you're better off casting a jig and letting it sink to their level.

Once the crappies leave the holding area and penetrate the shallows, you're in for some of the most exciting fishing of the year. Shallow crappies are generally easy to locate, but if you expect to catch fish, you still must match your presentation to the areas being fished. The easiest way to do this is to tailor your approach to the type of cover the fish are using. Here's how to catch shallow-water crappies using the tips and techniques described in Chapter 14.

Crappies in meso lakes usually spawn in the reeds. At this time of year you'll find that the ice has bent or broken many reeds. Mixed among these are the straighter stalks of reeds which are beginning to grow. This jumble of reeds provides cover and indicates a prime crappie spawning area.

A bobber and jig set-up is the best way to fish reed clumps. Place the bobber approximately 2 feet above the jig. You seldom need to add a minnow to the jig, because pre-spawn crappies in these areas are generally quite active and will readily strike a plain jig.

We prefer to use a long 9- or 10-foot rod when fishing reeds. The long length serves a dual purpose. First, it allows for easy casting of the light jig/bobber combination. A nice, slow, even arm motion is all it takes to lob the jig out. It should enter the water with minimum splash to prevent spooking the fish.

Second, and very important, the long rod will give you increased leverage

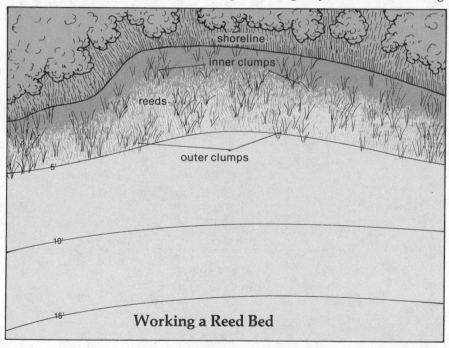

**Working a Reed Bed**

*It's usually best to work the outer reed clumps first, and then move into the reed bed. This allows you to catch the outer fish first and then go after the ones inside. If you just shoot right inside, you run the risk of spooking many of the crappies. Work the edges first.*

on the fish. You'll be able to lift even the largest crappies to the surface and drag them across the tops of the broken reeds. Shorter rods don't allow you to do this; they force you to fight the fish down in the reeds. With light, 4- or 6-pound-test line you'll break the fish off repeatedly unless you bring them to the surface.

The first reed clumps that crappies use are generally located on the outside, deeper edge of the reeds. Many anglers fish only these outer areas, because they occasionally catch fish there. These outer spots are excellent areas during the early pre-spawn, but later most of the crappies generally penetrate the main body of the reeds. They'll spread out and relate to the thickest reed clumps, and it's not unusual to catch several fish from a single heavy clump.

The best way to catch these fish is to cast the jig and bobber to the windward side of visible reed clumps. Allow the wind to drift the lure into the clumps. It doesn't take long to learn if the fish are present.

In order to take maximum advantage of an area, first work the outer reed clumps. After they've been fished thoroughly, proceed into the reeds and work the inner clumps. This is better than blasting your way right into the reeds and spooking the fish. Use your electric motor to slowly and effectively work the area, and you'll catch plenty of crappies.

Stumps provide a somewhat different situation and need to be approached in a slightly different manner. Many stumps hold one or two fish, but you'll seldom see a large concentration of crappies in one spot. This tends to make

**Crappies Relating to Stumps**

*Crappies often relate very closely to stumps in early spring. It's common to find small groups of fish down among the washed-out roots. They're not too anxious to leave the protection of the roots, and usually you're forced to fish them very slowly and carefully in order to entice a strike.*

them spooky and more reluctant to feed. Stump crappies don't exhibit the tight schooling behavior and competitive urge that reed crappies do, so you're generally forced to fish stump areas more slowly and carefully in order to catch fish.

Since stump crappies are often spooky it pays to approach stumps with the sun in your face to prevent throwing your shadow across the water. You can use the same jig and bobber set-up as in reeds, but fish slower. Cast three feet upwind of a stump and let the wind drift the jig past one side of the stump. Then cast again and let the jig drift by the other side. Stump crappies seem more prone to contemplate your offering, so it pays to fish your way very slowly and quietly through the area.

## COMPARING SPRING CRAPPIE LOCATION ON LAKES, RIVERS AND RESERVOIRS

While we've keyed on natural lakes thus far, pre-spawn crappie behavior is strikingly similar in reservoirs, as well. As the water warms, crappies will begin shifting into shallow cuts and coves in search of warmer water.

Since fluctuating water levels often prevent or hinder substantial weed-growth from developing in impoundments, you can expect crappies to relate heavily to "wood"; stumps, timber, brush, fish attractors, etc., are all potential areas if they lie at the proper depth. Chapter 13, "Reservoirs," describes this aspect of spring crappie movement in detail.

River crappies generally move into shallow backwater (non-current) areas in spring. Their behavior is almost a carbon copy of that displayed by crappies in impoundments. As the other areas warm, they become productive, too.

Once you understand the available habitat, crappie behavior becomes predictable. For example, in the accompanying illustration, crappies are moving toward shallow, protected areas in spring. In the natural lake, they use canals; then bays; then shoreline reed beds; and finally, main-lake reed clumps. As each area warms, it begins to attract fish.

Note the parallels in the other examples. In the shallow reservoir cove, the crappies first use shallow, protected cuts; then cover in the general end of the cove; then shoreline "wood;" and finally, deeper brushy humps in the main cove. In the oxbow lake connected to a river, the fish first use shallow back-

---

## Spring Crappie Areas

*Back bays and shallow coves with sheltered cover typically provide the best pre-spawn/spawn crappie areas. Oxbow lakes or flooded river backwaters are classic examples. Crappies will hold along the edges of deep weeds or timber prior to spawning, and then move into the shallows to feed or seek nesting sites.*

*Large reservoirs and natural lakes usually have main-lake crappie spawning, too. All of the fish don't head for the bays or coves. Shallow, brushy humps in reservoirs, or main-lake reed beds in natural lakes, often host a portion of the spawn—particularly for the big fish. Since the water in the main lake typically warms more slowly than in back bays or coves, the best activity there typically occurs a week or two after the shallows start poppin'.*

### NATURAL LAKES

*In spring, natural-lake anglers often rely on three, shallow-crappie locational patterns: canals (AREA A), bays (AREA B), and main-lake reed beds (AREA C).*

*Canals warm quickly, and crappies may begin to use them shortly after ice-out. The best canals are wind-protected, have some water color, only one inlet as opposed to flow-through canals with two or more, and secondary arms. Good canals also offer cover, often in the form of boat hoists or docks.*

*A week or so after crappies begin to use canals, they may enter shallow bays. The*

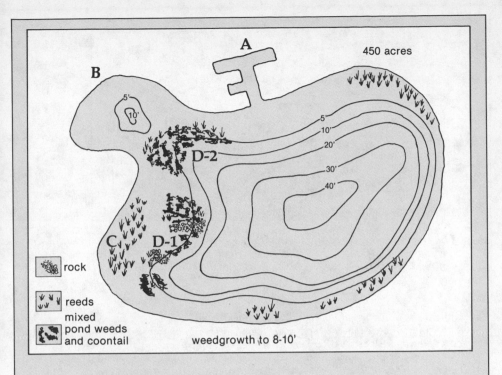

450 acres

weedgrowth to 8-10'

rock

reeds

mixed
pond weeds
and coontail

| AREA | CONDITION | | |
|------|-----------|---|---|
| A | canals, shallow cuts, or connected waters | C | main-lake, shoreline-oriented cover |
| B | back ends of bays, coves, or backwaters | D | shallow, main-lake hump with cover |

*best bays warm quickly and offer cover. A good bay usually also has a deeper hole in it. Holes offer refuge to shallow crappies when cold-front conditions strike.*

*Eventually, crappies begin to frequent main-lake reed beds. The best reed beds are usually the largest beds offering the most cover. Reed-bed activity usually begins 2 to 3 weeks after canal activity, and a week or so after activity in bays. To find crappies in reed beds, use your electric motor to quietly slide through the reeds and look for them.*

*A fourth, largely ignored pattern occurs in AREAS D-1 and D-2. Deep, 3- to 5-foot reed beds often host a portion of the crappie spawn—particularly for big fish. These are the last spawning areas to warm up and see the last spawning activity. They're often tough to fish due to their exposure to the wind, however.*

## RESERVOIRS

*Here's a typical, shallow-spawning cove in a reservoir. The spring-crappie areas may look different than those in a natural lake, but the principles are the same. Once you get the hang of it, you'll notice many similarities in how crappies adapt to available habitat.*

*AREA A is a shallow, protected, brushy cut, off the back end of the cove. It's probably the first area to warm and attract spring crappies. AREA B is the brushy end of the cove itself. The brush-lined shorelines are the next areas to attract shallow fish.*

*AREAS C-1 and C-2 are similar to B, but are more main-lake oriented. They'll attract fish, but usually later than A or B due to the deeper, cooler, slower-warming water at the mouth of the cove.*

*AREA D is a shallow, brushy hump along the main river channel. It's a big-fish spot. It's also the last spawning area to warm, and will see the last flush of spawning fish.*

*During cold fronts, crappies may pull off the flats, shorelines and humps and head*

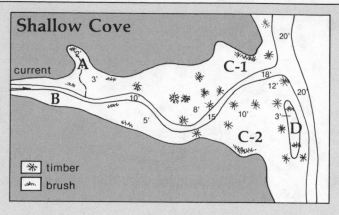

toward deeper water. Deep trees along the channel edge, the bottoms of the outside channel bends, and deep water adjacent to the hump (D) could all draw fish during frontal conditions. The more severe the front, the farther toward the main lake fish will retreat.

## RIVERS

Rivers aren't all current areas. There are backwaters, bays, cuts, etc. where crappies can get out of the current and spawn in slack water. Small, brushy backwaters or connected lakes like AREA A often see the first spring crappie use. Large areas like the oxbow lake shown here warm up slower. (The old river channel runs through the oxbow. When the river shifted course, the oxbow became a slack-water area connected to the river.)

AREAS B-1 and B-2 are brush-filled cuts or small bays in the back end of the oxbow. Great spots! C-1 is a brush point on an island. It's deeper, more exposed to the wind, and will attract crappies a bit later than AREA B.

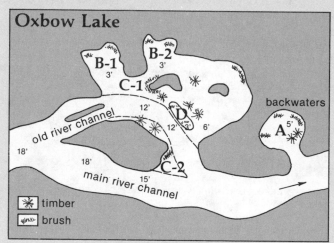

AREA C-2 is similar to C-1, except that it's more exposed to the river current. It's a late-spawning spot, but is a good choice if backwaters are absent or they lack suitable bottom content and/or cover. AREA D, meanwhile, is a shallow, brushy hump near the old river channel. It's also more exposed to the elements, and is a "late" spot.

During cold front conditions, crappies will pull out of the shallow cover and gather in deep timber, or lie in the bottom of the old river channel. Some fish may even school up at the intersection of the oxbow and the river if an eddy (calm water area) forms at C-2.

waters; then cuts in the oxbow itself; then shoreline brush near an island; and finally, a deeper, brushy hump. In each case, the pattern repeats itself. The environments may be a bit different, but the general principles still apply.

# THE SPAWN

As we've seen, crappies follow a predictable pre-spawn progression, using each available area as the water warms to the proper temperature (the low 50°Fs). As you might expect, they follow a similar progression at spawning time. As each area begins warming into the low 60°Fs, the crappies in that area will begin displaying spawning-related behavior.

There are several tip-offs to this transition other than water temperature. For example, note the appearance and mood of the fish. When crappies first penetrate the shallows, they are typically very light in color and spooky. However, the longer they are in the shallows, the more they change. Males begin displaying a darker color, triggered by hormonal changes, and become increasingly territorial and aggressive. Rather than just using a reed bed or brush pile, for example, they'll stake out a particular reed clump or brush pile, begin sweeping out a nest and defending it against intruders. They often become so fearless that they're extremely easy to approach and catch.

*Bingo, another crappie bites the dust! Reservoir expert Steve McCadams and Dan Sura team up to spank Kentucky Lake crappies. Their ammo? Light spinning tackle with a small jig tipped with a minnow fished around stake beds.*

# Crappie Spawning Depth

Water clarity has a distinct bearing on how deep crappies spawn. However, since water clarity varies from lake to lake and can even change from year to year on the same body of water, we must establish how fish react to water clarity before we can zero in on spring crappies.

In general, clear bodies of water permit deep sunlight penetration into the water; dark bodies of water, in contrast, have poor sunlight penetration. Stained waters fall somewhere in between.

In each case, the visibility is a good general indicator of fish behavior. You can estimate visibility by noting how deep you can see the bottom or how deep you can see a large, white lure lowered into the water on a calm, sunny afternoon. (Biologists use a white object called a Secchi disk as a standard measure of light penetration. In essence, it measures how deep sunlight can penetrate the water and reflect back up to the surface.)

In most reservoirs, crappies apparently prefer to nest slightly below this level if favorable conditions exist there. In general, if visibility is less than 10 feet, the level 2 feet below this depth is a typical nesting depth. If the visibility is greater than 10 feet, the depth range 4 to 6 feet below this level is a common nesting area.

Apparently, the amount of light available at that depth is favorable for egg development, and the crappies do no need to move shallower to spawn successfully unless the combination of conditions there are more attractive.

## THE PROPER COMBINATION

Crappie spawning depth does not depend on visibility alone; it actually varies according to the combination of how clear the water is; the bottom content; the depth, type and amount of cover available; competing predators; etc. For instance, in clear-water mesotrophic lakes, crappies often spawn in the deepest (4 to 6 feet), thickest reed clumps even though the water is clear enough to permit successful spawning much deeper. Apparently, the combination of depth, thick weed cover for protection, and suitable bottom content is so favorable that the crappies prefer to spawn at this depth level. While some fish may spawn shallower or deeper, you can expect the bulk of the population to use approximately the same depth.

Contrast this condition with a stained-to-dark-water reservoir. In this case, crappies generally relate to the best available cover at the "proper depth level." The proper depth level, however, can vary from year to year due to changes in water clarity. Variations in spring snowmelt and/or rainfall can create big differences in water clarity from year to year. Faced with these conditions, crappies adjust their spawning depth to match the prevailing conditions.

By comparison, natural-lake crappies generally experience far less severe changes in water clarity. Thus, you can expect most fish to spawn at approximately the same depth, in and around the same types of natural weed cover, every year.

Clear-water reservoirs, meanwhile, often permit crappies to spawn quite deep—20 feet is not unusual in the clear water of Table Rock Lake, Missouri, for example. The fish often spawn on minor ledges or on whatever timber is available in the proper depth range. Without the presence of natural weed cover (as in natural lakes) to draw them shallow, crappies react by choosing the best combination of elements at a favorable depth level.

Deep-crappie-spawning behavior in highland reservoirs is probably also due in part to competition with largemouth bass for limited spawning areas. Under such conditions, crappies often spawn deeper and later than largemouths. However, when you consider that the water at the 15- or 20-foot level takes longer to warm up than it does in the shallows, crappies may actually be spawning under the same temperature conditions as the bass; it simply occurs at a later time.

In general, then, water clarity provides a good guideline to begin your search for spring crappies. However, you must still locate the best combination of elements available to the fish for consistent springtime success.

## MESOTROPHIC NATURAL LAKES

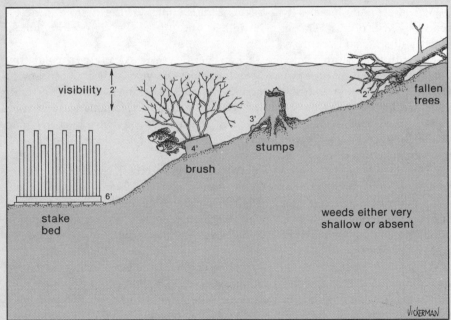

*Crappies often spawn in deep reed clumps even though the water is clear enough that they could spawn deeper. Apparently, the combination of thick cover and proper bottom content is attractive enough to draw them moderately shallow.*

## STAINED-TO-DARK-WATER RESERVOIRS, RIVER BACKWATERS OR STRIP PITS

*Crappies choose spawning depths depending on water clarity: In dirty-water years, they'll spawn shallow; in clearer-water years, they'll spawn deeper. In any case, they'll relate to the best available cover in the proper depth range. General rule: If the visibility is less than 10 feet, crappies often spawn about 2 feet deeper than you can see on a calm, sunny afternoon.*

## CLEAR-WATER RESERVOIRS OR STRIP PITS

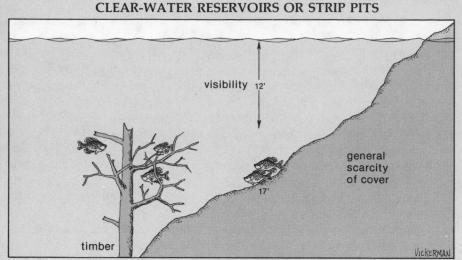

*Crappies relate to the visibility, and cover if it's available. General rule: If visibility is greater than 10 feet, fish usually spawn about 4 to 6 feet deeper than the depth you can see on a calm, sunny afternoon.*

At some point, females will begin joining males in the nest, and actual spawning will occur. Females will mill in and out of the area, although the males will stick stubbornly to their nesting sites.

The entire spawning cycle may take several weeks. At any particular time you might encounter pre-spawn, spawn or post-spawn crappies, depending on which spot you're in and how much the water has warmed. Eventually, only males will remain in the shallows, guarding the nests against attack from predatory panfish, while the females begin drifting out toward deeper water. While they're technically post-spawn fish, the crappies are still in the immediate general vicinity of their spawning sites.

Crappies can be extremely easy to catch while on the nest, which often creates a problem of overharvest. In waters with poor crappie populations and/or limited spawning areas, the fish can be devastated by intense fishing pressure. On the other hand, some huge reservoirs with excellent crappie populations are able to withstand the heavy spring harvest. It all depends on what is available.

We strongly encourage you to practice catch and release during the spring spawning phase (pre-spawn/spawn/post-spawn) unless the crappie population is exceptionally good. In that case, take a few fish to eat and perhaps a trophy for the wall. But, *don't* load up the freezer. In most waters, we'd recommend not taking fish off the beds at all—particularly post-spawn males. Letting them protect the developing eggs will help ensure a crappie fishery for the future. In this event, we recommend fishing other areas or other lakes where the fish have not yet spawned or have finished spawning and left the spawning area completely.

# POST-SPAWN LOCATION

Once spawning is completed, the search for post-spawn crappies begins. This isn't as difficult as you might believe, because the males remain fairly aggressive, and after only a few days of rest the females return to normal status.

The obvious place to begin searching for post-spawn crappies is just outside their spawning areas. Crappies don't instantly move to their summer areas once spawning is completed. You're dealing with an in-between stage, and the way crappies react depends upon what's available to them. Let's look at a few

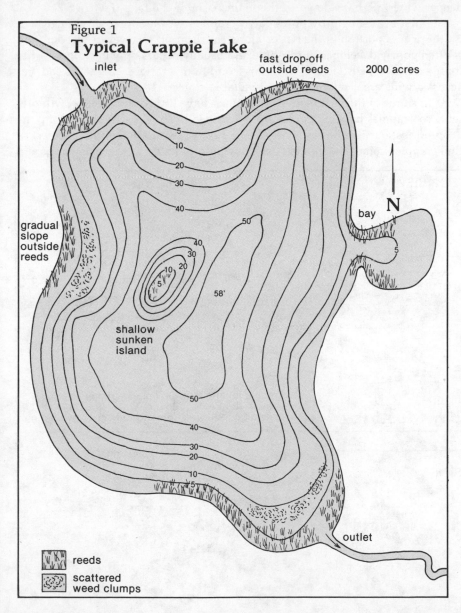

Figure 1
**Typical Crappie Lake**

inlet

fast drop-off
outside reeds

2000 acres

N

gradual
slope
outside
reeds

bay

shallow
sunken
island

58'

outlet

reeds

scattered
weed clumps

examples. Once again, we'll key on natural lakes for our examples. A detailed explanation of reservoir, post-spawn crappie movement is described in Chapter 13.

## BAY MOUTHS

Post-spawn crappies leave the confines of shallow spawning bays and congregate at the bottlenecks or just off the entrance to the bay areas. Such areas typically have a short, shallow flat just outside the bay that drops off into deeper water, perhaps down to the main basin of the lake (*FIGURE 2*).

The first area sought by post-spawn crappies is some form of weedgrowth on the deeper portion of the flat or along the drop-off. However, weedgrowth is often poorly developed at this time and usually occurs only in clumps rather than extensive beds. Faced with this condition, crappies might spread out across a wide area, relating to the available clumps.

At this time of the year, some bay mouths have little or no weedgrowth present, so crappies have no choice but to suspend. They'll school up along the drop-off just outside the bay. Early in the Post-spawn Period you can expect to find crappies immediately outside the bay mouth. Later, as the lake warms and

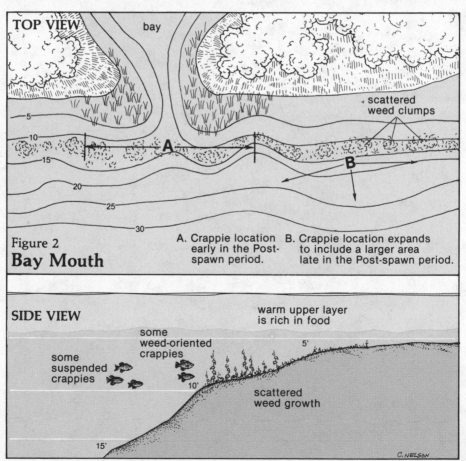

Figure 2
**Bay Mouth**

A. Crappie location early in the Post-spawn period.

B. Crappie location expands to include a larger area late in the Post-spawn period.

weedgrowth develops, they'll roam wider areas along the drop-off. Finally, when summer arrives and the weeds reach their full growth, the crappies might range far and wide and use a variety of places. But directly after the spawn, expect to find them just outside the bay.

The depth at which crappies suspend depends mainly on water color. The clearer the water, the deeper they'll move. In dark water they might be only a couple feet from the surface, whereas in clear water, crappies might be 6 to 10 or more feet down.

Another reason crappies remain near the surface is that the warm layer of surface water is rich in food. Small insects and minnows, particularly the small shiners that are often the crappies' main forage, inhabit this shallow zone. The crappies, understandably, remain very near to or in this feeding zone.

Since shallow bays are generally the warmest water available at this time of year, they generally host the best available food supply. The food chain here gets a head start on the rest of the lake. Wind currents will blow plankton, insects and minnows out of the bay, right to the waiting crappies. Therefore, any time you have a bottleneck situation, chances are you'll find a concentration of crappies. Remember, crappies will never be far from their food.

## CREEK INLETS AND OUTLETS

Creek mouths function much the same as bays, but have the added influence of current. The water flow means inlets and outlets are a perfect place to find food drifting by, making them particularly good attractors. Let's look at each.

Creek inlets generally find crappies spawning on either side of the current flow (*FIGURE 3*). Then as they leave the shallows, the fish once again set up on one or both sides of the current. They'll either relate to the best weedgrowth

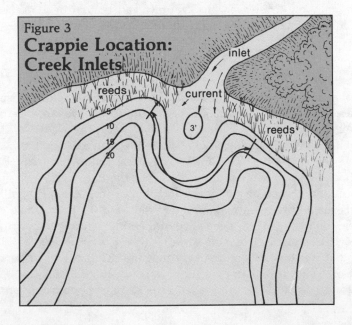

Figure 3
Crappie Location:
Creek Inlets

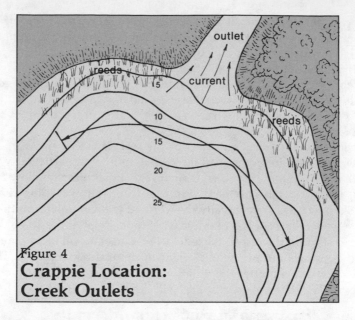

Figure 4
## Crappie Location:
## Creek Outlets

that adjoins the current flow, or simply suspend out in front of the main flow. If the force of the current is strong, they'll remain far out off the drop-off. However, if the current is mild, they'll be tight to the drop-off. Whichever the case, the creek is the main source of their food supply and they won't be far from it.

The main difference in an outlet area is that the current is less well defined and the crappies are more free to roam. They could be found along the drop-off on either side of the outlet (FIGURE 4). In years of low food supply, they'll roam longer distances from the spawning area. In years with good hatches of insects or minnows, however, the crappies can remain in the general outlet area for a long time, until the main lake weeds begin to flourish.

# SHORELINES

Reed-studded shorelines attract spawning crappies, so again it's logical to assume that post-spawn crappies will lurk somewhere nearby. Exactly how they relate to the area, once again depends on what's available. Let's examine two extreme cases.

The first area is a gradually sloping shoreline with a weedy flat between the reeds and the drop-off (FIGURE 5). The basic shallow layout of this area means that the water will warm up on top of the flat, weeds will grow fairly early, and there should be plenty of food. In particular, baitfish will work all along this shallow growth, making it a prime area for post-spawn crappies.

Crappies will hang off the deep edge of these flats during the day. If healthy weedgrowth exists, they'll hug the edge. However, since weeds are seldom well developed at this time, it's more likely that the crappies will suspend out, off the drop-off. They'll remain over deep water during the day and make brief feeding forays toward the food-laden flats during the morning and evening twilight hours.

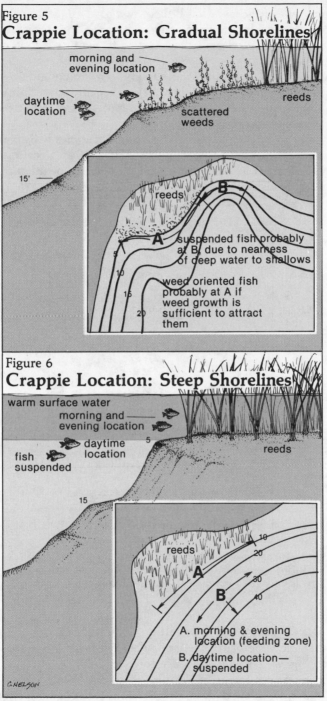

Figure 5
**Crappie Location: Gradual Shorelines**

morning and evening location

daytime location

scattered weeds

reeds

15'

reeds

B

A

suspended fish probably at B, due to nearness of deep water to shallows

weed oriented fish probably at A if weed growth is sufficient to attract them

5
10
15
20

Figure 6
**Crappie Location: Steep Shorelines**

warm surface water

morning and evening location

daytime location

fish suspended

5

reeds

15

reeds

A

B

A. morning & evening location (feeding zone)

B. daytime location— suspended

10
20
30
40

C. NELSON

Take a close look at the structural layout of the area. There's generally a sharp drop-off along some portion of it—usually to one or both sides. The proximity of the deep water to the flat makes *AREA B* the prime spot for crappies to suspend.

The second type of shoreline has little or no flat at all (*FIGURE 6*). The shore simply drops off quickly into deep water. This situation furnishes crappies an ideal spawning location without their having to venture a long distance into the shallows.

In these instances, crappies are more likely to roam up and down the entire drop-off. There's nothing to hold them in one specific spot. Baitfish roam the area outside the reeds, and once again the crappies move in to feed during the low-light periods of morning and evening.

The last areas to warm and the final place the crappies will spawn are reed-studded sunken islands out in the main lake (*FIGURE 7*). Locating post-spawn crappies in these areas is much more difficult because of the vast amount of open water for the fish to suspend in. And since these areas are slow to warm

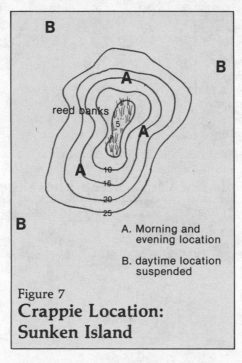

Figure 7
**Crappie Location:
Sunken Island**

A. Morning and
   evening location

B. daytime location
   suspended

up, the food supply is generally limited in spring. Consequently, the crappies are forced into longer forays when searching for food, and they might roam a few hundred yards out over deep water. This often makes locating them quite difficult.

Fortunately, the usable water is limited to the warmer, upper 10 feet or so, because that's where the baitfish will be. This fact helps you limit your search as far as depth goes, but you still have to cover a lot of water.

The most important factor in locating these open-water fish is prevailing winds. For example, a few days of strong winds from one direction will push suspended algae and plankton clouds (food for the baitfish) up against a shoreline. The baitfish, and consequently the crappies, will pile in along that shore to feed.

It's important to remember that the crappie is actually a confined open-water fish. It's not unusual for crappies to move long distances in the course of a few days as they follow their food. And these movements don't have to be in relation to any form of cover. Also, this roaming behavior points out a difference between shore-related crappies that spawn in shallow bays, shorelines, or creek mouths, as opposed to open-water fish that spawn on shallow, main-lake sunken islands.

Here's another interesting aspect of crappie behavior that occurs later in summer. In the course of their post-spawn roaming, fish often run across open-water rockpiles. Some of these rockpiles become prime attractors later, during the Summer Period. The best ones usually top off within 6 to 12 feet of the surface, where sunlight penetration striking the rocks produces a mossy growth that attracts minnows.

Don't expect to find crappies on these rockpiles too early in the season, though. Mid-lake post-spawners are far more likely to roam. The only time they use the rockpiles early in the season is in years of limited food supply.

In conclusion, there are several key features to look for when searching for post-spawn crappies. They shouldn't be too hard to find, because there are fairly obvious structural elements in a good crappie lake. Generally, concentrate your fishing in the warm surface layer of water within these areas. Crappies feed quite aggressively, even during their Post-spawn Period, so they are a fine, early season choice—especially at a time when other gamefish can be very difficult to catch.

The crappie's wide-ranging tendencies make it very difficult to stay on them. However, intense pressure during the vulnerable spawning cycle can take its toll. Once depleted, it takes a long time for the fish to refill a void left by over-harvest. Always exercise a conservation-minded approach when fish come in shallow to spawn.

# PRESENTATION

Presentation techniques for post-spawn crappies are basically the same as summer and fall tactics. In most cases, you'll be after suspended fish. Small jigs or jig and bobber combinations are the best choice.

The exact approach depends on conditions and how the crappies relate to a particular area. As we've already seen, different kinds of areas, types of weed-growth, etc., result in a different fish response. For instance, fish holding along weed edges can be easily caught by casting or bobber fishing. Open-water crappies, however, require covering a lot of water to locate them, so a trolling approach is usually more effective. Trolling lets you cover a wide area quickly and efficiently. You must attack each area in the most effective manner, depending on what you're faced with.

No matter which type of area you're in, however, one invaluable tool is your depth finder. It's very effective for spotting suspended fish. Once you spot the crappies and determine how they're relating to the available habitat, you can then determine your best approach, and 60% of the battle is already won.

Start your search near a bay mouth such as we described in *FIGURE 2*. Slowly motor back and forth across the drop-off where fish might suspend, and watch for suspended fish!

If there's some weedgrowth present, begin fishing there. Pick out the deeper stands of weeds, perhaps in 8 or 10 feet of water. Place a small 1/16-ounce jig about 5 feet below a thin, pencil-type bobber. Tip your jig with a tiny shiner minnow or, if you can't get small shiners, use a 2-inch fathead.

You can cast this combination, but you're usually better off slowly trolling it with your electric motor. Cast out perhaps 30 feet and begin a slow, S-shaped, trolling pass in and out of the weed edge. If crappies are in the weeds, they're usually scattered. That's what makes this trolling approach so effective. You cover a lot of water.

If the crappies aren't right in front of the bay, proceed up or down the drop-off area. Remember, they show a tendency to roam, and you might have to cover a wide area to find them.

Your next choice is between an open shoreline area or a creek mouth. Choose whichever you think has the warmest water. Let's say there's a shoreline area on the north shore that gets good sun exposure and has developed some good weedgrowth. Once again, begin working the weed edge in front of the reed bed. Troll in and out of weeds, keeping an eye out for suspended fish.

If the weedgrowth is poor, don't be afraid to troll out over deep water. Chances are the crappies are suspended. Again, pay careful attention to areas with a sharper drop-off. That's the choice location for suspended fish.

Position the boat just outside the drop-off and try casting a jig up over the weed edge and then swimming it back out to the boat, or cast all around the boat. You never know just where they'll be. Once you locate suspended fish, they're usually concentrated. Stay on them and experiment until you hit the right color pattern, depth and retrieve speed; chances are you'll catch a bunch.

If the shoreline has no weedy flat—just a steep drop like in *FIGURE 6*—it's a good bet that the fish will be schooled and suspended near the reeds. Try moving all along this area. Cast the jig and minnow combination to the reeds and swim it back.

Another deadly lure combo is a small floating jig with a split shot, 24 to 36 inches ahead of it. Hook a minnow and cast it like a regular jig. The drop speed is incredibly slow, even slower than a 1/16-ounce jig, so it works well on finicky fish.

After checking out the shoreline areas, take a look at the creek mouths. Again, the basic procedure is the same. Just remember that if the current is fairly strong, the crappies won't be right in it. They'll relate to the available weed cover on either side of the flow, or suspend off the drop-off where the current is weak enough to be comfortable.

Finally, check out the sunken islands. Use a silent electric motor/bobber trolling technique to cover the weed edge, the drop-off, and the immediately adjacent deeper water.

## Chapter 10

# SUMMER

### Warm-Water Crappies

Since summer is often the most difficult time to locate crappies, especially slabs, many anglers give up after the fish leave their easy-to-find spawning grounds. Crappies make a locational shift as spring progresses and warmer weather arrives; they begin to seek deeper water during the day. Unlike bass, crappies don't prefer shallow weedbeds, lily pads or grassy areas. Instead, they prefer confined open water or deep cover like brush piles, rock piles, deep weedbeds, or wherever schools of baitfish are found. First, we'll look at summer crappie behavior in natural lakes, and then we'll examine their reactions in reservoirs.

In northern mid-mesotrophic and some early eutrophic lakes that house slabs, the two major types of structure crappies relate to are rocks and weeds. Rock piles, without a doubt, are the best trophy spots. Small rock piles are especially good, since they confine the crappies to a much smaller area than a large weedbed. On many lakes, the rocks and weeds will be adjacent to each other, creating particularly attractive crappie sites.

# ROCK PILES

The best rock piles peak about 1 to 5 feet above the level of maximum light penetration. The level of effective light penetration usually corresponds with weedline depth. So, the better rock piles will top off slightly shallower than the weedline. These rock piles may drop off into depths of anywhere from 25 to 60 feet, depending on the lake.

During summer, sunlight encourages the growth of a light, green moss on the rocks. This moss, in turn, attracts small minnows, bullheads and other forage that feed on aquatic insects and other organisms attracted by the moss. Summer crappies usually feed at such sites from predawn through the mid-morning hours.

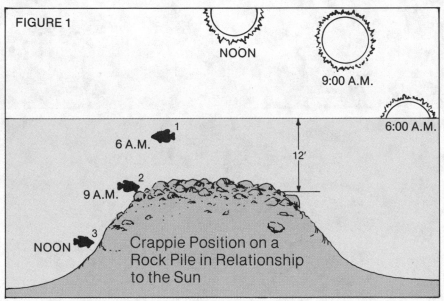

FIGURE 1

NOON

9:00 A.M.

6:00 A.M.

6 A.M. 1

12'

2
9 A.M.

3
NOON

Crappie Position on a Rock Pile in Relationship to the Sun

Let's go through a typical morning crappie movement on a rock pile as shown in *FIGURE #1.* Assume it's been three days since the last cold front. The sun is shining and there are a few, fluffy white cumulus clouds in the sky. In other words, the weather has been stable.

From predawn until about 5 A.M. or 6 A.M. the fish will be positioned over the rock pile as in *POSITION #1.* They may even suspend up to the surface. The crappies tend to be rather loosely grouped at this time of day, since they aren't affected as much by sunlight during these early morning hours.

As the sun rises (between 6 A.M. and 10 A.M.) the crappies will seek the shaded side (usually the west side) of the rock pile *(POSITION #2).* The fish will move to the first drop-off and group closer together. This position is generally about 2 to 4 feet above the depth of maximum light penetration. During the mid-morning hours, the fish are still relatively unaffected by the light and will continue to feed near the bottom.

As the sun's rays gradually become more direct, the crappies will congregate tight against the shady side of the drop-off *(POSITION #3)* and drop to a deeper level as midday approaches. The big crappies—lazy fish by nature—feed at their leisure on minnows that swim past the sharp breakline.

The outside or deep edges of the cabbage weeds on the drop-offs are also excellent crappie spots on these lakes. If rock piles are absent, the deeper cabbage beds will be the preferred midsummer location. The larger weedbeds—usually found on the edge of a shallow, sandy flat that tapers slowly from the shore—will inevitably hold the most crappies.

It is often difficult to find crappies along these big weedbeds, because there is just too much cover. Generally, they'll be located along the drop-off, but you'll still have to look for some irregularity (points or pockets) in the weeds that will attract and hold fish. The thicker cabbage patches are often key sites, since they provide more cover and usually more forage. There may be some weeds all along the entire shoreline drop-off, but they'll often grow thicker in certain places.

Small, isolated cabbage beds on drop-offs can also draw crappies. However, because of their small size they will not hold numbers of fish, but may concentrate a few, easily accessible fish.

Rock piles adjacent to weedbeds are often more attractive than a weedbed alone. The rocks may begin at the edge of the weeds (or even shallower) and extend down to 25 or 30 feet. Where the weeds end and the rocks begin is generally the best place to start. A bottom-bouncing jig or a finely tuned depth finder is the best way to find these rocky sites.

Once you locate a rock pile, scout around until you learn its shape. Then you'll know where to work the area and what part of the structure might hold fish. In fact, this is a good practice with any key spot such as an underwater rock pile or a large weedbed.

Sunken islands with weeds are also prime crappie locations, especially when rocks are present. Depending on the time of day, large groups of fish may work all sides of such an area, shading themselves from the sun. In the morning, the west side would shield them. Around noon, the only place to go would be deeper. Toward evening, the crappies may be up on the east side of the island.

Sunken islands vary considerably in size, shape and weed content. We've found the best ones have at least a hard, sandy bottom—and preferably rock or gravel. Sunken islands with muck bottoms do not seem to be as productive, probably because mucky bottoms do not support cabbage weeds.

Curly cabbage is the weed type most commonly used by crappies. However, coontail is also good. In fact, it often grows to a greater depth than cabbage. Since coontail is thick and spongy, the fish often lie buried in the weeds. Deep coontail serves as a prime holding spot for straggler crappies after a cold front has passed.

## CRAPPIE POSITION IN RELATION TO THE WEEDS

Let's look at a typical, shoreline, weedy drop-off. A weedy, sunken island would also produce the same reaction in crappies. *FIGURE #2* shows crappies

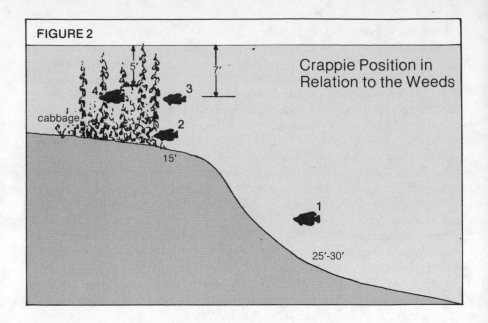

FIGURE 2

Crappie Position in Relation to the Weeds

at four different sites in relation to a weedline.

*POSITION #1* finds the fish suspended anywhere from 5 to 15 feet off the bottom in 25 to 30 feet of water. Crappies will often suspend off a lip like this during the middle of the day under direct sun. This position is also used during cold-front conditions when the fish have a neutral or negative feeding attitude.

*POSITION #2* shows the crappies at the base of the weeds. They will often take this position when feeding. Under favorable conditions the entire school may locate at this point, especially in the late afternoon as the sun becomes less direct and the fish no longer need depth for cover.

Schools of crappies feeding along the edge of the weeds often move horizontally along the weedline and suspend about 5 to 8 feet below the surface *(See POSITION #3)*. This usually will take place in the evening near sunset. Under ideal conditions, you'll see fish "popping" and feeding on the surface as far as 100 feet out from the edge of the weeds. They may cover a considerable distance in their search for food, traveling about 5 feet below the surface.

Under ideal conditions, crappies may move into the weedbed itself *(POSITION #4)*. You may locate some stray fish in the weeds under normal warming trends, but only after several days of warm, stable weather may you find any number of fish moving into the weeds. When they enter the weeds, they tend to be anywhere from near the surface, to about 5 feet down.

To further illustrate crappie location, let's zero in on a specific area in a mid-meso lake that contains several of the areas we've talked about. *FIGURE #3* shows a section of weedline. There are several holding areas that we will need to locate, identify and check.

*AREA A*, a rock pile sitting on the weedline, is the type of spot that will be a fish magnet for many types of fish throughout the season. It is a prime crappie spot, one that deserves concentrated effort.

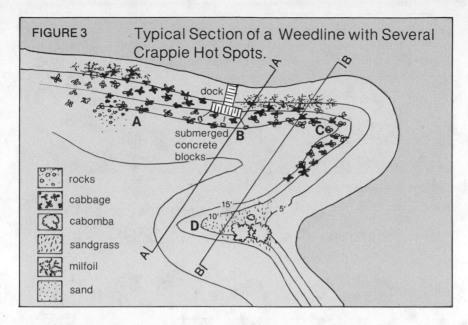

FIGURE 3 Typical Section of a Weedline with Several Crappie Hot Spots.

A dock extends out to the edge of the weeds at *AREA B*. This particular dock happens to be a floating dock with its deep end anchored by three large concrete blocks. The fish relate to these blocks. Large numbers of crappies could even mill around this spot long after the dock has been removed.

*AREA C* is a sharp inside turn in the weedline. At this point, a school of fish moving parallel to the weedline would be forced to do one of several things: Either they could take the turn and follow the weedline out to the weed-covered point, or they could stop and pause at the inside turn. If they stop, they could spread out into shallower water to feed. If they turn and follow the breakline, they would soon show up at the end of the point *(AREA D)*.

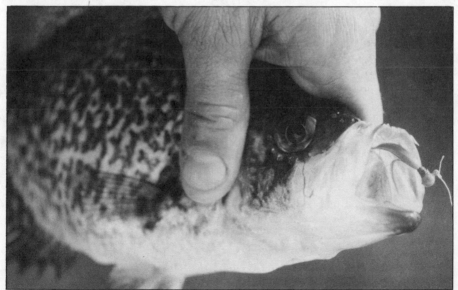

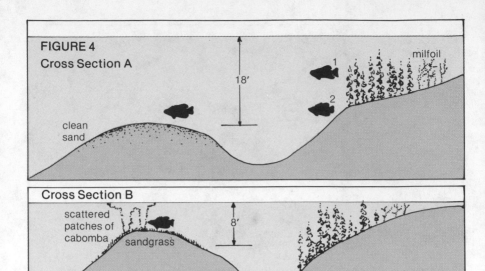

FIGURE 4
Cross Section A

18'

milfoil

1

2

clean
sand

Cross Section B

scattered
patches of
cabomba   sandgrass

8'

The *CROSS-SECTIONS A* and *B* in *FIGURE #4* show the bottom contours found along this stretch, as well as the breaklines formed by weedlines and bottom content. Generally, a school of crappies moving along the shoreline stretch will be found at the edge of the weedline—5 to 8 feet below the surface *(POSITION #1)*. On bright days, you'll find them deeper, at *POSITION #2*, over the edge of the firm bottom, very close to the base of the weeds. The weedgrowth along the shoreline drop-off is primarily a mixture of coontail in the shallows and cabbage in deeper water.

On the weedy point, at *POSITION #3* in *CROSS SECTION B*, the weeds are mostly sandgrass with a few scattered patches of coontail. If the crappies are actively feeding, they'll usually spread out on top and suspend about a foot or two above the sandgrass. They rarely move shallower than 6 feet. When they are less aggressive, they hold on the very end of the bar above the clean sand bottom, and hang about 15 feet under the surface.

The same pattern will hold true at the inside turn *(AREA C in FIGURE #3)*. When they are feeding heavily, they often move into the weedgrowth, or just over it. When they have a neutral attitude, they tend to remain outside the vegetation and suspend at about 15 feet, even though that's closer to bottom here than on the end of the point.

In fact, there often seems to be a "key" depth on various lakes at which crappies hold or move along weedlines. But, they will leave this depth when they're actively feeding in or around cover. The key depth varies from lake to lake, depending on conditions. By keeping an eye on the depth finder while moving around the lake (especially when you're in crappie areas), you'll often see suspended fish. Don't waste time trying to catch fish every time your depth finder shows some but, you will notice that the bulk of the fish are in a band

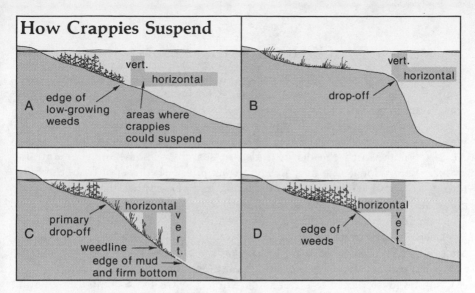

## How Crappies Suspend

**A** — edge of low-growing weeds · vert. · horizontal · areas where crappies could suspend

**B** — drop-off · vert. · horizontal

**C** — primary drop-off · horizontal · vert. · weedline · edge of mud and firm bottom

**D** — edge of weeds · horizontal · vert.

In natural lakes, crappies often relate to the deep edge of the weeds. But, they also use the edge of the drop-off, and even the breakline formed where hard bottom meets the muck bottom of the lake's deep-water basin.

Obviously, a sensitive depth sounder is an invaluable aid in locating suspended crappies, measuring their depth and how they're relating to a breakline. Knowing the relationship between a breakline and the path that a school of crappies is traveling is a must if you expect to stay in contact with moving fish.

POSITION A shows the fish in a fairly typical late summer position, assuming that they are in a lake in which there are some deep growing, low-lying weeds, preferably sandgrass. In a lake where this type of condition is common, the crappies might position themselves in this area frequently throughout the course of the season, although it seems to be much more prevalent at the tail end of summer and into the Post-summer Period.

POSITION B illustrates the common position of suspended crappies in lakes where the weedgrowth does not extend all the way to the drop-off. Depending on the type and location of their prime forage, crappies will usually relate to the drop-off either horizontally or vertically.

A similar situation is often found in extremely clear lakes, where the weedgrowth often grows well past the drop-off. This is shown in POSITION C. Note that there is a larger area for the fish to relate to, and finding them is that much more difficult. In a situation like this, they could suspend either vertically or horizontally from the edge of the drop-off or weedline, or relate to both breaklines simultaneously.

POSITION D shows two positions. It shows the fish suspended horizontally from the deep edge of the weedgrowth, and also suspended vertically from the breakline formed where soft and hard bottom meet at the edge of the basin area. Fish relating to the deep edge of the weeds could be just about any distance horizontally off the weedline. But, if they are at the approximate depth of the deep edge of the weeds, it's a good bet that they are relating to that edge and will follow its contours.

of a few feet. When you start looking for crappies, start at that depth range.

Be opportunistic and pinpoint the fish in areas where they are most likely active. For the most part, this means fishing schools which are either "holding" at one of the areas we've mentioned and/or have moved "over the cover" and are actively feeding. On the section of lake shown in FIGURE #3, A, B, C & D are such areas.

# FISHING THE AREA

Let's assume that during the course of the morning you've noticed suspended fish just outside the weedline at 12 feet. After lunch, you decide to give the crappies a go, so where do you start?

First, locate irregularities along the weedline. Then move the boat along the weedline, using an electric motor, while tossing a jig and "swimming" it back. At this point, watch the depth finder to search for some unusual bottom feature. Before long, you may locate a rock pile. Fish this spot from the bottom up to about 7 feet, using both casting and vertical fishing methods, and allow about ten minutes for some sign of activity.

If you don't make fish contact, move to the next spot, "fishing through" the intermediate area by casting jigs and watching the depth finder for additional areas. Once you reach the dock, just repeat the procedure you used at the rock pile. This process should be continued all along the weedline.

Crappies located between "hot spots" should be treated as a moving school. If you find them at the rock pile, on the other hand, assume that they are holding there. When dealing with a moving school, it's important to determine the direction they're traveling. Drop a marker when contact is made and then fish 30 or 40 yards past the marker in one direction. If no contact is made within 15 minutes or so, quickly check the marked spot again to see if the crappies might be holding at some overlooked feature. If the fish are no longer there, it would be safe to assume that they are moving in the opposite direction. Move down the breakline in that direction, fifty yards or so, casting ahead of the boat, and you'll make contact again.

Generally, moving fish are slightly more active and more prone to take a lure, but holding fish are easier to present a lure to. Each situation has its advantages and disadvantages, but crappies can be caught in either case. However, you must have an idea of what you're dealing with if you expect to score heavily.

During summer, active crappies seem to spend a majority of their time moving parallel to some type of weedline. Therefore, location becomes the key. Once the fish are located, presentation is generally not too difficult.

# PLAYING THE WIND

Another key to crappie location is the velocity and direction of the wind. Small minnows which are crappie prey, feed primarily on free-floating microorganisms and plankton. The plankton, which the minnows follow, is moved by wind-formed currents. Often, crappie fishing will be excellent on the side of the lake receiving the wind and poor on the protected shore. Apparently, there is a plankton buildup along the windward shore that triggers feeding activity.

Do the crappies follow the minnows around the lake? Probably not. Rather, the crappies in the wind-blown areas become active, triggered by the influx of an abundance of prey, while the crappies on the opposite shore turn off when their food supply temporarily disappears.

# PRESENTATION

One of the major thrills of catching big  slab crappies is landing them on light tackle. Because crappie lures are small, light tackle is necessary to work the lures effectively. Not only are you looking for fish that are larger than the typical panfish, but you're going to have a lot of fun catching them, as well.

No doubt jigs account for more crappie catches than all other methods combined. Jigs in the 1/16- to 1/8-ounce range are generally the most effective. They are small enough to appeal to crappies and heavy enough for easy casting or backtrolling.

By experimenting with sizes and styles of jigheads along with varieties of body dressing, you can achieve any type of action that the crappies may desire. One important fact to remember is that lures in the 1½- to 2½-inch range are generally the most effective. Don't overdo the action. Keep it slow and simple.

It generally pays to tip a crappie jig with a small minnow. Actively feeding fish may strike a plain jig, but neutral-attitude fish usually must be tempted. A 1½- to 2-inch fathead minnow, hooked upward through the jaw and out the top of the skull, is perfect. Small shiners are also good, although they require more careful handling than the durable fatheads. A small strip of pork rind or a 2-inch Twister-type tail is also a good substitute if bait is not available. In addition, you can add a scent product if it gives you confidence. However, experience has shown that scent products are more effective in cold water.

# TACKLE

Specialized tackle will help you present these small lures properly. Although you can get by with standard spinning equipment, a long, sensitive, ultralight rod will make crappie fishing much easier.

Light lures require long rods for casting. It's similar to casting a split-shot/nightcrawler combination for walleyes. You need an extra long rod to swing the bait out on a cast, rather than casting with a quick snap of the wrist, which usually rips the bait off the hook.

A good crappie rod is long, flexible and light enough to handle 2- to 4-pound-test line. It allows you to fight crappies without putting undue pressure on the line. Let the rod absorb the strain, not the line. And, since a crappie's mouth structure is quite delicate, it's best to use a soft rod that will absorb shock and prevent tearing the hook from the fish's mouth.

A quality, ultralight spinning reel is also recommended. The larger, standard-size reels are too bulky to efficiently handle 2- to 4-pound-test line.

# CATCHING CRAPPIES NEAR THE BOTTOM

The most efficient way of working crappie jigs in deep water is to slowly backtroll. This is extremely effective when the fish are near the bottom, such as at the base of a weedline or on the edge of a rock pile. The jig is constantly in productive water, as compared to casting, where the jig is in the fish zone for a relatively small amount of time.

The key to backtrolling 1/16- to 1/8-ounce jigs successfully is to move the boat very slowly. The best way to accomplish this is to drift and occasionally use an electric motor to keep the boat in proper position. Moving slowly lets you use a short line and fish vertically while keeping the jig in contact with the bottom. You also retain maximum lure control and are in an excellent position to feel a strike.

Crappies often hit the jig very lightly, so you must pay careful attention to any change in the feel of the jig. In fact, it pays to watch the line where it enters the water. Your only indication of a strike may be a slight twitch in the line when the crappie sucks in the jig; you may not even feel it. We strongly suggest that you rest your index finger on the line in order to enhance your sense of feel.

Working the jig with a slow, lift/drop action is very effective. Simply raise and lower the rod tip about a foot. This approach will maintain frequent contact with the bottom but reduce the tendency to get snagged. Try pausing occasionally, or even giving the jig a slight jerk once in awhile. It may trigger an inactive fish into striking. In general, though, keep the action to a minimum for crappies. Even a slow drag across the bottom can produce, providing the area is relatively snag free.

For example, to work a deep rock pile, slowly backtroll a jig around the top lip, and then progressively work your way down the shaded side in depth increments of two feet or so. Make a pass at 18 feet, then 20, then 22, etc. It's a very effective, thorough way to check an area. Backtrolling the base of a weedline or the adjacent drop-off would be much the same. We prefer not to anchor in these areas, because that will usually spook the school.

## LIVE BAIT RIGS

Another excellent way to take crappies that are near the bottom is with a live-bait rig with a very light slip sinker (preferably 1/8-ounce) or a slip shot. The rigs can be backtrolled or drifted along the weedline or the edge of a rock pile and are an effective way to present a small minnow in deeper water.

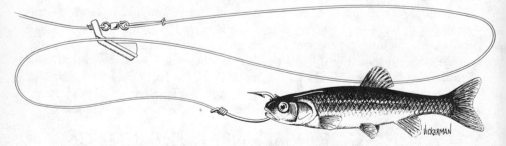

Again, the best choice is a 1½- to 2-inch fathead minnow. Shiners will work, but they tend to swim higher, while fatheads will try to duck down into the rocks and moss. This attempt to hide seems to trigger neutral crappies.

A long leader (4 to 6 feet) is preferable, especially if the fish are several feet above bottom. In this case, use shiners, and let them swim up to the crappies. Otherwise, stick to fatheads.

Pay careful attention to how crappies hit the minnow. If they run after a strike, it's an indication of a competitive, aggressive, feeding fish. In this case, switch to jigs which will allow you to fish faster. If the crappie doesn't run, it could indicate two things: You've either hit a straggler, or the school is inactive and not feeding; subsequent casts will determine this.

If there are more fish present, try removing the swivel from the live-bait rig, which will allow the slip sinker to slide down to the minnow. You can then jig the minnow, achieve a little more action, and perhaps trigger a few more fish. Should the fish turn on and start feeding, switch to a jig and minnow combination.

## SUSPENDED FISH

These are the ones you spot on your depth finder—the times when you're running across the lake, and suddenly your depth finder lights up like a Christmas tree. You have a huge school of fish from 12 to 17 feet suspended over 30 feet of water. How do you handle it?

First, remember that fish suspended near a weedbed or rock pile will tend to be much more catchable than fish that are seemingly unrelated to anything. Why? Because fish that are near their food source are usually there for a reason. They are going to feed or have fed recently. Those that have little inclination to feed can be suspended anywhere. Percentage-wise, stick with those that are near a food source.

You can catch these fish by placing a jig and minnow at the proper depth. Either lower a jig and hold it there, or suspend it with a bobber.

To keep a jig at the right depth without a bobber, place a rubber band around your reel spool when you've let out the proper amount of line. After you catch a fish, let the line out again and the rubber band will stop it at the proper depth.

When vertically jigging, always set your depth so the tip of the rod is only a few inches from the surface of the water when the lure is at its lowest point in your jigging motion. This allows you to keep the line out of the wind, results in better feel, and gives you maximum rod sweep when setting the hook. Also, if you place the line over your index finger as if you were backtrolling (but with the bail closed), you'll be able to feel the light peck of a crappie when it inhales the jig.

The most efficient way to present a lure to deep-water, suspended crappies is to fish vertically. But most lures are very difficult to work in this manner. With this thought in mind, who does more vertical fishing than an ice fisherman? Ice-fishing tackle provides one of the best vertical-fishing lures, the jigging Rapala. This lure hangs horizontal when stationary and swims around in circles when moved. Crappies prefer the two smallest (3 and 5 cm) sizes. Jigging Rapalas work best with either a very slow, rhythmic pumping action (1 to 2 feet) or by holding them still as possible while you drift.

Deep-water bobber techniques require a slip bobber. Place the bobber stop on your line at the proper depth, and you can backtroll, drift or even cast. The bait automatically returns to the proper depth. You'll have the same degree of control as with the rubber band/spool combination.

# CRAPPIES NEAR THE SURFACE

Most of the time, crappies near the surface are adjacent to a weedbed or brush pile. Such shallow depths (1 to 6 feet) allow you to cast as well as backtroll or drift. In fact, casting is the better technique, since it places the lures out and away from the boat which prevents spooking shallow fish.

The best way to check a weedbed is by swimming a jig over the tops of the weeds. Simply cast a jig over the weeds; let it sink to the approximate depth of the top of the weeds, and slowly reel in the line. Trial and error will determine how long to let the jig sink and how fast to reel in to get the right combination.

Crappies suspended just outside the weeds can also be fished by swimming a jig. Of course, you'll have to get the proper depth. And remember, the larger crappies are usually slightly deeper than the smaller ones. If you're catching small crappies, let your jig sink a little deeper. If the small crappies hit your jig before it sinks far enough, try casting past the school and retrieving a little deeper so the bigger fish will have an opportunity to hit it.

Use your electric motor and move down a weedline, casting ahead with the jig. Meanwhile, a second person can simultaneously backtroll a jig on the bottom. In this way you'll cover all depths. It's a very quick and efficient way to cover water and locate fish.

A bobber works well for fishing crappies near the surface. It's better when the fish are actually inside the weeds, since it's hard to swim the jig through heavy weeds by casting. When the fish are just beneath the surface (1 to 4 feet), you can get by with a standard bobber. If they're deeper, you'll need a slip bobber to cast effectively. In either case, rig the jig/minnow, or a minnow hooked beneath the dorsal fin with a number 6 or 8 hook, at the proper depth below the bobber.

When working these shallow crappies, remember to keep a low profile. If you stand up in the boat, you may spook the whole school. But if you stay low, you can work right on top of them.

# INSECT-FEEDING CRAPPIES

When the crappies are feeding on insects, use a tiny jig (1/32 or 1/64 ounce). Obviously, this small size makes casting, trolling, and general handling very difficult. Fortunately, crappies feed on emerging insects just as the insects emerge from the bottom, or just as they rise to the surface.

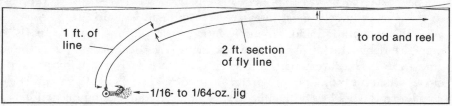

1 ft. of line

2 ft. section of fly line

to rod and reel

1/16- to 1/64-oz. jig

*Trim down a 1/16-ounce marabou jig so the chenille-wrapped jig has only a quarter-inch of marabou extending past the hook shank. The real key, however, is to tie a 2-foot section of floating fly line one foot above the jig. Splice this onto your main line. The secret is that the fly line acts as a super sensitive float. Work the lure with a series of slow twitches, never allowing the jig to sink more than a couple feet. The action is almost unreal, and produces slab crappies.*

*A tiny 1/64-ounce jig fished 2 feet below the surface tricked these insect-feeding crappies. Don't underestimate the value of small jigs when fishing crappies—they're dynamite.*

When crappies feed on insects near the surface, you can often spot these smaller insects on the surface. This is common in late afternoon or early evening during the summer period. The best way to take these fish is to use a small bobber and suspend a tiny 1/64-ounce jig, 12 to 24 inches below the surface, or use the tip shown in the accompanying illustration—using a piece of floating fly line. Move the jig in short, slow movements (a few inches at a time), and allow long pauses between movements.

The opposite situation would occur when crappies are feeding on emerging insects near the bottom. This commonly occurs several days after a severe cold front. It's not an easy time to fish for crappies, because they appear to be adversely affected by cold fronts. But, there are some things you can do.

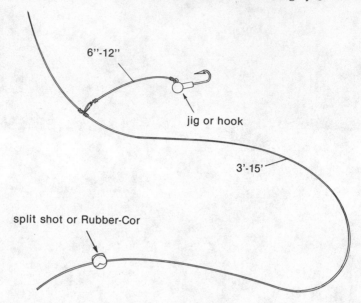

6"-12"

jig or hook

3'-15'

split shot or Rubber-Cor

*We've had considerable success with a light tackle variation of the tightline rig for backtrolling for suspended fish in summer. A single No. 8 hook or a 1/16-ounce jighead is tied on a short dropper at least three and sometimes as much as 15 feet from the end of the line. A big split shot is lightly crimped to the line beyond the dropper. The split shot (or a Rubber-Cor sinker) can be moved up or down the line to control the distance that bait is presented off bottom. When using this rig, the bait is lip-hooked, as opposed to the typical method of hooking minnows behind the dorsal fin.*

*This set-up allows you to keep your bait a specific distance above bottom, and the tight line maintained by the heavy split shot tremendously increases your sense of feel. It works well with just a plain crappie jig as well. Using this type of set-up allows you to backtroll slowly for suspended fish in open water and provides precise control over (and direct contact with) your lure or bait at all times. No other backtrolling presentation for suspended fish provides this.*

*Your hooking ratio will skyrocket with this type of backtrolling set-up as opposed to a slip-sinker jig with a long snell and floating jig.*

A cold-front dropper rig can be used to present a 1/64-ounce jig or a dull-colored trout nymph near the bottom. Tie the jig to a 3- to 6-inch dropper line about 18 inches above the end of the main line, and then place a #5 split shot on the end of the main line. It's sort of an ultralight version of the Wolf River Walleye Rig!

To retain maximum feel of the dropper rig, keep the line as vertical as possible, directly below the boat. Because of its light weight, drift or backtroll the rig very slowly, keeping the split shot in contact with the bottom. The split shot not only allows precise depth control with a tiny jig, but in the event of a hang-up, a firm pull on the line will release it, and all you've lost is a split shot.

# Chapter 11

# FALL

## Cold-Water Crappies

As summer winds down, autumn arrives bringing shorter days and cooler temperatures. Autumn includes two Calendar Periods: the Turnover Period and the Cold Water Period. In response to seasonal environmental changes, crappies make adjustments in their behavior.

The most drastic fall turnover situation occurs in bodies of water which stratify in distinct temperature layers during the summer. Since cold water is heavier than warm water, the warmer water stays on top and the colder water sinks and builds up on the bottom; in between lies a narrow band of rapid temperature change from warm to cold water called the thermocline.

In these waters, the thermocline condition usually remains in effect throughout most of the summer. But during the tail end of summer the angle of the sun to the earth becomes less direct, and the environment begins to cool. Additionally, seasonal, hard-driving, cold winds and rain begin rapidly chilling the surface temperature of the water. As the heavier (colder) surface water begins sinking, it comes in contact with the warmer water below. This action forces the lighter, yet warmer, deeper water back to the surface. Eventually, the thermocline layer ruptures, and a mixing or "turning over" process takes place. As the wind whips the water, the mixing action continues until it thoroughly homogenizes the water to a point where the whole body of water is the same temperature. This process also reoxygenates the deep water.

The actual turnover process itself takes place once the thermocline layer ruptures. But the turmoil (side effects) that results usually adversely affects the fish for a period of time before and after this event actually occurs. Fishing doesn't pick up again until conditions stabilize. In general, once the water temperature drops to about 55°F and the water clears perceptibly, cold-water fishing patterns emerge.

As a time of turmoil, the Turnover Period is relative. First, all bodies of water do not thermocline during summer, so many do not "turn over" as such. Most rivers are a case in point. Lakes and reservoirs, too, may or may not stratify. Usually, shallow bodies of water—which the wind periodically stirs up—or waters with a lot of current flowing through them, do not stratify. Consequently, the fish in these waters are not subjected to as much stress as fish in waters where the transition from a warm- to a cold-water environment is a traumatic event. Nonetheless, the change from a warmer- to a cooler- to a colder-water environment demands some adjustment by both fish *and* fisherman.

In any case, fishing during the Turnover Period on bodies of water that actually thermocline is tough, to say the least. However, since all bodies of water do not turn over at the same time, it is usually best to avoid fishing this condition by switching to: (1) waters which have already turned over, (2) bodies of water which have not yet begun to turn over, or (3) waters which don't thermocline at all—such as rivers or large, shallow, windswept lakes.

The entire time span from the end of the turnover to freeze-up (on bodies of water that freeze over) is termed the Cold Water Period. This period is characterized by a gradual slowing down of a fish's metabolism and stabilization process of the entire ecosystem.

As the days grow steadily shorter, weedgrowth, insect hatches and plankton blooms diminish. In addition the chemical characteristics of the water can vary considerably with the changing season, and this has multiple effects on plant and fish life.

Let's take a close look at cold-water crappie location and presentation on mesotrophic lakes, Canadian shield lakes, and reservoirs.

# MESOTROPHIC LAKES

As summer wanes and September arrives, the weather generally takes a turn for the worse. The wind switches to the north, delivering a week or so of icy blasts, heralding the end of summer and the arrival of the fall turnover. The sudden drop in temperature and strong winds churn the lakes into a state of turmoil, mixing the water and breaking up the summer thermocline. The locational patterns of the fish are disrupted, and feeding activity comes to a virtual halt. It's a tough time for both fish and fisherman!

After a week or ten days of this confusion, conditions generally stabilize. Fall has arrived. The weather takes on a more predictable pattern, although the general trend moves toward an increasingly cooler environment. The thermocline is gone, so both the temperature and oxygen content of the lake are virtually constant from top to bottom. This reopens a wide range of deep lake zones for fish use.

Under these conditions, smallmouths, walleyes and northerns generally begin to move deeper. Largemouths begin deserting the extreme shallows and pile up on the weedlines and weedy flats. Everything seems to be moving deeper. Everything, that is, except crappies!

## Cold-Water Crappie Location

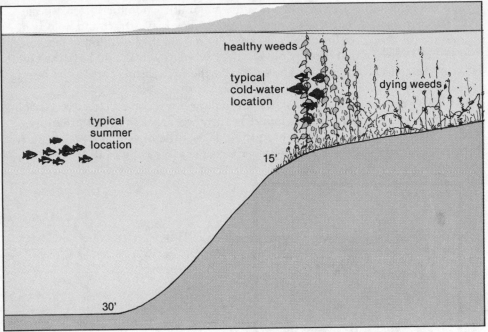

*Note the difference in fall crappie location as opposed to their usual summer pattern. During the summer, crappies spend a large part of the day suspended in open water outside the weeds. In early fall, however, they'll usually be right up against the weeds, or even a bit inside of them. A quick check of the weedline should tell you if there's any fish using the area.*

Strangely enough, at this time, crappies may move *toward* the shallows rather than away from them! *Toward* them, but not *into* them. It's an important point that requires explanation.

Early fall crappies generally remain in the same areas they inhabited before the fall turnover; however, now they'll move in much *closer to cover*. Rather than suspending 100 feet away from a deep weedline as in midsummer, they'll generally be right next to or even a few feet inside it. Similarly, instead of suspending well off the side of a rock pile or weedy sunken island, they'll remain very near the edge.

Fall crappies converge into smaller, more well defined areas than they did in summer. This naturally makes them a bit harder to locate than summer fish. Simply cruising along the deep weedline is no guarantee that you'll spot the fish on your depth finder. You'll probably have to fish weed edges or the rims of weedy sunken islands in order to locate crappies. Once you find them, however, their compact schooling tendency leads to fast action and lots of fish.

Fall crappies can continue to display this weedline-oriented behavior as long as the deep weeds remain green and healthy. How long does this last? Well, a lake's shallowest weeds characteristically begin dying early in the fall, giving off offensive hydrogen sulfide gas. This drives bass, bluegills and other fish out to the weedline. Yet, the deepest growing weeds generally remain healthy far into the Fall Cold Water Period and are a major attraction for various species of fish. As long as the weeds remain healthy, they may attract and hold fish.

Since the deepest-growing weeds generally remain the healthiest in late fall, it stands to reason that lakes with very deep weedgrowth should have the best weedline concentrations of crappies late in the fall season. Experience bears this out.

Smaller and/or dark-water lakes with shallower weedlines (8 to 10 feet) cool off faster and are less able to support healthy weedgrowth as fall progresses. Conversely, big, deep, clear mesotrophic lakes—the ones that usually grow trophy crappies—generally have deeper weedlines (typically 14 to 18 feet) that

*Gary Korsgaden displays a 3-lb.-class crappie. Monster crappies are Gary's specialty; he has contributed much to our knowledge of these elusive fish.*

remain quite healthy until the lakes begin to freeze. Therefore, it's easy to see that large lakes not only give you the best shot at trophy crappies, but also have the best concentrations of late fall weedline fish, as well.

## LATE FALL LOCATION

A time comes when even the deepest weeds begin dying off and become poor fish habitat. This occurs first in shallow lakes and eventually in deep, clear ones. Since the weeds are no longer suitable to the fish, something has to give.

It does. Once the deep weeds die, both the baitfish and the crappies leave the area. At this point, crappies may revert to their characteristic behavior and suspend again if there are no suitable deep-water structural elements available for their use. They'll move out over the deeper water in the lake, suspending near a food source at whatever depth is most comfortable to them.

Once you find them, crappies are still very catchable at this time, but rather than being on an edge (a weedline or a rock pile), the crappies could now be out in the middle of nowhere. It's back to the hunting approach of summer to locate crappies.

The best way to locate crappies under these conditions is to look just outside the areas which they used in early fall. Begin searching the adjacent deep water. Slowly cruise back and forth, watching your depth finder. Look for the telltale flashes that signal suspended fish. It may take awhile, but once you locate crappies, you can catch a bunch.

## ROCK PILES

A far easier condition to fish occurs when deep crappies congregate in the vicinity of deep structural elements. Deep rock piles are perhaps the most consistent, fall-crappie producers, yet they're usually the most ignored areas. That's because most anglers simply don't understand how crappies live. Many people think that crappies live in the weeds—which is quite the opposite of what actually occurs. Open-water rock piles attract crappies—often the largest ones in the lake.

Any time a rock pile is shallow enough to receive some degree of sunlight, moss (algae) will grow on the rocks. This kicks off a food chain of tiny organisms which serves as food for small minnows. And where there are tiny minnows, chances are that crappies are nearby. Inactive crappies suspend off the sides of such areas and move in to feed on the minnows.

Rock piles remain productive through the entire fall season, as opposed to weed areas which lose their attractiveness as the weeds die out. In fact, rock piles seem to get better as fall progresses, because as healthy weeds become more scarce, crappies shift location and many of these displaced fish relocate on rock piles. Late fall often finds massive concentrations of crappies in such spots, where they'll remain until just before the lake freezes. Then the crappies often move to open water to suspend for the winter.

In a nutshell then, crappies may relate to deep, healthy weedgrowth or rock piles during much of the early Fall Cold Water Period. As the weeds die, the fish shift toward other healthy weeds or onto the rocks. Or, in lakes with poor weedgrowth, crappies may shift deeper directly after the turnover. Finally, just before freeze-up, crappies often move out and suspend over the deepest water in the lake. That's where you'll find them during most of the winter.

## SUNLIGHT AND FISH POSITION

Crappies are by nature low-light feeders, so most anglers experience their best success during the morning and evening hours. It's at these times that summer crappies are nearest the weedlines and in an aggressive feeding mood. Many anglers think crappies live in the weeds, because that's the only place they catch them.

The few crappie anglers probing the lakes in fall usually experience improved fishing, because crappies remain near the weedline area and are accessible. In addition, the sun is lower in the sky, the days are shorter, and the crappies are more prone to feeding all day long, instead of just during morning and evening. All in all, conditions are ripe for consistent action.

Cloudy weather really triggers some superb crappie fishing. Photosynthesis slows down during cloudy weather, so the amount of oxygen produced by the weeds is reduced. Consequently, baitfish move outside the weed edge and become easy prey. Feeding occurs all day long, so conditions are perhaps best for taking fall crappies. Contrast this situation with deep-water, fall smallmouth activity, which is usually best on sunny days! Knowing how different species behave lets you adjust your approach to take advantage of weather conditions.

## EQUIPMENT

Catching fall crappies seldom requires more than a few, simple, jigging techniques; a handful of small jigs; a few bobbers; and a bucketful of small minnows. There's no need to invest in fancy equipment, because when it comes to crappies, the more simple your approach, the better.

## JIGS

The most productive crappie jigs are in the 1/32- to 1/8-ounce range. These lightweight jigs sink slowly and provide excellent depth control, which is essential when you're fishing for suspended fish. You can easily keep the smaller jigs at the crappies' level; heavier jigs tend to sink too fast. Crappies also prefer smaller jigs which match the small-sized food they generally feed on. If you place a larger, bulkier 1/4-ounce jig right on their noses, chances are they'll simply ignore it. It's simply too big.

Gary Korsgaden feels that the best, all-around, crappie jigs are 1/16- and 1/8-ounce marabou jigs. The slow-breathing action of the marabou is very enticing, even when the jig is motionless. He prefers to thin out the jig by shortening and pulling out about half the marabou. This cuts the bulk to a minimum. This may seem picky, but in the long run it makes a difference.

Is marabou the only jig style to use? Not necessarily. If the crappies are slightly into the weeds, the marabou feathers may pick up stringy moss and

The accompanying photo shows several of the more popular crappie jigs. First, (upper left) is a 1/16-ounce Bass Buster marabou. It's an excellent choice for most conditions.

In the center is a Lindy Fuzz-E-Grub and at the upper right is one of Gapen's Ugly Bugs. They're also good in most instances—especially in areas where moss tends to cling to a marabou jig.

At the lower left is Northland's Whistler jig. The tiny propeller makes it sink very slowly and helps it remain at a constant depth level when retrieved.

Finally, at the lower right is Grassl's Flu-Flu jig. It's only 1/32 ounce, but will catch fish under conditions when they ignore larger sized jigs.

Experience shows that light-colored jigs outproduce darker shades many times over when it comes to crappies. Crappies feed chiefly on small minnows, which are usually light or silvery in color. White, yellow or chartreuse jigs match this natural food best and are your top, color choices for crappies.

completely lose their attractiveness. You'd be better off with a rubber-bodied jig, because it will come through the weeds clean and is much more effective in this instance. It all boils down to matching your jig to conditions.

Finally, when using a jig and bobber approach, a 1/32-ounce Grassl's Flu-Flu jig or similar jig works very well. It's very light, tiny, and may be difficult to cast unless you have the extra weight of a bobber to help cast it. But for a bobber approach, ultra-small jigs are excellent.

# BOBBERS

There are several bobber styles to choose from, and naturally each has its strong point. Let's examine each of them.

A long, thin, quill-type bobber has the least water resistance and is a natural choice for finicky crappies. It works best in and around reeds for spawning crappies or when crappies are near the surface. It's an excellent choice, when there isn't too much wind. If the wind kicks up, though, these lightweight bobbers become very difficult to cast.

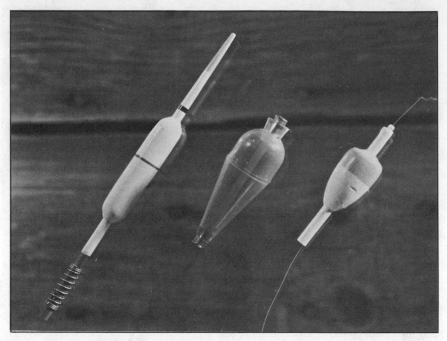

*Here are three types of bobbers that fit the bill for crappies. The quill type (left) has little water resistance and has the least spooking effect. The Adjust-A-Bubble (center) can be partially filled with water, giving you some added weight to make casting easier. At the right is the slip-bobber arrangement that allows you to fish at any depth. The small bobber stop placed on the line keeps your lure at the proper depth.*

For windy conditions, a plastic bubble like the Adjust-A-Bubble is dynamite. You can partially fill it with water, giving it added weight for casting into the wind. Its unique, thread-on, twist-tighten feature doesn't damage your line like most bobbers do. This is a real plus, because when you're fishing 4-pound-test line to begin with, there's no room for error. A damaged line doesn't last long.

Finally, when the fish are deeper than 4 feet, you'll probably need a slip bobber. A slip bobber and a bobber stop will let you fish the jig at any depth. It works as well in 6 feet as it does in 20, so you can fish wherever the fish are.

## TACKLE

The light line and tiny lures used for crappie fishing should be teamed with quality spinning gear. Although you can use standard spinning tackle, serious crappie addicts prefer to specialize a bit. A premium, ultralight spinning outfit is perfect for casting or trolling tiny jigs. However, a long, 8-foot fly-rod blank might serve your purpose better for casting small, lightweight bobbers. The extra length lets you lob the bobber out, instead of casting with a quick wrist snap. A spinning rod made from such a fly-rod blank is not a very versatile piece of equipment, but it really fits the bill for this approach. If you really get into fishing crappies, consider buying or making one.

# PRESENTATION

The best way to choose a jigging technique is to match each approach to the type of cover and fish's position. That's exactly what you do when you're on the water. Let's take a look at each of them and examine the strong points of each.

## WORKING THE WEEDLINE

Let's say you suspect that fall crappies are relating to a particular point or bar formation. The best way to check for the presence of crappies is to fish the weedline. Remember, late-summer or early-fall crappies are often so tight to the weedline that you can't count on spotting them with your depth finder. They'll blend in with the weeds. Therefore, you'll need to manually fish the area to see if they're present.

Begin at one end of the area and position the boat just outside the weedline. One person should cast a small jig into the weeds and then slowly swim it back to the boat. Adjust your retrieve speed so that the jig occasionally touches the weeds without fouling too often. The other person should cast parallel to the

## Typical Early Fall Crappie Locations in a Meso Lake

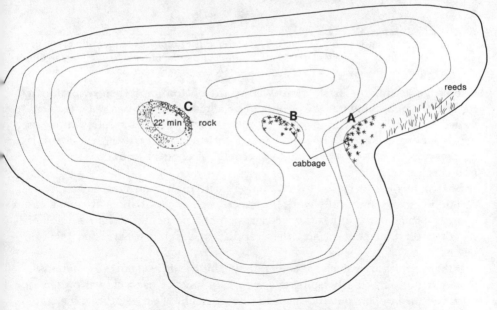

*A quick look at this lake map section gives you a pretty good idea where to begin looking for fall crappies. The major attractions would be the weedy point, weedy sunken island, and the rocky hump.*

*Since crappies suspend and have an affinity for deep, open water, you'd generally find them on the sides of these areas that have the fastest drop to deep water. Fall fish would typically be along the healthiest weedgrowth on the fast-dropping sides of the shoreline point (A) or the sunken island (B), or on the sharp, rocky deep drop-off (C) on the sunken island.*

*Small jigs are deadly on big crappies. This slab white crappie was caught by vertically fishing a 1/8-ounce jig tipped with a small minnow along the outside bend of a reservoir creek channel.*

weed edge, letting the jig sink part way to the bottom, and then swimming it back to the boat. How far the jig should be allowed to sink can only be determined by trial and error. Be sure to count the jig down so you'll know its depth. Crappies may be a few feet beneath the surface, or 6 to 12 feet down. It all depends on water color, cloud cover, etc. You never know for sure until you check it out.

Boat control is very important. Either drift or use an electric motor to carefully and systematically work the entire weed edge. Chances are you'll encounter a thick patch of healthy weedgrowth or a particularly sharp section of the drop-off that concentrates the crappies in a small area. Then the fun begins.

If the crappies are somewhat active, they'll hit the jig as it sinks or swims by. If they're not particularly aggressive, you may have to use a slower presentation. Get the bobbers out and suspend tiny jigs right at or just above the crappies' eye level. Once you trigger a few fish, the rest may become excited enough to improve their feeding mood. Then you can go back to swimming a jig. It's quicker, easier, and you may catch a bunch of fish in a hurry.

Weedy sunken islands are worked in the same fashion. Here, though, you may be able to use a short cut for locating fish. Crappies will generally be along the sharpest-dropping side of the sunken island. Concentrate your fishing along the side that has the fastest drop to deep water.

# FISHING ROCK PILES

In fall, rock-pile crappies are perhaps the deepest crappies that you'll encounter. Again, they can be very close to or right up tight to the rocks. This makes backtrolling a small jig a perfect approach.

Backtroll an 1/8-ounce jig very slowly across the rocks. Since the jig is quite small, you have to move very slowly to remain in contact with the bottom. An electric motor lets you move slowly and remain directly above the fish without spooking them.

## Jigging a Rock Pile

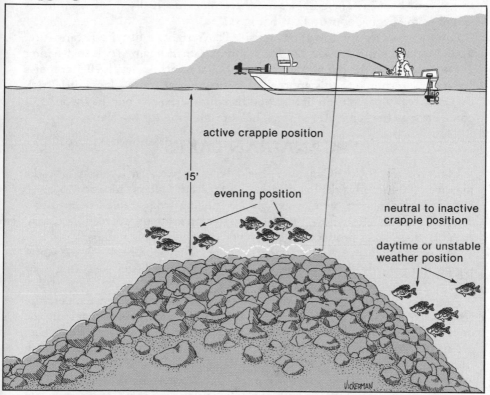

active crappie position

15'

evening position

neutral to inactive crappie position

daytime or unstable weather position

*Big fall crappies frequently relate to deep-water rock piles. They'll suspend off the edges during the day and move up onto the hump to feed on small minnows during the evening hours. Backtrolling a small jig is one of the top ways to catch them.*

If there are no fish present on top of the rock pile, progressively work deeper down the sides. When a fish hits, hover there with the electric motor. Don't drop anchor. The fish are spooky and the drop of an anchor will spook them. By carefully hovering above them, you can catch a lot of fish before they eventually spook.

# SUSPENDED FISH

As we've said, at some point in late fall, crappies will leave the cover they've been using and suspend over deep water. There are a couple ways to deal with this situation.

The first thought, naturally, is to use the sink and swim technique with a jig. It's effective until the water gets really cold. Then it may simply be too fast a presentation for the fish to respond to. Try switching to a stationary-slip-bobber approach. Let the jig hang motionless, giving the fish a chance to respond.

Let's assume that it's very late in the year, and you have to crack a bit of ice to get your boat in. The crappies are there, but they really don't seem to respond to the jigging approach. What next?

Drop a small ice fly down to the fish. That's right, a tiny ice-fishing lure. Sounds crazy, but it works! Use the standard, small jigging stick that winter anglers use. Drop the lure through the school at 6-inch intervals. Big crappies are quite susceptible to this approach, particularly at sunset. It's a little trick that may really pay off. So, if you find fish during the day but they won't hit, come back as the sun starts to set. That's prime time for big slabs.

# CANADIAN LAKES

Many of the rocky, Canadian shield lakes in western Ontario lack the massive, 100-foot-plus depths of deep, clear, trout waters. Instead, 25 to 40 feet is more common, with water clarity ranging from stained to medium-clear. Given enough shallow, reed-filled spawning grounds and plenty of small baitfish, these lakes produce huge crappies in unbelievable numbers.

The cooler nights of August signal a changing environment. As the water temperature slowly drops to the low 60°F's, crappies begin schooling very tightly, suspending 10 to 20 feet down over deeper water.

After the fall turnover—usually completed once the water temperature reaches 55°F—crappies drop even deeper. With plenty of oxygen in the depths, and a fairly consistent water temperature from top to bottom, there are no barriers to deep-water movement. Both crappies and the small baitfish they prey upon continue shifting deeper, to 25, 30, 35 feet or more by late fall. As the crappies continue grouping into huge "mega-schools"—hundreds of fish—they become extremely vulnerable, once you find them. Here are a few keys to locating fall crappies.

# GENERAL CRAPPIE LOCATION

Cooling water temperatures slow crappie metabolism, reducing the distances that fall crappies travel. They move slowly within a general area, foraging for food. But they won't range too far. They usually remain somewhere in the general vicinity.

As with many species of fish, fall location centers around quick access to deep water—in other words, sharp drop-offs rather than gradual-tapering flats. The sharp-dropping sides of shoreline points, the steep edges of deep (20-foot) rock humps, etc., are key areas to begin your search. Areas like these

# Typical Good Crappie Bay on a Rocky Canadian Shield Lake

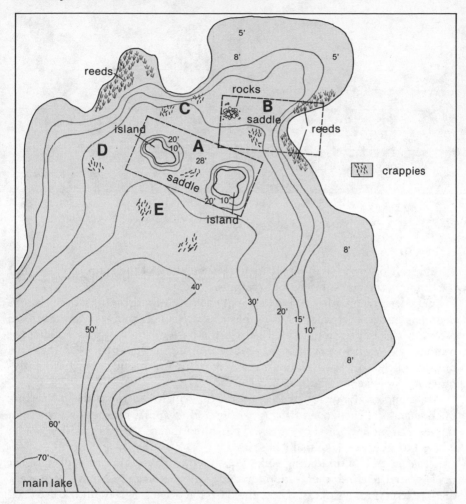

*The accompanying map depicts a good crappie bay on a rocky Canadian lake. Note the maximum depth of about 40 feet. If it were deeper, the amount of usable area would be decreased, and the bay would probably host far fewer crappies.*

*AREA A depicts a saddle area between two islands. AREA B is a similar saddle between a rocky hump and a shoreline point. Crappies would tend to lie in the saddle area during the day and move toward the drop-offs in the evening. AREA C shows a school of crappies that have done just this. Note that the fast taper of the shore gives the school quick access to deep water.*

*AREA D shows a school of fish suspended over the deep flat, halfway in relation to the drop-off. AREA E, meanwhile, has two groups of fish suspended in relation to, basically, nothing. Yes, D and E are very frustrating to anglers who want to nail down a rhyme and reason for every bit of fish behavior. In this case, it's easier to accept the fact that some of the fish might be very far away from a structural element, and not give yourself a headache trying to figure out why. It's much easier to concentrate on more predictable fish like those in AREAS A, B and C!*

Detail of Area A

Detail of Area B

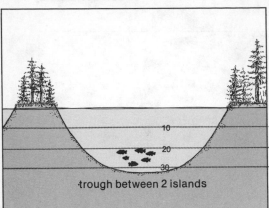

10
20
30

trough between 2 islands

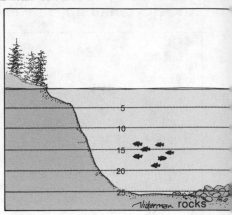

5
10
15
20
25
rocks

within bays or in the shallow (20 to 40 feet) portions of the main lake are your focal points for late-summer/fall crappies.

A key feeding area for active fish is at the base of a drop-off where it stops dropping and meets the lake's softer basin. A school of crappies using a sunken hump, for example, might slowly circle the base of the hump, searching for minnows. They'll follow this deep-water transition (edge) between the hard hump and the soft basin, like a road map. This is a particularly good early-morning/late-evening pattern.

Are crappies always on these edges? No, which brings up the interesting phenomenon of suspended fish. As we've said, crappies can be somewhere in the general vicinity of these areas. That often means off to the sides, somewhere out over the lake's soft basin.

If that sounds intimidating—like you have to cover hundreds of acres of open water to find them—don't panic. They're usually somewhere near distinct structural elements. Thus, the deep flat adjacent to (within 100 to 200 feet) a deep point, hump, etc. is a likely fish attractor. The saddle area between two islands or between the top of the shoreline point and an adjacent sunken island, for example, are key spots.

In the past, we've termed these areas confined open water, and it's a good concept. It's the open water near structural elements rather than out in the wide-open lake. If you keep this in mind, it takes the mystery out of searching for open-water crappies.

You can eventually contact these fish by drifting small lures across the adjacent, open water and waiting for a bite. However, when searching for suspended fish, it's much more effective to use a depth finder, graph or LCR to scout the areas adjacent to points and humps. Crappies show up as light flashes on the depth finder. Sometimes they're near bottom, and sometimes they're 5, 10, or 15 feet above it. Your depth finder not only tells you where they are, but how deep to fish your lures. You can't beat that!

# Circle the Wagons!

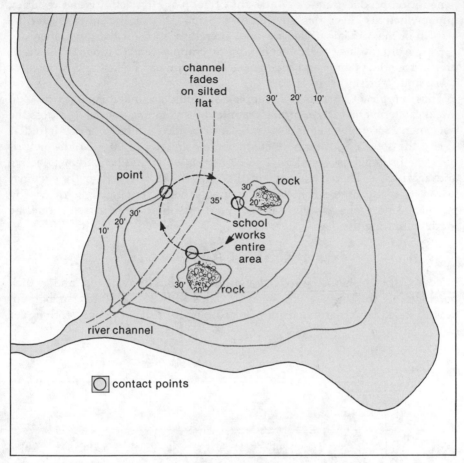

*That's what wagon trains used to do when surrounded by hostile Indians. In this case, it's a school of "hostile" crappies slowly circling a good feeding area. The area has several good humps and points with a 35-foot hole between them.*

*A crappie school might slowly circle this area, foraging for minnows, contacting each feeding spot every hour or so. If you're anchored on the point, you might pop a few fish every once in a while, and then deadsville. However, if you can predict their movement, jump ahead, and be ready for their arrival. You can catch 'em consistently!*

As a general rule, in early evening, fish tend to be nearer the drop-offs, and both morning and evening fish are fairly tight to bottom. On darker, cloudier days, they tend to hug tighter to the bottom for longer periods of the day. The fish tend to move less than they do on sunny days and are definitely a little finicky about what they'll strike.

On sunny mornings and evenings or during most days, crappies tend to rise off the bottom. They'll suspend 5 to 15 feet off the bottom over 25 to 40 feet of water, becoming extremely active and catchable.

This midday, sun-related activity is probably due to the stained or tea-colored water common to these lakes. The sun makes it easier for crappies to spot their food and may also slightly warm the water. The increased light penetration produces a greater amount of zooplankton activity and resulting minnow activity. Even this tiny increase in sunlight is sufficient to trigger the growth of microscopic organisms and, therefore, kick off the food chain.

By late afternoon or early evening, many crappies tend to move to the drop-offs surrounding points and rock piles. The action can be fast and furious for 1-1/2 hours, or so, before sunset.

Thus, a typical Canadian fall-crappie day would go something like this. You might catch several early-morning crappies by swimming a small jig across the bottom in 28 feet of water and never see a suspended fish on your depth finder. Yet, as the hours pass the school might begin rising. By 11:00 A.M. the majority of the fish might suspend in 12 to 18 feet of water and be extremely active and aggressive. They could remain that way most of the day. By evening, however, many of the fish would probably begin moving tight to nearby points and drop-offs. As you can see, your presentation approach should be modified during the day.

# PRESENTATION

Your first step should be to find a good lake map (if available) and to pick out bays off (or sections of) the main lake with 20- to 40-foot maximum depths. Begin your morning fishing by scouting for fish with your depth finder

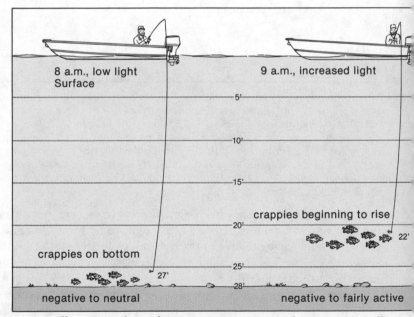

*The accompanying illustration shows how crappie position and activity typically changes throughout the course of a day. In early morning, they're tight to the bottom and inactive. As the day wears on, they eventually rise to an active position.*

*The suspended, active position is also more common on sunny, rather than cloudy*

and drifting the areas adjacent to sharp-dropping points or sunken islands. One angler should keep his jig right on the bottom, the other a few feet off bottom. If there are no results, keep lifting your lures up a few feet on each drift until you begin catching fish or spot fish on the depth finder.

Toss out a floating marker to mark the general area; it'll keep you on fish and help you plan your drift patterns. Concentrate your efforts at that depth until you stop catching fish. Then it's time to experiment with depth again or move to a different spot.

For best results, keep your equipment light. Anytime you're after panfish, a good ultralight spinning outfit is usually your best bet. If that doesn't fit your budget, you can get by with a regular, medium-action spinning rod like you'd use for walleyes. Just be sure the rod has a soft, sensitive tip. This allows you to lift up slightly and watch the rod tip to sense if a finicky fish has sucked in your jig, instead of having to pull up too hard and spook the fish. While 4-pound-test line is adequate for most conditions, you can go up to 6-pound test for snag-infested conditions, although it makes presenting a tiny jig in deep water much more difficult. If you're a sport and don't mind losing a few fish, you can even experiment with 2-pound-test line.

Without a doubt, there's no better lure to fish for suspended crappies than a tiny jig. Day in and day out, a 1/16- or 1/8-ounce, white or chartreuse jig is hard to beat. Other colors—usually light to imitate light colored minnows—will produce, but these two are superb.

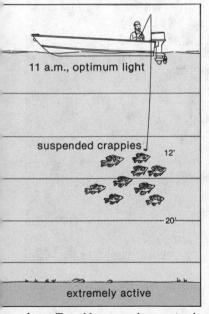

11 a.m., optimum light

suspended crappies 12'

20'

extremely active

*days. Tom Neustrom has noticed a correlation between it and the barometric pressure. Rising or fairly high barometers of 29.60- to 30.00-plus (typical of sunny days) generally show suspended fish. Lower readings of 29.2 to 29.6 generally indicate darker days and fish located more on the bottom.*

Small marabou, chenille-body/marabou-tail, or plastic-body/marabou-tail jigs are all dynamite. They have a natural-breathing action at rest and entice even fussy fish. Tip them with a small, 1-1/2-inch crappie minnow (if available) by inserting the hook up through the minnow's bottom jaw and out the top of its head.

If live minnows aren't available, fish the jigs plain—or use dead minnows. You can't transport live minnows across the Canadian border from the U.S., so pack dead minnows in a bag of ice (no water) if you can't buy live ones locally. They'll stay fresh and usable for days.

You can even add a sliver of throat skin cut from a crappie. It's a little trick that pays big dividends. At times, adding a drop of a scent product may produce even better results—especially when minnows aren't available. (In some areas of Canada, live bait is difficult to obtain or even illegal.)

As an alternate approach, try drifting a floating-jighead/sliding-sinker, minnow rig. Keep the snell short (2 feet or less) and use a sinker just heavy enough to scrape along the bottom on the drift. It's deadly for fish on or just off the bottom. Whatever the case, simplicity is the key. Whether it's a small jig or just a plain hook, always tie directly to your line. Adding snaps and swivels will hamper the natural action of these tiny lures.

## FISHING THE JIG

Jig presentation varies, depending on the activity and position of a crappie school, and also weather conditions. For example, let's say it's very calm and

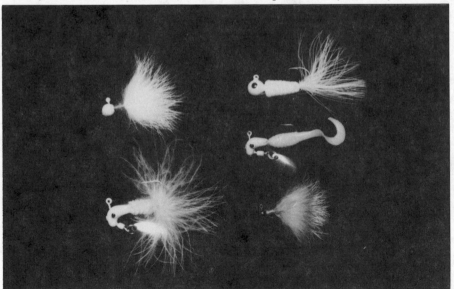

*Small and simple is the rule for crappies. Any attempt to exaggerate lure size or movement is usually counterproductive. A small assortment of 1/16- and 1/8-ounce, light-colored jigs usually does the trick.*

*Top row, left to right: A Cordell Doll Fly marabou jig and a Lindy Fuzz-E-Grub (plastic-body/marabou-tail).*

*Bottom row: Blakemore Road Runners with (1) a chenille-body/marabou-tail and (2) a plastic Twister tail, and a Windels Rabbit Hair jig.*

you've used your depth finder to locate a school of suspended crappies. Under these conditions, it's very easy to hover directly above the fish and vertically jig your lure right through the school. If there's a gentle wind, simply drift. If it's calm, you can fish a 1/16-ounce jig very effectively; there's no need to go to a bulkier, 1/8-ounce jig like you need to maintain "feel" in windy conditions.

With 4-pound-test line, the jig will sink approximately 1 to 2 feet per second, depending on the body style. Open your bail and let the jig sink to the approximate depth of the fish; watch the line for the telltale twitch of a fish hitting the sinking line.

Once your jig reaches the proper depth level, close the bail and place your index finger on the line to help detect soft strikes. Lift your rod tip 2 or 3 feet, hold it there for a few seconds, and then slowly drop it again. Pause between lifts for a count of about five, and watch that rod tip. Crappies generally hit a stationary or falling jig best. Since their eyes face upward, crappies feed most effectively in that direction. But, it's not a vicious strike! Instead, it's more of a subtle twitch—a slight pressure you detect by gently lifting the rod tip.

When you hook a fish, make sure your partner casts or drops a jig in the vicinity of the hooked fish. Often, several fish will be excited by the hooked crappie and follow it. You can catch another fish by simultaneously reeling a jig past them. In fact, if you can, try to keep a hooked fish struggling, say halfway to the boat, until your partner hooks one. Then reel yours in. It'll keep 'em in a frenzy. Take turns!

*Pausing before you set the hook, especially on cloudy/windy days when the fish are fussy and you have a hard time feeling a strike, is very essential. A soft, rod tip is critical in these conditions to help sense the strike.*

If you can, work above or right at the top of a crappie school. Keep drawing the fish up rather than dragging hooked fish up through the entire school. That might spook 'em eventually. By using this trick, we've caught many slab crappies off a deep rock pile before spooking them.

Another variation to fishing suspended crappies is a swing and drop method. It works well in areas with a large concentration of fish that are not tightly schooled. Cast the jig out 10 to 15 yards. Close the bail and place your index finger on the line. The jig will swing and drop back below the boat in an arc, while covering a range of depths. You can even just cast out, let the jig sink to the proper depth, and slowly reel in.

This method is particularly deadly with an action jig like a Twister Tail or a spinner jig like a Blakemore Road Runner. Watch your rod tip and line closely, because crappies will follow, suck in the line, keep swimming, and create slack that's very difficult to detect. Pay attention!

# FLATLAND RESERVOIRS

Flatland reservoirs are some of the finest, multi-species fisheries in North America. Depending on the region, they may 'host bass, crappies, saugers, walleyes, catfish, and even a big musky or two.

An important key to fishing flatland reservoirs is realizing their commonly stained or off-colored water tends to keep fish shallow much of the year. Granted, the water is usually clearer in the main reservoir, and it's possible to catch fish deeper there. However, creek arms, where a major segment of the fish are located, are usually darker than the main lake. The crappie populations found there tend to remain shallow. To be more specific, for most of the season the crappies in creek arms may be spread out on shallow, massive flats, often relating to flooded cover like brush piles, stump beds and fallen trees. Such is the case on good, multi-species, flatland reservoirs like Kentucky or Barkley Lakes in Kentucky and Tennessee.

# THE FALL DRAWDOWN

About October, the Corps of Engineers commonly finishes dropping the lake level of these reservoir types about 2 to 6 feet to winter pool. This strategy builds a "cushion" so heavy spring run-off won't overrun the capacity of the reservoir and helps minimize ice damage to shorelines on lakes that freeze. If you think this fall drawdown has a big effect on the lake, just think what it does to the fish!

The fall drawdown effectively "pulls the plug" on many shallow, summer-fishing spots. As the water drops, those beautiful, 2- to 6-foot-deep brush, stump and fallen tree areas on the flats begin drying up, or at least become too shallow for fish to use consistently. The fish have no choice but to vacate these areas for deeper water.

As the water recedes, it literally sucks the fish off the flats, concentrating them in specific kinds of deeper spots.

# FALL CRAPPIES

During spring and summer, a portion of the crappie population often uses similar (but deeper) areas as largemouth bass. After the fall drawdown, they tend to prefer a different kind of area than bass. Rather than moving to steep shoreline points, crappies generally move to deep outside bends in the creek channel, usually somewhere in the 10- to 20-foot range. In moderately stained water, 10 feet is sufficiently deep. However, since the water color tends to clear somewhat in fall, 15 to 20 feet is more typical.

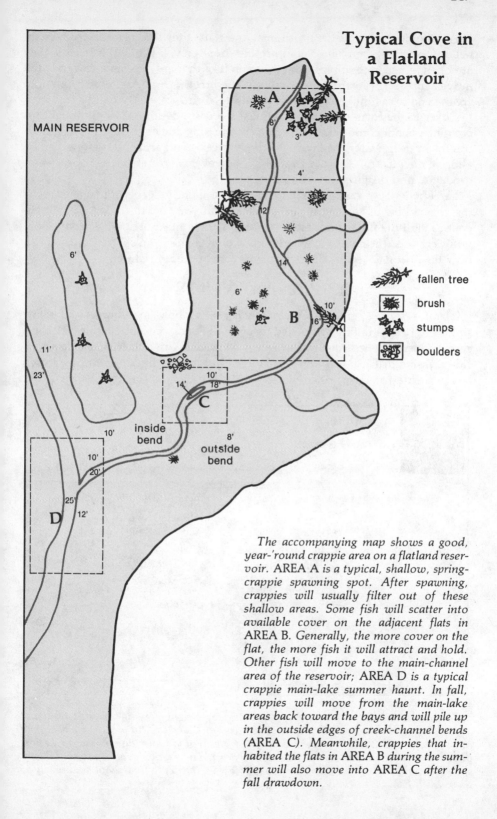

# Typical Cove in a Flatland Reservoir

MAIN RESERVOIR

A

B

C

D

inside bend

outside bend

fallen tree

brush

stumps

boulders

The accompanying map shows a good, year-'round crappie area on a flatland reservoir. AREA A is a typical, shallow, spring-crappie spawning spot. After spawning, crappies will usually filter out of these shallow areas. Some fish will scatter into available cover on the adjacent flats in AREA B. Generally, the more cover on the flat, the more fish it will attract and hold. Other fish will move to the main-channel area of the reservoir; AREA D is a typical crappie main-lake summer haunt. In fall, crappies will move from the main-lake areas back toward the bays and will pile up in the outside edges of creek-channel bends (AREA C). Meanwhile, crappies that inhabited the flats in AREA B during the summer will also move into AREA C after the fall drawdown.

As crappies move off the brush piles and flats, they'll follow the creek channel out to a creek bend at a "comfortable" depth level. While this occurs, they are often joined by crappies from the main lake that are making a "reverse" fall movement back toward the mouths of the creek arms. As the fish pile into creek-bend areas, huge fall schools begin to form.

Cover in the form of brush or sunken trees is a definite plus, although this condition is not common unless some enterprising angler sinks his own fish attractor in deep water. Many of the best, creek-bend areas, therefore, can be almost devoid of wood. Crappies, however, are effective open-water predators and do just fine without it.

Large schools of crappies will gather in the slightly deeper, outside edges of the channel bends, and you can spot them on your depth finder. They'll appear as multiple flashes, generally within the first 4 feet or so of bottom. Once you've cruised the channel, scouted a few creek bends and spotted signs of fish near the bottom, you're all set for some fast and easy fishing.

# PRESENTATION

Many, reservoir, crappie anglers rely on heavy line, large hooks and heavy sinkers to drop a minnow (hooked through the back) into brush piles. While a case can be made for such a heavy-duty approach when the fish are down inside massive brush piles, don't make the mistake of thinking you need such heavy tackle for deep, open-water fish in the channel bends. An ultralight

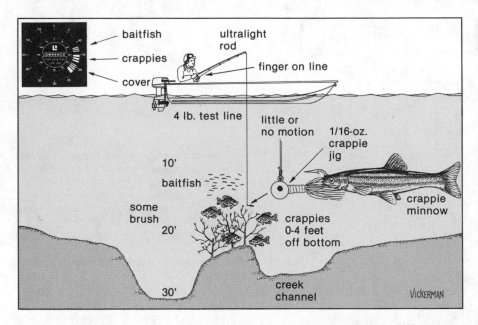

*Slow and simple is the rule for deep crappies. Hover right over the fish and let out just enough line to hit bottom. When the line goes slack, engage the reel and place your finger on the line. It'll help you detect "soft" strikes. For crappies, use minimum motion in your presentation. The best jigging motion is often no motion at all—just hold the jig still. Since crappies often suspend, try to spot 'em on the depth finder and hold the jig at their depth level. It's deadly.*

spinning outfit with 4-pound-test line gets your bait down deeper, easier, and the fish put up one whale of a fight to boot!

Tiny crappie jigs in the 1/16- to 1/8-ounce range are deadly for these conditions. One favorite is the pink and white Lindy Fuzz-E-Grub—a real killer in both clear and stained water. However, pink, white, yellow and chartreuse are all superb color choices. Small marabou- and chenille-bodied jigs are productive, too.

*Feast your eyes on these monster fall black crappies. How big are they. Believe it or not the three largest fish weighed in at nearly 11 pounds! The fish were caught from a northeastern, natural lake on a 1/8-ounce chartreuse Charlie Brewer Crappie Slider.*

Southern anglers seem to fish a jig or a minnow but seldom fish the two together—a common "Yankee" technique. Simply insert the hook beneath the minnow's lower jaw, poking it out the top of the head. Tipping a jig with a minnow is deadly on cold-water crappies.

Lower your jig to the bottom; close the bail on the reel; pick up the line with your index finger, and simply hold it there. After a few seconds, lift the jig up 6 inches to a foot. Again hold it steady. Don't jig it up and down. Crappies prefer a steady lure rather than a wildly hopping one. Use your electric motor to slowly cruise along the channel basin, sometimes holding it 1, 2 or 3 feet off the bottom—particularly if you spot fish suspended above the bottom.

Strikes are light, so pay attention to any little twitch or change in the feel of the jig. Stick 'em hard and then enjoy the fight of a big crappie bulldogging around 15 or 18 feet down. It takes a long time to get 'em up from that depth, especially on ultralight tackle.

Throw out a floating marker; get your jig back down; and do it again. Redrift and work the school over and over. A good channel bend can attract hundreds of crappies by fall and perhaps even thousands by mid-winter. Talk about the mother lode: all the fish you could ever want and probably few, if any, anglers fishing them this late in the year. The term "like shooting fish in a barrel" is appropriate!

The fall drawdown on flatland reservoirs is not a calamity! In fact, it's an eagerly awaited event for those in-the-know. The reduced water level concentrates fish in easily identified spots, and you can get on them if you know what to look for.

Frankly, we're astonished by the lack of anglers on many mid-South impoundments in November and December. The fishing's just getting good. Don't pass up this incredible opportunity to enjoy fall crappies.

# Chapter 12

# WINTER

## Coldest-Water Crappies

Because of the crappie's wide range, winter creates two extremely contrasting fishing situations: ice fishing in the North and open-water angling in the South. For both areas, this time frame encompasses the coldest water temperatures of the year.

Even during this Coldest Water Period, crappies feed actively and are very catchable. In fact, some real trophies are caught during early winter in northern lakes and southern impoundments. December may be the month for trophy fish throughout the South.

## FIRST ICE

Crappies are light sensitive, and in clear bodies of water they often bite best during twilight hours, after dark, or in deeper water during midday; ice fishing is no exception, although you can experience good, daytime angling, too. During first-ice, you can almost always catch some midday crappies in clear-water lakes from cover such as weeds or timber. And, of course, the heavy ice and snow cover of late season cuts light penetration and may intensify midday feeding.

In lakes with a bit of color, crappies often bite consistently in shallower water right through midday. However, even on these lakes, look for twilight activity. Changing light intensity at dusk and dawn often triggers crappie and other gamefish activity.

Most consistent fishing patterns key around the location of forage. Zooplankton and minnow concentrations often mean crappie concentrations. To illustrate this concept, let's examine one area that usually concentrates zooplankton and draws minnows during first-ice.

When any relatively large, shallow bay or creek arm freezes, a good portion of the baitfish present will be sucked out toward the main body of water. We're not exactly sure why this happens, but we have seen the phenomenon enough to be sure it occurs. When conditions stabilize, the baitfish may move back into the bay or creek arm.

After the baitfish make a mass exodus from a shallow bay or creek arm, they hold for a time in the first main-lake or reservoir cover they encounter. Cover might be either weeds, timber or brush on an adjacent main-lake or reservoir flat; weeds or timberlines near the edges of the flat; the deeper-water drop-off area, etc. When the bait moves out, the crappies move in—not into the shallow bay or creek arm but into areas *adjacent to* the mouth of the bay or creek arm. Crappies head 'em off at the pass, and the collision of bait and crappies can produce some of the finest crappie fishing of the year.

By now you should have a clear picture of a general type of area to look for. Let's get more specific. As you might expect, large bays or creek arms generally offer more potential than small bays or creek arms, because large areas generally attract more bait. However, whatever size the bay or creek arm is, it must be shallow enough so that freeze-up (or very cold weather prior to freeze-up) causes bait to migrate from the shallower areas.

A bay or creek arm with a deep hole or channel may upset this pattern, because the bait may not move all the way out. Still, the flat or drop-off at the mouth of the bay or creek arm would be worth checking. In the case of a creek arm, check the flat or drop-off next to the channel. A better option in this instance is fishing either the hole in the bay, or the fringe of the creek channel. If these areas attract and concentrate forage, they likely will also hold crappies.

The more the mouth of a bay or creek arm narrows down, bait and crappies are more likely to be channeled into a specific area. Obviously, this is an advantage. A wide bay or creek-arm mouth can be a problem, because bait can leave the area anywhere. The crappies will also spread out. Excellent fishing usually results when conditions funnel baitfish, and subsequently predators, into a confined area. Such perfect conditions frequently exist in lakes, but only seldom in reservoirs.

As bait vacates a bay or creek arm, it contacts the flat immediately outside the area. Some flats are better than others. First, a good flat should have cover like remaining stands of leafy pondweed, or timber, or both. A flat without cover will not hold fish very long.

The flat should also be deep enough to contrast with the depth inside the bay or creek arm. In other words, for a flat outside a bay or creek arm to hold fish for long, it should be at least as deep as the bay or creek arm it is adjacent to.

# "Bait Out/Crappies In"

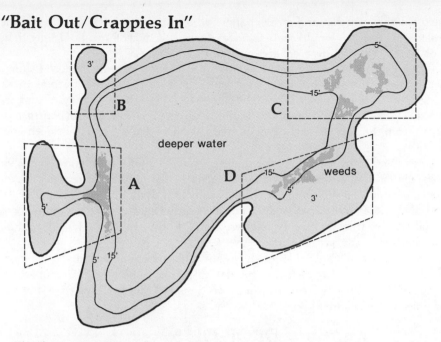

The "bait out/crappies in" pattern is based on the movement of bait out of relatively shallow bays into main-lake areas, where they are intercepted by crappies. Although we observe this happening at first ice, it probably occurs before then. In other words, hardy, late-season boat anglers can also key on this pattern.

The best crappie fishing usually occurs outside large, relatively shallow bays with narrow, main-lake openings. The narrow, main-lake opening should lead to a fairly deep, and moderately sized flat, with cover extending all the way to the drop-off. None of the areas on our test lake exhibits perfect conditions, but they all may still attract crappies. Let's look at each area.

AREA A—A relatively shallow bay with a narrow opening to a cover-filled, main-lake flat. Everything you're looking for except a distinct area on the flat or drop-off to concentrate fish. One of the best (perhaps the best) first-ice areas on the lake.

AREA B—The bay is too small to hold much bait, and the flat is too small to hold many crappies for long, but any crappies attracted to bait moving out of this bay will be in the clearly defined area of the inside turn just outside the bay. If this inside turn was at the mouth of AREA A, you'd have a tremendous spot!

AREA C—The opening at the mouth of the bay is too large, and the flat outside the bay is too large, to really concentrate fish, but there will be crappies here. The drop-off is a big plus in this area. The 15-foot water juts into the bay and creates a clearly defined holding area.

AREA D—There'll be plenty of bait and crappies, but everything will be spread out, making fishing more difficult.

If we had to choose between the four areas, we'd fish AREA A first, followed by AREA C. Actually, we'd probably check AREA B quickly before moving to AREA C. AREAS C and D would probably offer the most sustained crappie activity over the entire winter season, but that, too, is another story.

The same principles apply to reservoir creek arms, as well.


Of course, it's better if the main lake or reservoir flat is deeper. In a lake, a good situation would occur where a 7- to 15-foot-deep flat adjoins a bay with depths from 3 to 5 feet. A good creek arm situation would have 7- to 15-feet-deep water on the flat and creek channel adjacent to the creek arm. Inside the creek arm, the flats would run 3 to 5 feet deep, and the channel no deeper than 7 or 8 feet. These, however, are optimum conditions.

Obviously, these examples are relative to the type of water you're fishing. For example, the bays on shallow eutrophic lakes are seldom as deep as those in deep, clear mesotrophic lakes. The same would be true if you were comparing this pattern on hill-land and flatland reservoirs. The key is *contrast in depth* from the interior of the bay or creek arm to adjacent structural elements outside.

Does the size of the main-lake or reservoir flat make a difference? Yes, it does. But it's not as simple as "large-flat-lotsa-fish/small-flat-few-fish." Actually, a small flat adjoining a big bay can host a dynamite fishery. After all, once the bait leaves the bay and the crappies move in, there are not many locational choices for crappies, or anglers. You'll know where the fish should be and that can mean great fishing.

Small flats don't hold many fish for long. Expect good fishing to be short lived. The opposite can be true of big flats. Big flats (with cover, of course) adjacent to large bays or creek arms may hold many fish for a long time, but the crappies may be spread out.

## DROP-OFFS

If a flat holds crappies, the drop-off will *definitely* hold them. But even when flats hold few fish, drop-offs may still hold crappies. Expect the most consistent crappie activity to take place in: (1) the confined open water just outside the drop-off, (2) on the drop-off itself, or (3) on the first part of the flat

*Many reservoirs don't freeze over but still experience a Winter Calendar Period comparable to lakes which freeze up. Remember, this period features the coldest water of the year. At this time, the most effective presentation is usually an ultra-slow and simple one similar to ice-fishing techniques. Here's a slab 2-pound crappie caught from a deep, timbered point on a small jig fished nearly motionless near the bottom.*

immediately adjacent to the drop-off.

The drop-off area must be distinct, although it does not need to fall into the deepest water in a body of water. A distinct drop-off has either a quick depth change or an abrupt halt to cover. Thus, a drop-off created by a flat that slowly tapers to 7 feet and then suddenly drops into 18 feet of water will often hold fish. Usually, however, this condition offers short-lived fishing, just as a small flat does.

*"Hey, Mom and Dad, look what I caught!" Modern, warm, winter clothing has made ice fishing an angling adventure for the entire family.*

# FLATS AND DROP-OFFS

The best type of drop-off has a depth change and cover that extends all the way to the drop-off. A timber-covered flat adjacent to a drop-off into the main reservoir is a good example. In a lake, weedgrowth should extend all the way to the drop-off.

## Good Time Flats and Drop-offs

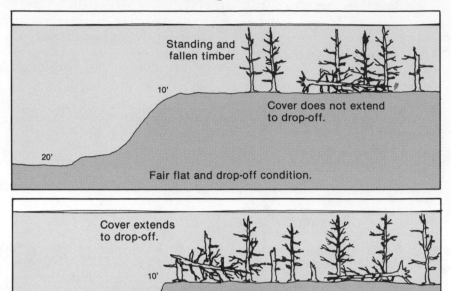

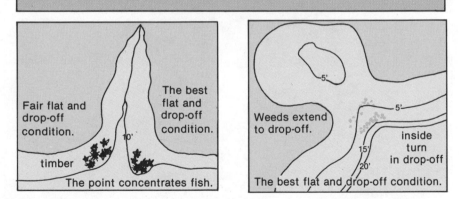

*The best flats outside relatively large, shallow bays offer plenty of cover extending all the way to the drop-off. The best drop-offs have points or inside turns to help concentrate fish.*

One final thought before proceeding: The mouths of canals, necked-down areas between different locations on a body of water, or even small feeder creeks may also attract bait and crappies. These situations are different, yet akin to the pattern we're keying on.

# LIGHT INTENSITY AND CRAPPIES

Some lakes develop distinct patterns at certain times. While we can't tell you ahead of time exactly *when* crappies will bite in the bodies of water you fish, we can talk about *tendencies*.

There are four major fishing zones: (1) the flat, (2) the small slice of flat immediately adjacent to the drop-off, (3) the drop-off, and (4) confined open water near the drop-off. On all bodies of water, crappie activity is possible in all four areas during the twilight periods of morning and evening. Changing light intensity often triggers crappies just as it does walleyes.

In dingy waters, crappie activity usually occurs during the day. Where? Any of the four areas may hold fish if the prerequisites are present. However, in dingy water, the confined-open-water zone is the most marginal pattern. In dingy lakes, crappies tend to relate to something definite. We have not done well fishing at night in these waters, but we admit that our night fishing has been limited.

In clear water, look for daytime activity on the flat only if there is good cover. Even then, expect the fishing to be sporadic because the fish are likely to be scattered. A better chance for schooling-fish is possible on the drop-off or the flat area immediately adjacent to the drop-off. Confined open water will usually hold many fish. Expect intense night feeding to take place on the drop-off and the flat. Nighttime activity may occur in confined open water but is more common later in the season.

Crappie activity often occurs at evening twilight, then shuts off abruptly, and begins again in a hour or two. Crappies have a vision advantage over minnow prey during the twilight hours. They also have an advantage after dark—when their eyes have readjusted. In our experience, things usually slow down for a short time just after dark.

# LATE SEASON LOCATION

By late season, many—probably most—crappies and plenty of baitfish have been sucked into deep water. The reason may be no more complex than that the water is comparatively warm and stable there. Water is most dense at about 39°F, so the temperature in deep water is probably around 39°F. Water just below the ice is near 32°F. The temperature rises toward 39°F as you proceed toward the bottom.

There are some crappies on shallow bars, and some move shallow from deeper water. But, the percentages are for finding the most crappies by using three types of areas: (1) the deep-water edges of prominent structural elements such as bars, points, sunken islands, or shoreline inside-turns; (2) the confined open water off these edges; and (3) the true open water of deeper-water holes in (A) shallower bays, and (B) small, shallow, dishpan-type lakes.

Structural elements in deep lakes include, for the most part, prominent points or inside-turn areas. Keep the "U-factor" in mind. A U-shaped turn in the drop-off can represent either a big inside turn or the opposite—a point. Look for U-factor spots to find crappies.

Look for U-factor spots on a grand, not a small scale. It's the general area off

# Crappie Location in Deep Lakes and Bays

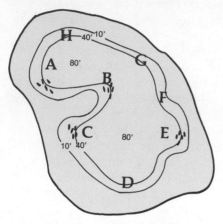

# Crappie Location in Shallow Lakes and Bays

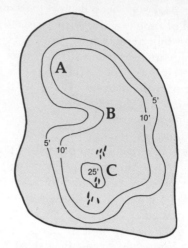

Take a big "U-turn" when you're looking for crappies in a deep lake or bay. A right-side-up "U" represents a big inside turn, and a turned-over "U", a point. Look for U-turns.

In our Deep Lake, spots A thru H are all U-turn areas. Spots A, B and C are the most distinct and, therefore, the most significant areas, but the others may also attract crappies at times. Crappies may indeed be roaming over the deepest-water sections of the lake, but your chance for finding them are better in U-turn areas.

Yes, yes. Most crappies are deep, but some will be using the shallows in spots like A, B and C.

Crappie location can be much different in shallow, dishpan-type lakes or bays. While crappies may use points and inside turns such as A and B, they are more likely to relate to the deep water surrounding deeper lake holes. In shallow lakes and bays, it's not uncommon for crappies to completely ignore points and inside turns.

the tip of a major point that's important. Small projections (points) off a major point are fairly insignificant. Likewise, small "U" spots (inside turns) on prominent bars are also insignificant to general crappie location. Large U-factor spots tend to gather crappies relating to confined open water, so a huge inside turn, formed where the base of a major point turns, is a good crappie spot. Crappies often use confined open water, but only occasionally use true open water. However, late winter is one yearly period when they do.

In large lake or bay areas, look for crappies to suspend off but near obvious points or inside turns. However, in smaller bays that have enough deep water (25 to 45 feet deep) to hold crappies, conditions are slightly different. More of the crappies may relate to the deepest water area in the lake or bay area, to the obvious disregard of shoreline points and inside turns. The same may hold true in smaller, dishpan-type lakes up to about 400 acres in size.

When crappies first start to appear in deeper water, there's a tendency for deep suspension. In a 40-foot hole, it's common to find crappies at the bottom

*A light-action, ice-fishing rod combined with a small minnow and bobber means crappie fun. This young fella has found a hot hole.*

or at least suspended within 1 to 10 feet off bottom. It's uncommon for them to suspend halfway down from the surface.

By late season, crappies tend to suspend at many different depths. Yet the best chance to find them on any given night is still 1 to 10 feet off bottom.

Here are good tips for locating crappies: Look (1) in or near a deep hole in a smaller lake or a bay, or (2) in the confined open water off a large main-lake or bay point, or an inside turn. When they are schooled deep, they usually spread out horizontally. Taking a few crappies at 4 feet above the bottom often means most of the fish will be caught there.

When schools suspend higher, they tend to spread out both horizontally and vertically. Larger-size, deep-water crappies are only occasionally tightly schooled. Large, loose schools are more common and, at other times, many small schools seem to take the place of large schools.

Crappies in deeper holes in small, dishpan-type lakes or in bays off a large lake are not always over the deepest water. Simply picture a school or schools somewhere in the lake near the deepest hole. Schools roam but tend to stay in

## Suspension Tendencies

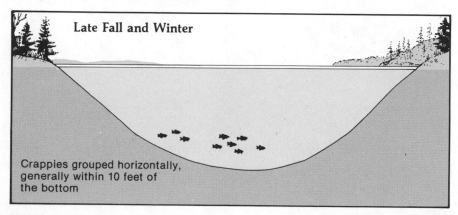

Late Fall and Winter

Crappies grouped horizontally, generally within 10 feet of the bottom

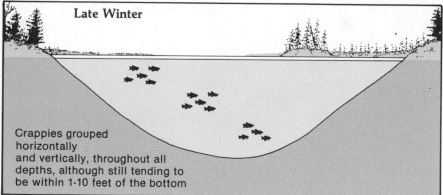

Late Winter

Crappies grouped horizontally and vertically, throughout all depths, although still tending to be within 1-10 feet of the bottom

*Crappies begin to use deeper lake areas during late fall or early winter. Although it's impossible to make hard/fast rules about how crappies suspend when they're in deeper water, here are two general tendencies.*

*When crappies first begin to use deep water, look for them to suspend horizontally, and near the bottom. As a rule, through most of winter, we find crappies within 10 feet of the bottom.*

*As ice-out approaches, this may change. Crappies may still be found near the*

this lake or bay region. Schools sort of "drift", rarely making drastic locational changes, although they may drift several hundred yards or more from one day to the next. But again, drifting will probably take place near or around the deeper water in the open-water portion of the smaller lake or bay.

That's general location. Specific location is a matter of looking with a depth finder and fishing in the general areas where crappie schools are working. At times, crappies tend to stay over harder-bottom areas off points or inside turns. Usually, however, you'll see nothing particularly different about an area, but the fish will tell you *that's the spot* by consistently being there.

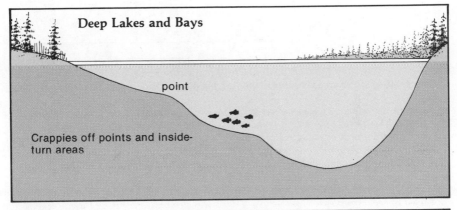

Deep Lakes and Bays

point

Crappies off points and inside-turn areas

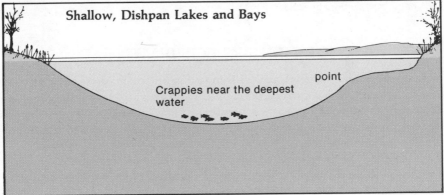

Shallow, Dishpan Lakes and Bays

Crappies near the deepest water

point

*bottom, but there is a tendency for them to suspend both horizontally and vertically. This suspension is often from the bottom into the upper half of the depths, although the percentage is still for fish to be within 10 feet of the bottom.*

*Where crappies suspend in deep water often differs from one type of lake to another. In deep lakes and bays, look for crappies off points and inside-turn areas. In shallow, dishpan-type lakes and bays, look for them near deeper holes, often to the obvious disregard of points and inside-turn areas.*

It's best to attach hooks and lures to 4- or 6-pound-test line when you're fishing for crappies, but that doesn't mean you have to fill an entire reel spool with it. In fact, that's counterproductive, because monofilament is hard to handle if you're hand-lining crappies.

Dacron's the answer. Fill your reel with 27- or 36-pound dacron and you have a line that's easy to handle and see. It'll mean more fish, because you can get back down faster. Attach your 4- or 6-pound-test line to a loop or swivel on the end of the dacron.

This shot also shows one of the 39-inch, graphite, H.T. Enterprise rods (a GJL-31) that we prefer for crappie fishing when we fish outside. A buoy-type bobber is also pictured.

In case you're new to the ice-fishing scene, the plastic reel is a line storage device and isn't used to reel crappies up and down. That's too slow. After setting the hook with the rod, hand-over-hand 'em in.

## ICE-FISHING EQUIPMENT

There are many varieties of ice-fishing rods on the market; obviously, it's best to have a rod that's strong enough to whip good fish yet is light and sensitive. Sticks (rods) with pegs for hand-wrapping line work well in many instances. However, we prefer a reel so it's easy to store line and to fish in both deep and shallow water.

For panfish, the reel should be light. Choose one with a reliable drag system because a 2-pound crappie can put quite a strain on light line.

Light line? For crappies, 2- or 4-pound test is usually sufficient, unless you're fishing in timber. Six-pound-test line is adequate in most cover situations.

## LURES AND BAITS

The standard rig and bait for catching crappies through the ice is a small minnow on a size 6, 8, or 10 hook held at an appropriate depth by a small split shot. Often as not, this arrangement is suspended below a bobber. This ap-

*It's hard to beat the standard minnow-on-a-small-hook rig held in place by a split shot and bobber, but there are other options that work better on occasion. Starting in the upper left hand corner and moving clockwise, other crappie ice-fishing lures include: our "search lure" (a Kastmaster plus a suspended leadhead jig); two lead-wire-wrapped hooks; a small leadhead jig; two daphnia-imitating concoctions from H.T. Enterprises; a Swedish Pimple; a jigging Rapala; and, in the center, two teardrops. Grubs or bits of fish flesh are usually added for triggering power, although minnows also work great on the search lure, teardrops or the small leadhead jig. You may need to add a split shot for extra weight when using a minnow (hook it under the dorsal fin) on a teardrop.*

proach to triggering winter crappies is the standard that other methods are judged by. However, this doesn't mean other methods won't work better at times.

A versatile angler pursuing crappies through the ice should also carry an assortment of teardrops or ice flies, jigging lures that swim when jigged, and jigging lures that flash (to attract fish) when vertically raised and dropped. All of these lure options have their moments. As a matter of fact, these options outproduce the standard minnow-on-a-small-hook rig on many occasions.

Crappies, even the large ones, often feed on tiny creatures (zooplankton) no bigger than a pinhead. Small, plain (no hair or other dressing) teardrops, ice flies, weighted wire hooks, and small leadhead jigs dressed with grubs probably all do a good job of imitating zooplankton.

Leadhead jigs are one of your best options when searching for fish. A jig dressed with a grub or two is easy to move from hole to hole without fuss; there's no hooking and unhooking minnows or sticking your hand in the bait bucket (we invariably forget a small minnow net). Once you find fish, you can continue to fish the jig and grub, switch to a teardrop and minnow, work a plain minnow, or try another jigging lure.

# A SEARCH LURE

Some lures attract fish, some trigger fish, and some do both in certain instances. We'd like to highlight an effective compromise lure. The lure is good

## Lures/Rigs

### SEARCH LURE

To make a search lure, remove the treble hook from an Acme Kastmaster. Add a drop-line of about 2-1/2 inches, and hang a small leadhead jig, teardrop or plain hook on the dropper. The flash attracts fish, and the small lure or hook dressed with grubs, fish flesh or a minnow triggers them when they're drawn close. This lure can be fished effectively in deep (down to 60 feet) or shallow water.

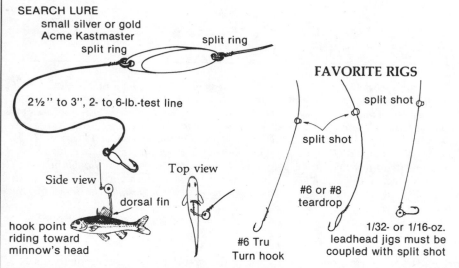

SEARCH LURE
small silver or gold
Acme Kastmaster
split ring
split ring

2½" to 3", 2- to 6-lb.-test line

Side view

dorsal fin

hook point riding toward minnow's head

Top view

FAVORITE RIGS

split shot

split shot

#6 or #8 teardrop

#6 Tru Turn hook

1/32- or 1/16-oz. leadhead jigs must be coupled with split shot

### HOOKING MINNOWS ON LEADHEAD JIGS

Most anglers assume that minnows can only be hooked through the lips when they're used on leadhead jigs. And, as an alternative, some anglers also hook a jig under a minnow's dorsal fin, perpendicular to the backbone.

We believe that hooking a minnow under the dorsal fin parallel to the backbone results in more consistent hooking. Make sure that the hook point rides toward the minnow's head. Teardrops can be used the same way.

when you're on fish, but it is especially effective as a "search lure" when you're probing for fish.

The search lure is a small Acme Kastmaster with the treble hook removed. Tie a small piece of light line on the bottom split ring. Add either a small 1/32- or 1/64-ounce, plain leadhead jig or a small teardrop to the end of this line. The bait should hang below the Kastmaster about 2-1/2 to 3 inches. If the line is too long, it'll tangle when you jig the lure. If it's shorter, you'll lose some of the lure's triggering power. Add a grub, minnow, fish meat, or a fish eye to the jig or teardrop.

This lure gets deep fast and can be effectively fished at any depth. It also has flash, thereby extra attracting power, and offers a small morsel as a triggering device once fish have been attracted. Again, once you find fish, you might consider switching to another lure with more triggering power.

## JIGGING OPTIONS

The type of ice-fishing lure and the jigging motion you should use may depend on the type of zooplankton that panfish are feeding on. Two typical zooplankton options are daphnia and copepods. Daphnia bob and flutter but rarely move horizontally unless they're swept by current. Copepods, on the other hand, make quick darting movements and usually remain in the upper-water layer. Daphnia imitations usually work well at all times, while copepod imitations usually work best during midday.

Because daphnia exhibit an almost constant fluttering motion that rarely

*You should have a variety of different lures like spoons and jigs—some with long-shank hooks (for adding larger grubs) and others with short-shanks hooks. Stick with 3 basic color approaches: (1) subdued colors such as black or purple, (2) bright colors such as fluorescent orange or chartreuse, or (3) subtle colors such as white or yellow. Colors are probably more important for attraction than for close-up triggering effect. Note the small size of the lures and bobber.*

moves them horizontally, a slow or rapid jiggling motion (the bait vibrating vertically about 1/16 to 1/8 inch) is a proper presentation with a teardrop and grub. To imitate copepods, your jigging approach should be more aggressive.

Most ice-fishing presentations should be a mixture of: (1) *attraction jigging* to get the fish's attention, and (2) *enticement jigging* to get fish to strike. Thus, make larger, intermittent jigging movements to draw attention to the presence of your bait. But, frequent pauses are also necessary in order to detect panfish bites. Thus, the basic jigging motion becomes jiggle-jiggle-jiggle (1/16- to 1/8-inch moves), pause, jiggle-jiggle-jiggle, pause, hop-hop (1-foot moves). Repeat the procedure.

Obviously, you should experiment by deviating from this basic pattern. Especially, try lengthening the pause. You're rarely able to hold a bait perfectly still, and on some days such slight movement may be the trigger. A small bobber allows you to suspend a bait nearly motionless. Studies show that panfish seldom take dead daphnia, so baits should rarely be still all the time.

# THE HOOK SET

Some anglers are puzzled by when to set the hook. Should you let a crappie take the bobber under 6 inches, a foot, or 2 feet?

Often, when a crappie inhales an entire minnow, the bobber will distinctly "pop" up or down an inch or two. If you see this "pop," and your bobber doesn't return to its exact former position, set the hook.

Crappies that swim up to take a bait often make the bobber float up as if there were no weight on it. Set the hook. And, crappies that hit a bait and immediately move off (the bobber moves down) with it, usually have it, too. Set the hook.

A hook set should be a firm, steady lift and not a jerk; a crappie has a tender mouth. We try to make the initial hook set using the flex in a light rod to be sure the hook doesn't tear out. If you're not using a spinning rod and reel combo, the set is followed by immediately hand-over-handing the fish up firmly and quickly. Don't allow any slack line or the fish is likely to come off on the way up.

# FLORIDA LAKES

Now it's time to look for some winter open water, and that leads us to the speckled perch (black crappies) of Florida. W. Horace Carter has fine tuned a system that takes black crappies year 'round on Florida's natural, shallow lakes. This entails trolling a neutrally buoyant lure in the deepest areas of the lake. In most Florida lakes, the deepest water is often only 10 to 16 feet deep.

The neutral-buoyant approach consists of the following: a 12- or 14-foot cane pole or telescopic crappie rod; 8- or 10-pound-test monofilament line a foot or two longer than the pole or rod; a 2- to 2-1/2-inch-long, oblong-shaped styrofoam or cork bobber; a Garland Mini Jig or Hal Fly jig; two or three medium-size split shot, about 8 inches apart, the last one about 8 inches above the jig; and one or two minnows tipped on the jig.

With Carter's system, the fastest action comes by trolling across the deepest areas of the lake about a foot off the bottom. When motionless, the lure will

# Typical Florida Lake

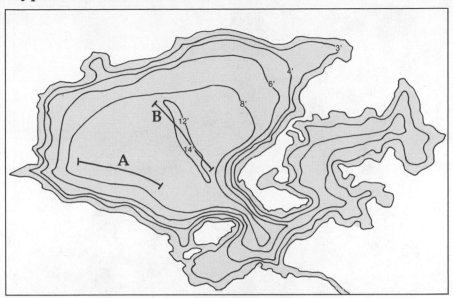

This is a typical Florida lake that normally contains a mixture of freshwater species. Usually largemouth bass, crappies and other panfishes are present. Hydrilla and hyacinth may be present along with lily pads and some reeds.

The two main areas for open-water trolling are: AREA A is usually most productive during spring and summer. AREA B is trolled during late fall and winter. Troll with the wind in both areas.

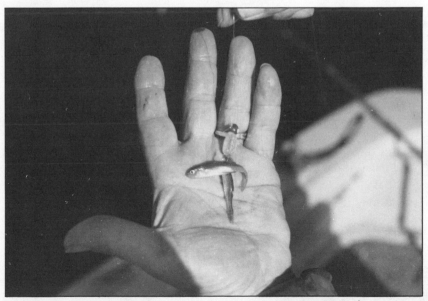

Carter uses 1-1/2-inch minnows tipped on a Hals Flies. Smaller minnows produce more fish and two can be used under tough conditions. Hook the first one through the eyes and the second one in the dorsal fin. It looks like a tiny windmill propelled through the water.

W. Horace Carter hits the Florida black crappies year-'round by trolling the open water.

Rod holders keep the poles parallel to the water. Notice the bobber just breaking the water at a 60-degree angle.

sink to the bottom, but trolling will incline your line at about a 60-degree angle and hold the jig up off the bottom. The poles or rods are held in holders perpendicular to the boat and parallel to the water. The best pole position is off the sides of the bow and stern.

Using the pole holders is necessary, because the fish are hooked when they hit. The bobber rides in the water and a hit can be seen immediately. Also, the pole or rod tip will hit the water, giving you another clue.

Look for the open-water stretches of the lake and troll with the wind. Best action occurs during early morning hours and again at evening. An electric, bow-mounted motor helps control the boat and keeps your trolling rate exact.

# RIVERS

River crappies often display distinct movement away from strong current areas in late fall/early winter. The types of slack-water areas available determine exactly how crappies respond to the cooling environment.

For example, small, shallow rivers typically have few, if any, deep backwater areas for crappies to use during fall or winter; the only non-current areas adjacent to the river might be only a few feet deep, choked with weeds or brush, or prone to freezing solid. Faced with such conditions, crappies may have no choice but to retreat to deeper holes and channel bends where the current is reduced or minimal. It's the only type of area that offers security in the form of depth, reduced current and sufficient depth under the ice.

## Late-Fall/Early-Winter
## River Crappie Hot Spots

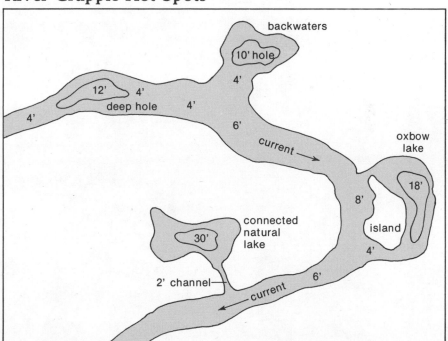

Larger rivers, however, usually offer a wide variety of locational options. They often feature deep backwater areas or connected oxbow lakes anywhere from 6 to 20 feet deep. Crappies may even have direct access to adjacent natural lakes connected to the river by creeks or channels; in each case, crappies may leave the river in favor of deeper, non-current areas of 10, 20, 30 feet or more.

In short, crappie location depends on what's available for fish use. However, anytime there are non-current or minimal-flow areas adjacent to a river which are deep enough so they don't freeze solid, chances are they'll attract crappies during fall and winter.

Faced with such conditions, simply approach them like you'd approach a natural lake. If there is open water, drift the deeper holes or backwater areas and drag a jig and minnow along or near the bottom. If the backwaters freeze, use the same types of ice-fishing techniques we described. There's really no mystery to catching the fish once you understand where they are and how they react to the seasonal conditions.

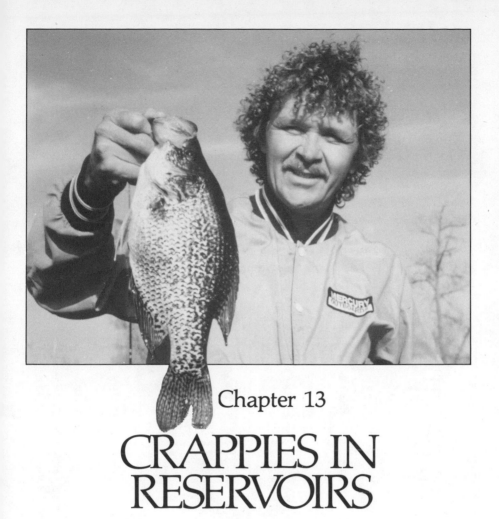

## Chapter 13

# CRAPPIES IN RESERVOIRS

From the Rockies to the Blue Ridge Mountains and on both sides of the Mason-Dixon Line, sprawl large reservoirs that satisfy man's demand for energy, flood control, or a dependable water supply. One by-product of these impoundments is a fantastic crappie fishery. A little versatility and a bit of crappie savvy will yield consistent stringers of "slabs" all season long from these big waters. This chapter will familiarize you with crappie behavior in several types of reservoirs.

Every impoundment has a unique personality, and no two are exactly alike. However, there are common features which are shared by most. What does a large lake in Kentucky have in common with a Wisconsin, South Carolina or California impoundment? For starters, there are submerged creek channels, cuts and coves, secondary bays, islands, and a main river channel. The anatomy of reservoirs is further broken down into both visible (above water) and submerged structural elements like brush or flooded timber. In addition, there's usually a direction of water flow with a prevailing current. A quick review of Chapter 8 (Reservoirs) will give you a detailed description of impoundment characteristics.

Highland, hill-land and flatland reservoirs usually provide the best crappie fishing, so we'll key on them. Let's begin with the highland category.

# HIGHLAND/HILL-LAND IMPOUNDMENTS

Typical characteristics of highland impoundments generally include clear water, hard bottom, and steep, rocky shorelines that drop quickly into deep water. Other common features are narrow and even non-existent flats between the base of the shoreline drop and the edge of the river channel, and a relative lack of cover. Highland reservoirs, because of their clear water and low surface-acreage to volume ratio, also tend to be cooler than hill-land or flatland types. Which of these features makes the highland type impoundment a seemingly more hospitable environment for black crappies than whites is up for question. In all likelihood, a combination of several of these features is important.

## UNITED STATES RESERVOIRS*

| RANK | STATE | NUMBER OF RESERVOIRS | TOTAL AREA IN ACRES | RANK | STATE | NUMBER OF RESERVOIRS | TOTAL AREA IN ACRES |
|---|---|---|---|---|---|---|---|
| 1 | Texas | 193 | 1,547,000 | 28 | Nevada | 10 | 108,000 |
| 2 | Oklahoma | 57 | 590,000 | 29 | Colorado | 52 | 101,000 |
| 3 | Tennessee | 31 | 475,000 | 30 | Virginia | 16 | 97,000 |
| 4 | N. Dakota | 11 | 469,000 | 31 | Ohio | 41 | 92,000 |
| 5 | S. Dakota | 15 | 454,000 | 32 | Michigan | 42 | 84,000 |
| 6 | Alabama | 35 | 432,000 | 33 | Nebraska | 19 | 82,000 |
| 7 | Montana | 44 | 424,000 | 34 | Pennsylvania | 31 | 77,000 |
| 8 | California | 143 | 370,000 | 35 | New Mexico | 16 | 66,000 |
| 9 | S. Carolina | 16 | 356,000 | 36 | Iowa | 8 | 51,000 |
| 10 | Washington | 43 | 351,000 | 37 | Minnesota | 11 | 49,000 |
| 11 | Arkansas | 58 | 338,000 | 38 | Indiana | 20 | 43,000 |
| 12 | Georgia | 27 | 262,000 | 39 | Florida | 8 | 43,000 |
| 13 | Idaho | 42 | 248,000 | 40 | Massachusetts | 5 | 32,000 |
| 14 | Louisiana | 34 | 245,000 | 41 | New Hampshire | 18 | 30,000 |
| 15 | Utah | 19 | 222,000 | 42 | Connecticut | 12 | 16,000 |
| 16 | Kentucky | 19 | 202,000 | 43 | Maryland | 8 | 16,000 |
| 17 | Oregon | 51 | 196,000 | 44 | New Jersey | 11 | 14,000 |
| 18 | Wisconsin | 71 | 182,000 | 45 | West Virginia | 7 | 11,000 |
| 19 | Maine | 21 | 180,000 | 46 | Vermont | 9 | 8,000 |
| 20 | Missouri | 25 | 178,000 | 47 | Alaska | 2 | 4,000 |
| 21 | N. Carolina | 37 | 169,000 | 48 | Rhode Island | 2 | 4,000 |
| 22 | Kansas | 29 | 148,000 | 49 | Delaware | 0 | 0 |
| 23 | New York | 51 | 131,000 | 50 | Hawaii | 0 | 0 |
| 24 | Mississippi | 15 | 131,000 | | Interstate | 1,520 | 9,693,000 |
| 25 | Wyoming | 25 | 128,000 | | Duplications | –40 | |
| 26 | Illinois | 38 | 121,000 | | | 1,480 | |
| 27 | Arizona | 22 | 116,000 | | | | |

*Reservoirs greater than 500 acres at average pool levels, ranked by total area at mean annual pool levels. Interstate reservoir areas are apportioned to the respective states. (As of January 1, 1976.) Source: *National Reservoir Research*

Impoundments which harbor strong populations of white crappies are typically flatland to hill-land in their overall characteristics. Black crappies are frequently common in reservoirs that range more toward highland characteristics, even though they also do well in certain hill-land impoundments.

Black crappies seem somewhat more adaptable than whites. When the two species coexist in a body of water, it's almost always in an impoundment that's more suited to the needs of white crappies rather than black crappies. Therefore, where they coexist, the whites usually dominate. Yet impoundments which are extremely well suited to blacks usually have no white crappie population at all. Since white crappies tend to dominate shallower, more turbid reservoirs, and blacks thrive in deep, clear reservoirs, it makes sense to plan your fishing accordingly. Fish for whites in dirty-water impoundments and for blacks in clear-water reservoirs.

While the techniques used to catch black and white crappies are almost interchangeable, the environmental conditions present in their prime reservoir types vary. This creates subtle differences in each species' seasonal movements and habits. Simply put: *Habitat affects habits!* The behavioral patterns of black crappies in deeper, clear-water impoundments are markedly different than those exhibited by white crappies in shallower, turbid environments. Black crappies in highland-type impoundments display similar behavioral tendencies to those they exhibit in mesotrophic natural lakes, with the exception that weeds aren't usually a key factor in reservoirs. While weeds aren't common in most highland impoundments, when weeds are present, crappies may use the confined open water zone adjacent to them.

One of the major differences in behavior between the two species of crappies is centered around spawning activities. It's not so much a difference in spawning activity as it is a condition dictated by the environment in which each lives. Most white crappie spawning takes place in bays, while most black crappie spawning, at least in highland impoundments, often takes place along main-lake shorelines.

In many highland impoundments which are "home" to viable populations of black crappies, "prime" spawning areas are at a minimum. Most sunfish species like largemouth bass and crappies nest in relatively shallow water on moderately firm bottom. Given the opportunity, they'll also spawn in areas protected from heavy current and main-lake wind and wave action. Because the ideal spawning temperature and habitat requirements of largemouth bass and crappies are similar, competition for spawning sites can take place.

When a shortage of prime spawning spots occurs, the largemouth population in many highland impoundments typically "owns" the prime area for an extended period of time. In these impoundments, more than in most environments, largemouth bass tend to spawn in "waves". Rather than a massive spawning movement occurring when the water temperature reaches the high 60°F's or low 70°F's, spawning often starts in approximately 63°F water in early May and continues into the mid-70°F's—well into summer.

Many highland impoundments can support more bass than there is habitat for all the bass to spawn in at one specific time. In addition, highland reservoirs warm more slowly than shallow, turbid waters, and this also tends to extend the spawn. Consequently, the crappies don't get a chance to use those same bays for spawning! In competition for territory between largemouths and crappies, the largemouths are likely to win most of the time. The end result is that most of the crappie spawn takes place in "unusual" habitat along main-lake shorelines.

## The Crappie Shuffle

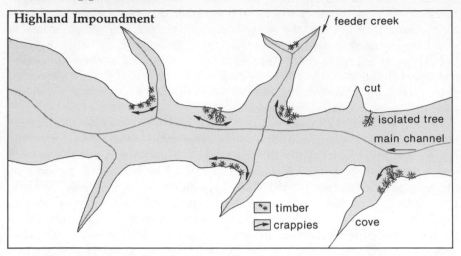

In many highland and some hill-land reservoirs, crappies use the main lake area extensively, all season long. Many times, competition with largemouth bass for spawning sites pushes the crappies out of any shallower bays and coves and into the main lake. During spring, crappies may spawn in fallen trees, on broken rocks or in flooded bushes along shorelines in the main lake and major feeder-creek arms.

In summer, the crappies usually suspend near the fast-dropping shoreline in the main-lake area. Typically, they'll suspend in water from 15 to 40 feet deep—the "crappie zone" in these waters. Fallen or standing timber will provide a holding spot for crappies.

During early fall, crappies may move shallow. Then, in late fall, they'll drop into deep cover. Depending on the environment, timber along the creek channel, a deep ridge or a rocky stair-stepping ledge may hold fish.

The key to locating crappies is finding the multi-seasonal habitat areas in the main lake and larger creek arms. Crappies will shuffle along horizontally and vertically in these areas seeking habitat and food.

What about black crappies in canyon and plateau reservoirs? In general, they're not the best crappie environments because of their extreme depth and lack of cover. However, some creek arms may provide environmental conditions similar enough to a highland impoundment to support crappies. The key to fishing canyon or plateau reservoirs is to consider each creek arm as a localized crappie area, and approach it just the way you'd fish a highland impoundment. Look for fish suspending near the shoreline. Any submerged trees could be superb crappie hot spots.

With the abundance of rock along these typically steep shoreline slopes, there doesn't appear to be much spawning habitat for crappies. Yet many highland impoundments host thriving black crappie populations. So how do they adapt to this seemingly inhospitable environment? Find a lake with a good crappie population, and fish it during the prime spawning period (water temperature 62°F to 66°F) and you'll have a hard time finding a crappie on a "bed." However, try looking in fallen trees along the steep rocky banks and inundated brush along the shorelines, and you'll find crappies.

Yup! They're spawning *on* the cover. Instead of creating a recognizable "bed," crappies often drop their gelatinous eggs on whatever cover exists to keep them elevated off the bottom. In fact, some crappies will spawn in the shallowest branches of fallen trees that are hanging over 35 feet of water!

## "TREED" CRAPPIES

In many reservoirs, the forest of flooded timber can be mind-boggling. Where do you start? Which trees are best? While we can't detail every situation, we can give you a couple guidelines for identifying which trees are potential crappie hotspots. Depending on the local environment, the areas with productive standing timber can vary. River and creek channels, ridges, humps, depressions and other terrain changes are all possible locations for standing timber. Seasonally, crappies will utilize different areas of the reservoir, and timber can provide a "holding" spot for the fish.

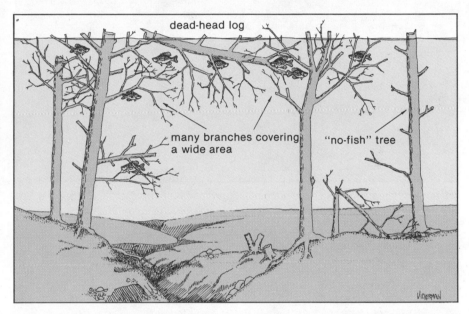

*The most productive "crappie trees" supply plenty of cover. They provide an "umbrella effect" with many branches of all sizes poking in all directions. Find a couple of these adjacent to each other and you've found a crappie paradise.*

Normally, the most productive trees have a maze of branches that provides cover. The best trees have many large and small branches covering a wide area and depth range. Normally, bigger is better. In addition, any floating, dead-head logs that get wedged into the branches are frosting on the cake.

In reservoirs with fast-dropping, main-lake areas, fallen timber can provide cover. Crappies may use the shallower branches to spawn on in spring and then move out and relate to the branches in deeper water during summer. While crappies will often suspend away from cover, when contact is made, many will hold around the branches of a fallen tree. If cover is sparse, even a

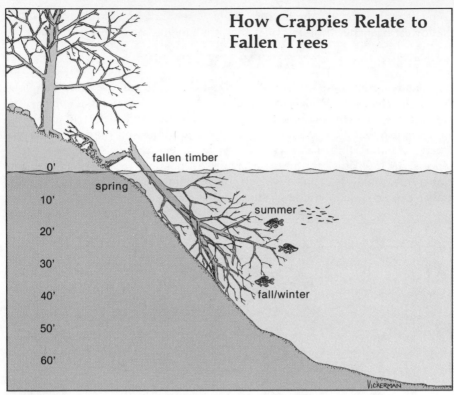

## How Crappies Relate to Fallen Trees

fallen timber

spring

summer

fall/winter

0'
10'
20'
30'
40'
50'
60'

VICKERMAN

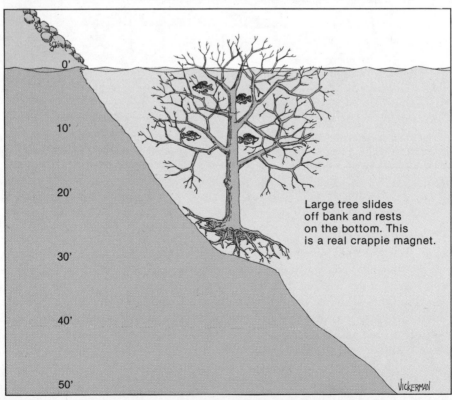

0'

10'

20'

30'

40'

50'

Large tree slides
off bank and rests
on the bottom. This
is a real crappie magnet.

VICKERMAN

single tree will hold fish. This condition often occurs on highland, hill-land and some canyon reservoirs.

All this isn't to say that blacks in highland impoundments *never* spawn in protected shallow bays, or that whites in flatland impoundments *never* spawn in main-lake areas among the branches of brush or timber. Certainly there are impoundments in which those options may be the rule; but the tendencies outlined here are more typical, and help to illustrate how the available habitat can affect crappies' habits.

End result? Fishing during the Pre-spawn Period can be a totally different ballgame for blacks in highland impoundments than it is for whites in flatland impoundments. Keep in mind that this difference will also dictate (or at least influence) the location of crappies during all Calendar Periods. Blacks in a highland-type impoundment move into shallow "backwater areas" early in the season to feed. However, they often must move out of those areas and back to main-lake shorelines before spawning. Not so with whites, because they can remain in shallow, protected areas until spawning time. Also, blacks in a highland reservoir usually spawn in the area of their summer habitat, so there's no true Post-spawn dispersal.

# SUMMER

In summer, the behavior of black and white crappies in reservoirs isn't too dissimilar. However, the differences in the physical characteristics of the typical black crappie impoundment and the typical white crappie impoundment tend to create the *appearance* of substantial behavioral differences.

Traditionally, most anglers consider crappies to be cover-oriented fish. That's actually misleading because both species of crappies spend *most* of their time suspended in confined open water. In natural lakes, highland reservoirs, and even tidal rivers, summertime crappies spend a majority of the time suspended. On Kentucky and Barkley Lakes, KY/TN, many locals believe that white crappies seldom suspend. During the summer, crappies are caught almost exclusively from brush and timber along the channel drop-offs. Of course, that's where most of the crappie anglers ply their trade. However, crappies frequently suspend—and they are catchable.

On a recent trip to Kentucky Lake, KY, we found crappies suspended at an outside turn in the main river channel. We caught a mess of slab whites by swimming a 1/16-ounce jig approximately 12 to 15 feet down over 25 feet of water. Yes, the fish were suspended but still catchable.

Over three days, we were able to find that same school of whites every day, always in the 12- to 15-foot-depth range. They spent most of their time over 20 to 25 feet of water on top of the flat, but each day at around noon, they'd move out over the creek bed. We won't begin to try to figure out why.

The behavior of these crappies was similar to that exhibited by summertime blacks in many waters. For example, in many northern, natural lakes, crappies typically spend 90% of their time suspended 12 to 20 feet down, and they rarely venture over water more than 40 feet deep. In highland reservoirs, the amount of water between 15 and 40 feet is normally a relatively narrow band around the perimeter of the main lake. Only in coves and creek arms do you

# Rule of Thumb: The "12 to 22" Crappie Zone

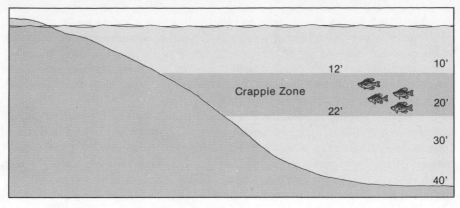

*During the Summer Calendar Period, the best crappie fishing is usually in the 12- to 22-foot range. Yes, there are many exceptions, but the "crappie zone" is a good place to start your fishing on many waters.*

find any considerable expanse of water in this depth range.

So blacks *seem* to be more shoreline related because they don't normally roam over extremely deep water. Even though they're suspended, crappies are usually within 100 feet or so of shore. However, in shallower hill-land and flatland impoundments, crappies have *much more water* within the 15-to 40-foot-depth range, and will roam over more wide-open spaces.

There are few generalities that apply to any fishing situation. Here's one as close as you'll ever find to an axiom: The best daytime crappie fishing during the Summer Calendar Period is *usually* within 5 feet of the 17-foot depth! That's 12 to 22 feet deep.

Certainly the rule can't be applied to bodies of water in which there is little or no water of that depth. With few notable exceptions, lakes and impoundments that *don't* offer deep water aren't the *best* places to fish for crappies. Florida's natural lakes are the most notable exception to this. Typically, very shallow impoundments and eutrophic lakes in many areas of the country can hold tremendous numbers of crappies, but they're often small and paper thin, averaging a few ounces in weight and topping out at well under a pound.

In a quality crappie lake, there's plenty of open water adjacent to cover. There's also an abundance of open-water preyfish. For best crappie growth, it's important that a year-'round supply of forage fish exists in the 1- to 3-inch range. In some natural lakes in the North, the baitfish requirement is filled by landlocked alewife populations; throughout the South and in most flatland and hill-land reservoirs, it's threadfin shad. A variety of minnow species, including common shiners, spot-tail shiners and dace fill the bill elsewhere.

These prey species are plankton feeders. In most lakes, the heaviest plankton layer during the summer (when the water is stratified) is located from the surface down to approximately half the distance of the deepest level of light penetration. Plankton feeders tend to congregate just *under* the heaviest layer of plankton, and crappies will concentrate below these plankton feeders.

Wind is an important factor in open-water crappie fishing. A steady breeze out of the same direction over a period of several days will "push" plankton clouds, and the fishing will usually be better on the downwind areas. A heavy blow, however, churns the water and disperses the plankton, which tends to break up the schools of baitfish. The end result is poor, open-water, crappie fishing. Immediately following a severe windstorm, most crappies will be caught in and around cover, yet usually within the same depth range that they had been using.

In summary, depending on wind, water clarity, density of the plankton and species of prey following the plankton, crappies will be found between 12 to 22

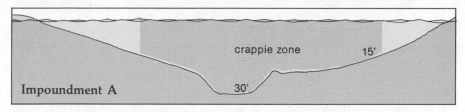

*Impoundment A is a flatland reservoir which is a classic white crappie environment. Here the "crappie zone" is extended because of the amount of shallower water and the normally dark water color. Crappie movement can be in any direction.*

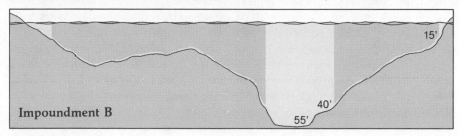

*Impoundment B is a hill-land impoundment typical of those where white crappies flourish. The shaded zone represents the area 15-40 feet deep—the crappie zone. Note that the water is slightly deeper and clearer than the average flatland impoundment.*

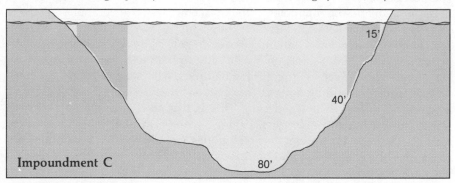

*Impoundment C, a clear-water highland impoundment, is often dominated by black crappies. Notice that there is less area of 15-40 foot water. Crappies exhibiting typical behavior here would appear to be shoreline oriented because the crappie zone is much narrower. Cover is usually scarce, and even a lone tree within this zone may attract fish.*

feet down most of the time. Remember, the rule of 17 includes the 12- to 22-foot depth range.

The most common exception to the 12- to 22-foot-depth-range guideline occurs just before dusk on calm, midsummer days. At this time (twilight), many light-sensitive organisms migrate toward the surface. In response to this movement, plankton-feeding baitfish and crappies may follow.

This is also a peak period of insect hatches. Areas of organic bottom are especially conducive to this, but during certain hatches, gravel bottom areas are also very productive. Just by being aware that late afternoon hatches are always a possibility during the summer should make you aware of the potential. Under these conditions, keep your eyes open for surface-feeding crappies.

Even the most minnow-oriented crappies will take advantage of this "bonus" food source. We're not really sure why, but crappies will almost always take the emerging insects at or just under the surface, even though the bugs may be coming up quite a distance from the bottom. The result is that the crappies will remain near the surface and can provide some mighty fine fishing.

If crappies spend so much of their time suspended, how did they ever develop such a strong "cover-oriented" reputation? The answer lies as much in traditional fishing techniques as it does in crappie behavior. While suspended *away* from cover, a school of crappies is seldom stationary. However, a school of suspended, moving crappies may pause when they make contact with some type of cover. When you find a school of crappies suspended away from cover, staying on them can be a chore. But when you find crappies suspended around a standing tree or mingled among the branches of a fallen tree that's hanging out over deep water, odds are they'll hold there for awhile.

In addition, any "stragglers" seem to hang around cover at the depth range that most crappies are using. Find crappies moving and you're usually lucky to catch more than a few before losing contact; find 'em at a tree and you'll likely catch a dozen or more before they move on. Why? Well, you have a specific area (tree) that will hold fish, instead of trying to cast to a moving school that you don't really comprehend the boundaries of!

On a highland impoundment, the movement of the crappies tends to roughly follow the bank. Remember, they seem to stay in that 15- to 40-foot-deep band of water. On a flatland impoundment, however, movement can be in any direction, and it's much more difficult to maintain contact with a moving school. Thus, given existing fishing methods, percentages dictate that most crappie fishing should be done at the "breaks" that hold a school of crappies temporarily during their wandering. This is true to a degree on all types of water, but on flatland reservoirs, fishing "cover" is usually the name of the game. It's either this or adopt new techniques that allow you to maintain contact with a moving school and more precisely control the depth of presentations in open water.

The growing popularity of chart recorders will have considerable influence on this factor. With a graph, it's much easier to visualize the actual location of the school and estimate its boundaries. With a school of suspended crappies moving across an open flat, if you can graph 'em two or three times as they move, dropping a marker buoy each time, you can fairly accurately predict their path, making it much easier to stay in contact with them. Certain adaptations of backtrolling techniques may also come into play as a means to maintain contact with a suspended school of open-water crappies.

The summer movement patterns also hold into the Turnover Period in most reservoirs, as long as the lake remains stratified and plankton "clouds" remain surface oriented—not necessarily *near* the surface, but some distance away from the surface. Even though adult crappies in the best impoundments rarely rely on plankton as a direct food source, it remains the key to locations of open-water, prey species which crappies relate to.

*Black or white? Two species of crappies are common in some reservoirs. Note the characteristic color variations between white (left) and black (right) crappies.*

After the fall turnover, in most reservoirs both species of crappies exhibit behavioral traits more in keeping with their "cover oriented" reputation. As the water temperature drops from the 50°F's and into the 40°F's, impoundment crappies spend less time roaming over open water. In highland reservoirs, crappies appear to migrate toward any cover in or adjacent to the deepest available water. In a highland reservoir, one or two good fallen trees reaching into 45 or 50 feet of water along a bluff bank may draw large schools of black crappies by the time the water temperature is about 45°F.

Whether you call it an aggregation or a "mega-school," it's a huge quantity of crappies in a confined area, and it's a fishing goldmine. Actually, it's the best crappie fishing of the year. Similar behavior exists on typical white crappie reservoirs, but the aggregation isn't usually as strong because prime cover isn't nearly so scarce in most waters.

While the 15- to 20-foot-depth range in highland impoundments remains productive, everything from the top edges of cover down to the bottom (yes, even 50 feet or more) becomes potential crappie-holding water. There are so many crappies jammed into such a limited area, especially on deep, relatively cover free impoundments, that crappies have to stack over a wider vertical range.

# FLATLAND IMPOUNDMENTS

Although many deeper, highland or hill-land reservoirs generally contain clear water, popular flatland impoundments have shallow basins with large bays and numerous feeder creeks where stained or dark water is common. In flatland impoundments, the average depth of the coves might only range from 5 to 10 feet. The lake probably has deeper channels, but the calling card seems to be plenty of *cover* at all depths.

Crappies thrive in such environments, and dingy water allows them to stay relatively shallow (less than 20 feet). The abundant cover provides excellent habitat, and a slight current flow creates a flushing effect which ensures good water quality. Reservoir crappies do best when their food supply (usually shad) is plentiful. Shad numbers often suffer when the water becomes polluted, but when the shad population is healthy, crappies thrive.

Impoundments more conducive to white crappies usually offer many acceptable spawning areas. Most importantly, the largemouth spawn is more compacted, timewise, than on highland impoundments. There are far fewer "early" spawners, because there's enough suitable spawning environment to serve most of the bass population in a shorter span of time. Also, there are plenty of suitable spawning sites for bass and crappies when co-use enters the picture.

After spawning, the crappies' requirements are no longer fulfilled by shoreline habitat. In flatland impoundments, warming surface temperatures combined with a slightly lower lake elevation (after spring run-off) move the fish to a different depth zone. The key here is "move"; the crappies are moving to their summer areas.

Threadfin shad is often a reservoir's most abundant crappie forage, and schools of this baitfish retreat to deeper areas also. These areas are located away from the shoreline. The prime areas are flats and submerged creek channels in secondary bays and coves. The fish are on a "stair-stepping," post-spawn pattern, moving toward deeper water in the main lake areas.

In short, as the summer sun heats the backwaters of shallow, secondary, coves and bays, and drawdowns begin to make shoreline habitat too shallow

## Spring vs. Summer Areas

*Crappies usually do not live in one bay or cove all year long. Seasonally, their habitat requirements change and so does their location. AREA A is a secondary cove attached to a main cove and is a prime spring area. However, during summer a majority of the crappies will move to main-lake AREA B.*

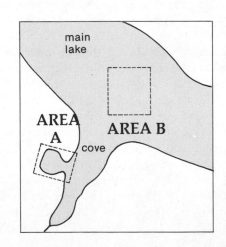

to hold fish, a deep-water pattern emerges. The crappies slowly filter out of the shallows and stack up in deeper areas. Most large, flatland reservoirs start annual drawdown in early to midsummer in anticipation of fall rain. This lowering of the water pulls crappies away from shorelines and out to drop-offs and sandbars adjacent to deep, river channels.

Summer crappies may suspend or school around areas of submerged cover like timber, stump rows or brush, which lie on or near the edge of the creek channel. For example, the top of a bar might be 8 feet deep and then abruptly break to a depth of 25 feet with cover scattered along the break. The key area is on the edge, in between the two extremes. Crappies like this environment because they have easy access to both deep and shallow water. It's a perfect area to intercept roving schools of shad.

At this time, small, underwater points or lips on such bars or humps are key crappie spots. Quite often, crappies reside on the down-current side—par-

## DETAIL OF AREA A
## Secondary Cove or Bay Attached to a Main Cove

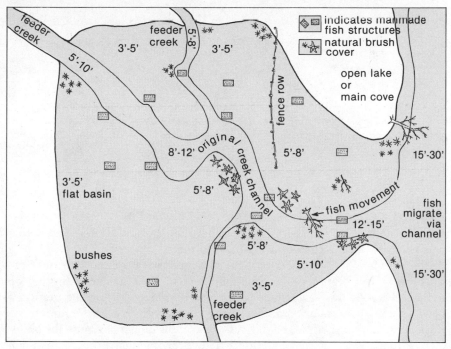

*Spring and early summer find crappies moving in and out of shallow, secondary spawning coves that are attached to larger, main coves or to the main lake itself. While the fish tend to follow flooded creek channels, shallow channels are often silted in and are very indistinct. Thus, you can't rule out the possibility of crappies crossing large flats, either. Therefore, your first choice is to look for flooded cover along channel edges and bends. If that option fails, look for flooded brush or manmade fish attractors up on the shallow flats. Even a small, 4' x 4' fish attractor can hold 15 to 20 nice crappies for awhile as the fish cross large flats.*

*DETAIL OF AREA B*
## Open-Water, Main-Lake Crappie Areas

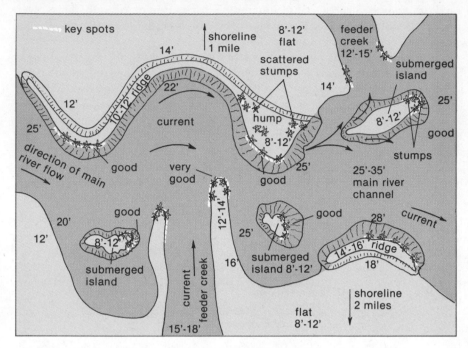

*Summer and fall crappies tend to relate more to cover along deep channel edges. On large reservoirs, such spots are often located a mile or more from shore, and depth finders are invaluable for finding them. Pay careful attention to channel bends, humps, and the intersections of two creek or river channels. The best areas usually have some sort of wood cover present.*

ticularly at times when the lake level is dropping and the current is at maximum flow. Crappies are basically lazy. They'll lie motionless in the eddy that forms here and let the current bring food to them.

Early summer finds crappies holding near mainstream bars. Not only are shad present, but crappies sometimes supplement their menu by feeding on mayfly larvae. As this early stage of the mayfly emerges from the mud in a wiggly, aquatic procession, crappies gorge themselves on nature's buffet.

This period can sometimes be difficult for crappie anglers because the abundance of food means stiff competition. However, keying in on mainstream points where the current has washed in mayfly larvae can put you on schools of feeding crappies.

Lake elevations are important to crappie movement. Rising water can scatter fish as they attempt to move toward the newly flooded, virgin territory. Just the opposite situation exists when a dropping water level pulls water from bays and creeks. In this instance, the fish often seek deeper water.

Experience has shown that water level changes of 2 to 3 inches affect fish

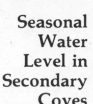

## Seasonal Water Level in Secondary Coves

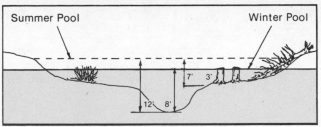

location. A daily monitoring of the pool elevation will give you a valuable clue to probable crappie location. In addition, the speed of the crappies' response to the changing water level is directly linked to the rate of increase or decrease in pool elevation. For example, if the fish were holding at 15 feet on a ledge and the lake level started dropping, on the next day's outing you would likely find crappies 17 to 20 feet deep.

A stable lake elevation is good, but a rise or fall in water level can actually help you establish a pattern. You can capitalize on the crappie's habits and key in on areas which draw crappies during a change in elevation.

Most big flatland impoundments have sufficient cover in deeper water where wind and ice erosion cannot reach. Although some siltation takes place, deep cover is usually present. A real change, however, occurs in the shallows where annual drawdown exposes shoreline areas. It is here that natural cover disappears over the years due to the forces of nature. Ice erosion, flooding and wind all contribute to loss of shallow habitat.

In contrast to the spring, post-spawn patterns of flatland reservoir crappie dispersal, fall movement takes place back *toward* the secondary channels and humps near the main stream. The fish slowly migrate back into the mouths of coves and bays as the water cools and fall arrives. Why in the world do flatland reservoir crappies move back in fall toward the mouths of the coves?

First, once the fall drawdown of 3 to 5 feet (typical of flatland reservoirs) is complete, the strongest current will be along the main river channel. Cold-water (fall and winter) crappies don't like to fight current, and they'll move toward the mouths of secondary coves. They'll still use relatively deep water (8 to 20 feet), but will move out of the main current.

Second, the cooling process of fall reoxygenates all the water in the lake. Due to the dark water, lack of weedgrowth and/or wind exposure, some shallow coves experience severe summer oxygen depletion in water deeper than 6 or 8 feet. The crappies may literally be chased out of the shallow coves in summer into deeper-water, main-lake areas, even though largemouth bass may remain in the shallow, 1- to 6-foot, flooded cover in the backs of coves. Now, however, they're able to return.

And third, late summer/early fall often finds a *second spawning* of threadfin shad taking place in the secondary coves on these impoundments. Studies show that threadfin shad may experience two spawning peaks on some southern waters—spring and fall. This phenomenon creates a bounty of small baitfish at a time of year when the spring hatch of threadfin and gizzard shad are growing too large for crappies to eat. This abundant, shad forage draws

# Crappie-Go-Round

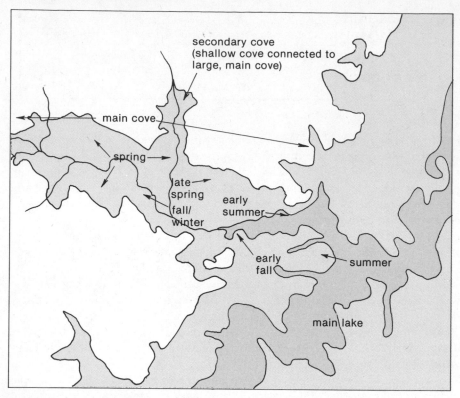

secondary cove
(shallow cove connected to
large, main cove)

main cove

spring

late
spring

fall/
winter

early
summer

early
fall

summer

main lake

Flatland-reservoir crappies display a predictable cycle of movement throughout the year. The accompanying map shows a portion of Kentucky Lake along the Kentucky/Tennessee border and describes this movement in detail.

The spring spawning season finds large numbers of crappies in the mid- to back-sections of shallow, secondary coves. After they spawn, the fish begin slowly dropping back toward the main lake. Steve McCadams calls it a "stair-stepping" effect. They don't race to deeper water; rather, they gradually migrate toward their summer habitat. During this movement, the fish will be spread out, although natural and manmade cover will hold fish. All of the fish do not do the same thing at the same time, but the bulk of the fish in that portion of the lake will be relating to the general areas indicated here.

Summer crappies relate primarily to the drop-offs along deep creek channels and the main river channel, so you should concentrate your efforts in the main portion of the lake. Then, as the water cools in early fall, the crappies begin moving back toward the large coves again. There is a definite, threadfin shad movement back toward the coves at this time of year, and the crappies follow close behind.

Fall and winter finds huge schools of crappies gathering along channel edges in the center to outer portions of the coves. They don't move as far back into the coves as they did in spring, largely because the drawdown has typically lowered the lake level 3 to 5 feet.

Crappies will relate to cover along the edges of the channel, and to the deep, bottom portions of channel bends and intersections that contain wood for cover.

Get the picture? Following the seasonal cycle of crappie movement on a mid-South, flatland reservoir will keep you on the majority of the fish population. Then it's simply a matter of trying several techniques until you locate and catch fish.

crappies back toward the cove mouths, although the crappies probably won't penetrate all the way to the shallow, back ends.

Fall crappies will continue to mass in these cove-mouth areas. As the water continues to cool (late fall), a collision of hungry predators and easily available prey begins and lasts well into the winter months.

Crappies in most lowland impoundments will behave similar to those in flatland impoundments. However, the species of crappies present should tip you off to some subtleties in their seasonal movements.

The presence of white crappies indicates a warmer environment and the likely presence of a shad food source. Given this environment, you can probably expect the same, classic movement patterns described for flatland reservoirs: namely, seasonal use of all parts of the reservoir and long-distance crappie movement. However, since most reservoirs are constructed by flooding natural swamps, you'll find a lack of natural cover in the deeper areas of the impoundment, and crappies will tend to roam a great deal.

The strong presence of black crappies in a lowland or even flatland impoundment indicates a cooler-water environment which probably lies in the northern half of the United States. In such impoundments, shad are probably minimal or absent, and the crappies will rely more on minnows, insects and small fish for food. Such shallow impoundments will generally have stained-to-dark water, although they seldom warm up to the same extent as the South's famous crappie impoundments. If the water is clear enough, significant weedgrowth may develop since this type of reservoir usually experiences minimal water fluctuation.

Given these conditions, black crappies are much more likely to relate to cover in the bays or shallower parts of the reservoir for a *longer* portion of the season; there's no major incentive or poor environmental conditions to *drive* them toward the deeper areas. Thus, shallow (6 to 10 foot), flooded brush and trees, or the deep edges of weedgrowth are good crappie attractors for much of the year, and you should concentrate your efforts in and around these areas.

Once the fish drop deeper in these impoundments—usually in fall—they'll relate to bends in the river channel or to deep holes. These areas are often silted in and may be only slightly deeper than the surrounding territory. Yet crappies will locate these subtle areas and stack into them. Find such an area with a bit of flooded cover and you have a real crappie magnet.

Interesting, isn't it? Subtle differences in the environment often trigger differences in crappie behavior. Yet when you're able to analyze the conditions, you can often predict the behavior of the fish.

# COVER

Although crappies suspended in open water can be taken, this situation is normally less effective than working cover. It's not that you can't catch them; it's just more difficult. In summer, some crappies will suspend in the main river channel! When open-water contact is made, it's usually an indication that crappies are on the move and you may have found them in transit. They are in between stops, and this pattern isn't likely to last. While you may catch some suspended fish, it's tough to stay on fish in a huge body of water.

The most catchable reservoir crappies are often cover oriented. The fish like to hide in cover and let prey come to them. Cover comes in many forms. It may be a weedbed adjacent to deep water or it can be other natural cover like fallen trees. Flooded trees, old stumps, rock piles, and riprap areas are other examples.

Other natural features worth noting are submerged creek channels and sand bars where some natural cover might have been left when the lake was flooded. Deep depressions, humps, ridges or other bottom elevation changes can all draw crappies.

Key areas are points falling off into mainstream or deep bays, as are islands near the mainstream. Down-current sections of submerged islands surrounded by deep water are also prime areas. These are natural crappie spots. They are even better when covered or dotted with debris like brush or original fence rows where trees were cut during the lake building process. In general, on huge impoundments, topographic maps will help you find structure like submerged brush tops and stump rows. Check with local marinas or lake officials to obtain a map before you even launch your boat. Pay attention to the elevation markings and key in on extreme depth changes. Doing your homework will help you locate and visualize bottom contours when you're on the water and will result in more fish.

# MANMADE FISH ATTRACTORS

Creating "homemade" crappie spots, where legal, has been the bread and butter of professional guides for years. These are especially effective in older reservoirs where much of the natural cover has disappeared after decades of wind, rain, siltation, and ice erosion. This is particularly true in shallow areas

*In reservoirs where shallow-water cover is sparse, artificial fish attractors are the answer. Manmade attractors are easy to build and they will draw lots of crappies.*

that dry up during the drawdown. The idea also works well in newly formed lakes where little or no cover exists.

Manmade fish attractors give fish a place to hide; they're a refuge—cover. Some anglers call them crappie "beds or hides." Other popular terms are "mats or huts." They all have the same goal: bringing the fish and the fishermen together. These brush piles attract and concentrate fish. In addition, fish attractors can become mini ecosystems providing crappies with feeding stations.

Many state and federal wildlife agencies are implementing programs of building and marking public fish attractors. Check with local reservoir authorities for maps showing the specific locations of such structures.

Building fish attractors sweetens the "crappie pie." Your effort gives existing fish populations a place to reside and also provides potential spawning habitat. In flatland reservoirs, crappies usually lay their eggs on the roots of bushes and trees. In addition, weedbeds or rock piles may also serve the purpose. However, in some older, flatland reservoirs, shallow-water cover is at a premium and crappies will use the manmade structures to spawn on.

Some of the most popular synthetic attractors are sunken treetops, tires wired together, and wooden "stake" beds built on shipping pallets or driven into the mud. The structures are simple, but effective. The main ingredients are time and labor.

How do you construct them, and where do you put 'em? Trees like willow, birch, ash, and cedar are popular woods. Leftover Christmas trees are good, too. Size can vary, but usually, trees in the 10- to 15-foot range are large enough to hold fish and small enough to transport.

Sometimes, several small trees or bushes can be wired together to form a crappie bed. Use copper wire and a concrete block or rocks as a weight to hold your structures on bottom. Also, standing trees upright in buckets filled with concrete is good for deeper areas, because the trees provide cover and appear to be growing on the lake's bottom.

Wooden stake beds are also super fish attractors. A series of wooden sticks or slabs can either be driven into the shallow mud, or nailed to shipping pallets for sinking in deeper water. The wooden stakes usually run 3 to 5 feet long and are 1 to 3 inches wide.

To place the beds in shallow water, use hip boots or chest waders. Drive the sticks into soft mud or gravel bottoms with a heavy pipe or small sledgehammer. Many anglers choose to build such structures during late fall and winter seasons when reservoir water levels are at their minimum elevation. When spring and summer arrive, the structures—then several feet deeper—hold fish until fall.

For sinking homemade beds in deeper water (12 to 15 feet), you'll need to wire concrete blocks to the wooden pallets after you've nailed 10 to 15 sticks to the studs of the pallet. For shallow stake beds, construct about a 4- to 8-foot square and use as many as 50 stakes. Since deeper structures are usually about 4 feet square, you'll likely have to drop a couple in one spot to create the desired bed size.

Many state agencies use old tires with holes punched in them to facilitate sinking. The tires can be wired to form a teepee image. Brush can also be added to the tires before sinking them to increase their attractiveness. These types

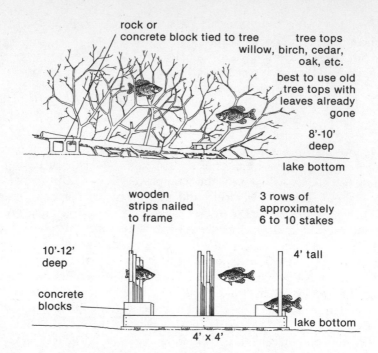

## Crappie Attractor Food Web

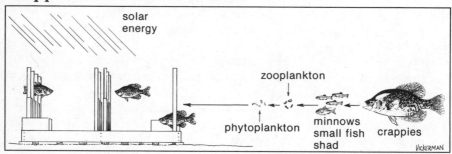

*Besides providing cover, crappie attractors are prime habitat for plant and animal communities that live in and around them. Small fish will eat these organisms and crappies will feed on the small fish, minnows, and shad. This is a classic example of a predator/prey relationship.*

of beds are quickly and easily put in place, and tires last forever. However, most anglers prefer just plain brush top and stake beds. Although fish seem to hold better in brush cover, tires will still improve a potential spot. In case you're wondering, crappies haven't shown a preference for either bias ply or radial tires.

In summary, the total surface area of your homemade structure will, to a degree, determine how effective it is. More surface area means more nutrients which will draw more fish. That's why brush is better than a single log—more surface area.

On some reservoirs, fish attractors function mainly as cover; however, in others, attractors can be crappie feeding and holding stations. This is especially true in clear-water reservoirs that contain a minimum amount of cover and prey. To be most effective, at least part of the crappie attractor should be placed above the depth of maximum sunlight penetration. The more surface area exposed to the effects of solar energy, the more "food" the attractor can produce. Here, plants (algae) will grow and attract minnows which feed upon the microscopic organisms that live on the structure. Eventually, crappies will locate and use this food source. Remember, while crappie attractors will draw some fish on any body of water, they are ideal in waters (or areas) with limited cover and baitfish. In many impoundments with a plentiful, suspended, shad-forage base, attractors probably serve more as temporary holding stations that crappies wander into in search of shad than as feeding stations. In summary, on many waters, crappies and attractors go hand-in-hand with on-the-water success.

Now, the question of where to place your cover comes up. Place the structures of your choice on the top of a ledge, along the break, and also on the deep side of the bar or ledge. Let the fish decide which depth best suits their needs. Just be sure to place them deep enough so they're not a hazard to navigation at low water. In addition, this also prevents other anglers from spotting your honey holes when the water level drops!

Place your structures in several different locations and depths with different wind directions in mind. Ask yourself where a likely spot with a strong west wind would be. East? North? South? By building a few structures in every situation, you'll be able to launch your boat and string some slabs when the rest of your buddies are back at the boat dock whining and waiting for the wind to subside.

Also note that changing lake levels can trigger seasonal and even daily locational changes. Deeper structures will hold fish when the lake is falling, and the shallow ones will produce best during rising water. During stable water conditions, you might find a few fish at several different depths.

How soon after you place structures on a spot will they yield fish? Sometimes crappies will invade the beds overnight, while others require a few weeks to draw fish. Usually, a structure improves with age.

Older structures allow algae to form. Various types of aquatic plankton utilize the growth, and shad often are attracted by this mini-ecosystem. Guess who follows the shad to these structures? You guessed it! Mr. & Mrs. Crappie are close behind. So the older beds are likely to hold more fish because they offer quality crappie habitat—cover and food.

Depending on the location and size of your structure, a dab of additional cover every 2 or 3 years might be necessary. Limbs break off and siltation occurs. You'll be able to determine the extent of deterioration by feeling the cover below with a "tightline" rig.

## TIPS ON FISHING RESERVOIRS

The best lake with "prime structure" will show you no fish if your techniques are wrong. It also holds true that the best bait catches no fish unless it's presented properly. So, to prevent the "no fish" blues, learn to match your tactics to the conditions you're faced with.

# Typical Cross-Section of River or Creek Channel

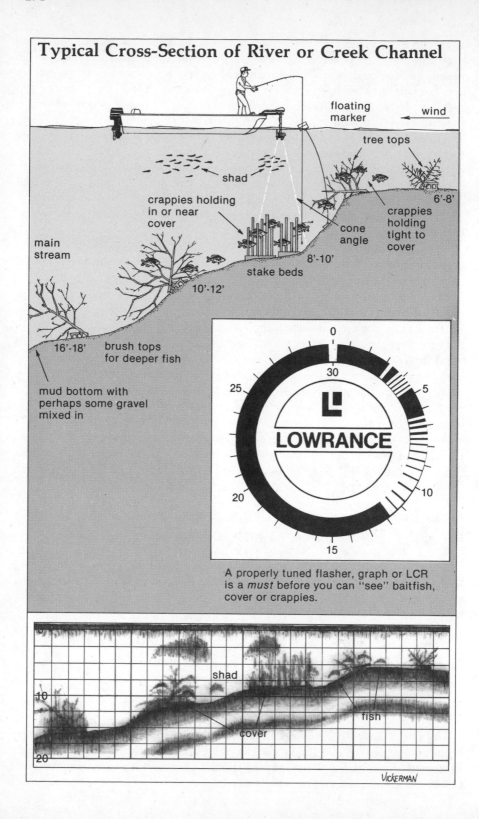

floating marker

wind

tree tops

shad

crappies holding in or near cover

crappies holding tight to cover

6'-8'

cone angle

main stream

8'-10'

stake beds

10'-12'

16'-18'

brush tops for deeper fish

mud bottom with perhaps some gravel mixed in

LOWRANCE

A properly tuned flasher, graph or LCR is a *must* before you can "see" baitfish, cover or crappies.

shad

fish

cover

VICKERMAN

On some reservoirs, prime crappie cover is visible. Fallen or standing timber and bushes are examples. However, in deep or dark water, submerged cover can be hard to locate. Just how do you find sunken cover?

Your best bet is to use your depth finder and tightline rig to locate cover. Watch your fish locator signals closely, and simultaneously feel for the cover. Once your bell sinker strikes wood, toss out a marker, back off within casting range and start fishing. In addition, your fish locator will also show the presence of baitfish and suspended crappies. Here are a few tips to help you plan your strategy.

The anticipation of seeing a bobber disappear with a slab crappie tugging on the other end is a lot of fun. At times, bobber fishing can be your best presentation option. Always carry a selection of styles. Bobber fishing allows you to fish over, around and through cover with minimum hang-ups. It's just the ticket for non-aggressive crappies holding tight to cover or for suspended fish.

In spring and fall, when crappies migrate from the deeper, open-water, river bars into shallower secondary creeks, look for them near cover. Crappies may relate to fallen trees in highland reservoirs, standing timber in hill-land impoundments, and manmade fish attractors in flatland reservoirs. When fishing cover, the situation may dictate positioning the boat several feet away from a structure and casting to it. Use a floating buoy marker to pinpoint the cover you want to fish. Presentation options include: (1) using a slip-float, casting bobber, and (2) counting your lure or minnow down into the strike zone.

Pitch a slip-bobber rig baited with a minnow over the cover. See what happens. If you get an instant strike, the fish are probably active and you can cast a jig to them. This is typical on cloudy days. When they're not active, though, they'll hold down and into cover (typical on sunny days), and you must extract them with the bobber rig.

If the crappies are active, simply cast a 1/16-ounce jig or jig & minnow combination across or alongside the cover. Let it sink to different levels on different casts, and slowly retrieve it. Count the jig down so you know the level you're working at, and experiment with retrieves to determine the most productive depth and speed. Bump the wood! Sure, you'll snag and lose jigs occasionally, but you won't catch fish if you're too timid to cast into cover. Continue this approach until the action slows.

Before you leave, drift or use an electric motor to position yourself directly over the cover. Drop your tightline rig directly into it and dig out an additional fish or two. If you snag up, a strong pull will straighten out the light-wire, Aberdeen hook. Bait up and repeat the process.

The old reliable, cane pole/bobber style of fishing for crappies can also be used here. A pole rigged with heavy braided nylon and fished with a slip float and a minnow or jig, is popular. A short, monofilament leader may be used to attach the hook (via a barrel swivel) to the heavy braided line. Hoisting the fish from heavy cover is important, and this simple and easy method works fine.

If you don't have a flasher or graph to help you locate crappie cover, slow trolling is a sure-fire way to find fish. Spider (tightline) rigs allow you to set out several poles at different depths. Then slowly troll or drift across flats or creeks. Scattered crappies are taken this way quite effectively. Consider anchoring your boat over likely spots, but be cautious when you position your anchor so you don't spook the fish.

# ROAMING THE RESERVOIRS

Large, sprawling reservoirs appear awesome to many anglers. How do you locate the productive spots with miles of open water staring you in the face? Ask any reservoir angler worth his grits and he'll tell you to get a good topographical map. A map will give you an overview of the reservoir. Channels, creeks, bays and coves plus depth contours are all easy to spot. Many times, detailed maps of the larger creek arms are available at marinas. Be sure to take time to study the map and the map's key because it'll help you locate potential fishing areas. In addition, you'll be gadding about the reservoir like an old-timer in no time.

General areas can be marked at home and checked out once you're on the water. Just apply the location strategies presented in this chapter and you'll be well on your way to becoming a crappie pro on any reservoir.

*This braggin'-sized bunch of white crappies was taken from Kentucky Lake, KY/TN. These slab crappies were caught while fishing a small jig tipped with a minnow around manmade fish attractors (stake beds).*

## Chapter 14

# SNEAKY TRICKS FOR CRAPPIES

### Tried And True Tips

How would you like to get the inside scoop on some of the nifty tricks that top crappie anglers use to catch fish? You would! Great, because we've picked the brains of several crappie experts and have assembled a number of hot tips to help you catch more and bigger crappies. These are tips that elite, crappie anglers use day in and day out to locate and catch fish.

Many times it's the little things that make a big difference in fishing. It's the subtle differences in equipment, location or presentation that really pay off. There are tips to help you trigger reluctant, non-aggressive fish; other techniques to use when they're biting ten-on-a-hook; plus inside information on location; and tips to help you catch more fish all season long.

The following information is a potpourri of little-known, productive secrets which you can add to your crappie fishing repertoire. Most of the tips and techniques can be applied to lakes, rivers and reservoirs. So, regardless of where you fish there will be many you can use. In essence, crappie fishing is simply matching your tactics to conditions.

# TACKLE

Selecting the proper rod and reel combo or crappie pole is important because a balanced outfit will maximize the effectiveness of your presentation. While almost any outfit will work, it's normally a good/better/best situation as far as crappie tackle goes. You can catch fish by using casting or spinning equipment, a fly rod outfit or a trusty cane pole. Be certain that the type of paraphernalia you choose allows you to use a presentation to match the conditions.

To sharpen your ability to feel the bottom or a bite, choose a casting or spinning rod with a sensitive tip. Then spool the reel with quality monofilament line. Use heavy line (10- to 30-pound test) and casting tackle for bouncing through heavy cover in dark water. For fishing sparse cover or clear water—the extreme opposite condition—use lighter, 2- to 4-pound-test line and spinning gear.

Another option is a 9- to 10-foot, graphite, fly rod (#5 weight). Spool the reel with 4- to 8-pound-test mono instead of fly line. A small jig on this set-up can be worked vertically in and around cover at all depths with maximum sensitivity and minimum hang-ups. A scrappy crappie is the ultimate challenge on this outfit—fun!

*A jig worked with a fly rod can be an effective way to catch crappies at all depths.*

Ultralight and light spinning tackle are very important in overall crappie presentation. Lighter tackle is a rule of thumb if the water is clear. A 5- to 6-foot, light-action, spinning rod with an open-bail, spinning reel spooled with

*Super crappie tackle!*

4- or 6-pound-test mono is ideal. Today's emphasis on super-light, leadhead jigs further complements the use of such tackle. The light jigs can be cast either around or over cover, or vertically fished through it.

Casting crappie jigs with weights of 1/16 or 1/32 ounce is best done on 2- or 4-pound line. The wind can play a role in the *feel* of your jig, and tiny split shots or a heavier jighead may be needed to get the lure down to the fish. When working the thick stuff, be prepared to cut and retie often. Decorating the snags with several dozen colorful jigs is common on some waters.

## CRAPPIE POLE

Millions of crappie anglers catch tons of crappies using a simple, 10- to 12-foot pole. An inexpensive cane pole works fine, but technology has developed sophisticated, ultra-sensitive, fiberglass and graphite, crappie poles.

For landing big crappies, the most popular pole is a 10- to 12-foot, fiberglass

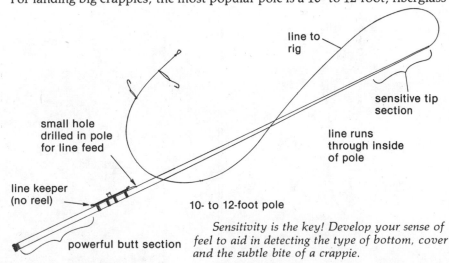

line to rig

sensitive tip section

small hole drilled in pole for line feed

line runs through inside of pole

line keeper (no reel)

10- to 12-foot pole

powerful butt section

*Sensitivity is the key! Develop your sense of feel to aid in detecting the type of bottom, cover and the subtle bite of a crappie.*

or graphite model with a sensitive tip and a strong butt section. The pole telescopes and is hollow on the inside where the line is threaded through and out the tip.

A line keeper is attached near the butt end of the pole where a tiny hole lets the line come up to the keeper. Depth can be regulated easily, because the line feeds (unwraps) off the keeper in one-foot increments. Some poles use a reel fixed to the butt end while others expose the line through eyelets on the rod. They all work, but with the line on the inside of the pole, there seem to be less tangles and more sensitivity.

The heavy-line, tightline, crappie rig is, of course, most effective in dark or stained water. However, by scaling down on the line size (10-pound vs. 30-pound test), the rig can be quite effective in clear water, too.

## 2 + 2 = CRAPPIES

Always cover water efficiently as you search for crappies. In the shallows, that can mean using a 2-rod/2-bobber approach.

Say you're fishing the shoreline of a bay, or using waders and a float tube (or a boat). You need to cover the shallowest water around the perimeter of the bay as well as the slightly deeper water offshore.

Rig a long, 6-1/2- to 7-1/2-foot, ultralight or light-action rod with 4-pound-test line. Slip a casting bubble such as the A-Just-A-Bubble onto your line. Slide it up to the desired depth and twist the top to hold it in place. Now tie a small, leadhead jig on the end of your line below the bobber. By adding a bit of water (weight) to the casting bubble you can cast this rig a mile. It's perfect for fishing the shallows.

This casting-bubble system fishes most efficiently with 1 to 2-1/2 feet of line

## A-Just-A-Bubble Rig      Slip Bobber Rig

A-Just-A-Bubble Rig: 1 to 2½ feet

Slip Bobber Rig: bead — option: place sinkers at 6'' intervals to reduce bow in line while retrieving — 2 to 5 feet — split shot — 12'' to 18'' — hook

VICKERMAN

hanging below the bobber. The more line dangling below the bobber, the more difficult it becomes to cast.

The other rod can be a short or long, ultralight, rigged with 4-pound-test line. Add a slip bobber to this rig and it becomes your "little-bit-deeper" rod. You'll lose some casting distance, but that's OK because little-bit-deeper crappies aren't quite so spooky.

You'll usually fish this combo in water from 2 to 5 feet deep, although you can fish it deeper or shallower by simply adjusting the bobber stop. Ready? Then step into your float tube and wade in. Pop a few casts out to the deeper water in front of you. Retrieve the bobber a foot before stopping it to let the jig glide back below it.

Now cover the shallow water parallel to shore. Lay your "short" rod across your tube or prop it in a rod holder and fire a cast out with the long rod. Sure, send the bobber out 60 feet. It's amazing how easily a long, light rod casts a casting bubble on 4-pound-test line.

Use this system anytime crappies are relatively shallow. When they drop into slightly deeper water, switch the slip bobber to the long rod and go without a bobber on the shorter rod. The longer rod with a slip bobber will allow you to probe the deeper areas more efficiently. In addition, the shorter, ultralight rod can be used to pitch either a small, subtle jig or an action jig along the deeper edges of a weed- or brushline. By using the countdown technique to control the depth of the lure, a jig can be fished above, through or parallel to cover or a drop-off.

## MINNOWS, JIGS AND BOBBERS

Crappies are among the least confusing of all species from a presentation point of view. Since most crappies worth catching are basically minnow- or fish-feeders, most of their feeding is done at mid-depth ranges, among schools of baitfish. Therefore, the range of potentially productive presentations is rather limited.

Normally, live-bait anglers can limit themselves to the most predominant open-water baitfish in any given body of water. Preferred bait size is almost always between 1-1/2 and 3 inches.

Sure, there are exceptions. A few crappies are caught on nightcrawlers. Also, during certain specific periods when crappies are feeding on emerging nymphs or insects, baitfish can go untouched. But for pure productivity, you're still better off with the most common baitfish within the preferred size range in the lake.

Minnow type and size are important factors in crappie fishing. Day in and day out, minnows in 1- to 2-inch lengths seem to produce best with both bobber- and jig-fishing presentations. Remember, match the minnow size to the size of the hook you're using; *don't* impale a small bait on a large hook. Simple and natural is usually best when dealing with crappies.

What are crappie minnows? Well, depending on where and when you buy them, crappie minnows are usually a real hodgepodge of different types. Shiners, fatheads, dace, chubs and shad are all typical varieties that show up in your minnow bucket. In addition, usually a few less desirable minnows like sticklebacks, suckers and carp have a habit of appearing, too; these are *not* preferred types. Know your minnow types and use the best local bait available; it pays!

Normally, you'll catch more fish on fresh, lively bait than on half-dead or unhealthy minnows. Therefore, take special care of your bait; baitfish must be kept cool and well oxygenated. In addition, don't overcrowd minnows. As a rule of thumb, 2 or 3 dozen minnows per gallon of water is about right. A few dozen, lively minnows are a lot better than a ton of dead, smelly bait.

Hooking the minnow is simply a matter of common sense based on the presentation. For example, when you're stationary-bobber-fishing, hook the minnow lightly in the back just behind the dorsal fin, taking care not to break the spine. When trolling, hook the minnow through the lips from the bottom upward so it trails naturally as it's moved along. When jigging, hook the minnow upward through the lower jaw and out the skull, or hook it through the eyes. Hooking the minnow properly will ensure a natural-appearing bait and will make catching crappies much easier.

Hooking minnows properly is important. Although we don't have research evidence, it appears that crappies often take their baitfish sideways or tail first. So, when you're bobber fishing, hook the bait just behind the dorsal fin and above the backbone. A minnow hooked in this manner will stay alive and move around actively. This movement is important in luring the crappie to take the bait.

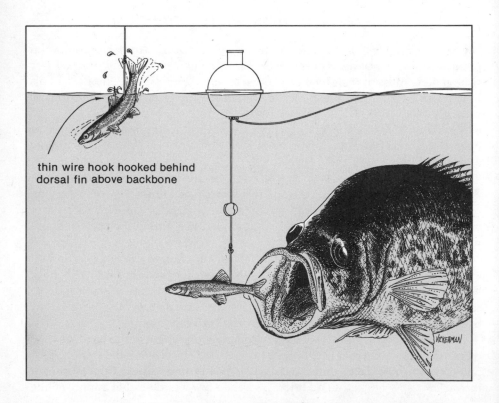

thin wire hook hooked behind
dorsal fin above backbone

In early spring when crappies are bedding in very shallow water, use this method: With the minnow just several inches under the bobber, slowly move the boat (or wade) along the shore, continually dropping the bait into likely spots. The trick is the presentation of the minnow. Reach out with your pole and slowly drop the minnow until it is partially under the surface. It will wiggle frantically, trying to get into the water. Hold it this way for several seconds before dropping it all the way in. Nearby crappies will have a tough time resisting.

Here are a couple tips to use when casting a crappie jig or jig/minnow combo. The drop rate of some jigs can be controlled by trimming the hair or feathers. In addition, tipping the jig with a minnow will add buoyancy. By experimenting with sizes and styles of jigheads, along with varieties of body dressing (plastic, feathers or hair), you can achieve nearly any drop-speed and/or action the fish desire.

Color? Crappie jigs are available in a zillion colors, but a couple basic colors will usually suffice. In clear water, white, yellow, pink and chartreuse seem to work best. However, black, purple and light fluorescent colors can produce in dark-water conditions. In stained water, trial and error will be necessary to determine a color preference. The pinky jig (pink jighead with white hair or feathers) is normally a good choice in clear water, while a pink jighead with yellow hair or feathers is a good pick for stained or dark water. While our general tendency is to try light-colored jigs first, recent experiments with the Color-C-Lector have shown that darker lures are productive at times. Thus, the rule is, *experiment!*

A last minute tip: Try a small loop knot when trolling or casting tiny crappie jigs. The loop gives the jig better action.

Finally, check lighter lines regularly for wear by passing the line over your lips. This technique is more discriminating than eyeball or finger checks and should be used routinely—especially when fishing around cover.

# JIGS

Miniature-size plugs; small, straight-shafted spinners; and a variety of other artificials will all take crappies, but jigs are the most productive artificial lures. As with live bait, keep the size small. In fact, for all practical purposes, you can eliminate almost anything over 2 inches long.

# SUBTLE JIGS

Subtle jigs also work well in the same areas as action jigs. They simply have less action and are better choices when the fish are less aggressive. Their true strength, however, is that they are deadly when retrieved with minimum movement or even held at rest! Bucktail jigs are buoyant (slow drop speed) and have very subtle action. Marabou "breathes" in a tantalizing fashion even when the jig is motionless. Plastic bodies only transmit the subtle motion *you* place on them. Plastic-body/marabou-tail combinations display the best aspects of both.

In general, most jigs are designed to be fished without a minnow and are somewhat bulky. When you tip a jig with a minnow, it's usually best to thin

out the jig by trimming down or pulling out some of the dressing. This reduces
the bulk of the combination so it's more appealing to crappies.

*Column 1: Knight Tiny Tube, Gopher Mushroom Head, Jack's jighead; Column 2: chenille/marabou jig, Lindy Fuzz-E-Grub, Windels Rabbit Hair Jig.*

# ACTION JIGS

Action jigs have spinners, wiggling tails, etc., and work better in motion
than at rest. They're great for swimming retrieves or when active crappies hit a
jig as it falls to the bottom. Action jigs work best for mid-depth retrieves, such
as along the edge of brush or a weedline. They are excellent choices before
crappies move in shallow (before pre-spawn) or after they leave the shallows
(after post-spawn).

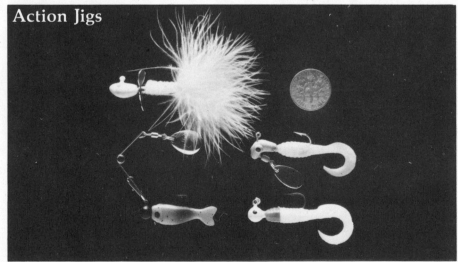

*Clockwise from upper left: Northland Whistler, Blakemore Road Runner, Mister Twister Teeny, Bass Buster Chumm'n Minnow.*

# JIG FISHING TIPS

Here are a couple tricks that'll increase your jig-fishing catch. When fish are aggressive, use an action jig like a Bass Buster Beetle Spin, Blakemore Road Runner or Northland Whistler Jig. For casting a light jig, 4- to 6-pound-test line on an ultralight to light action, 5- or 6-foot rod is preferred. Position the knot on the front of the eye of the jig; it's perfect for swimming retrieves.

However, a slightly different approach works better when subtle jigs like a Knight Tiny Tube, Lindy Fuzz-E-Grub, marabou/hair jig or plain jighead are fished either vertically or below a float. Simply position the knot in the center or slightly back of the jig's eyelet. This allows the jig to remain in a horizontal position and not just hang at an odd angle.

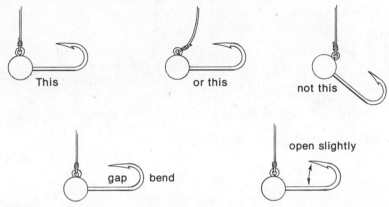

Remember to re-adjust the knot after catching a fish. An additional tip that will help you hook more crappies is to open the bend of the hook slightly to increase the gap and increase hooking ability.

# CRAPPIE JIG BRUSHGUARD/WEEDGUARD

No doubt about it, fishing for crappies in many waters means fishing cover. Whether you fish standing timber in a reservoir, flooded brush in an oxbow lake or heavy reeds in a natural lake, snags and crappie fishing go hand-in-hand. Here's a neat little trick that some good ol' southern boys have used to minimize jig loss. However, the tip can be used anywhere.

Place a small rubber band or dental elastic over the jighead and hook. Put the rubber band over the hook barb and then carefully pull it over the eyelet of the jig. Bingo—a simple yet effective guard.

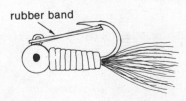

# WHY KNOT?

Tying a strong knot is a *must*. Because many crappie presentations require the use of 2-, 4- or 6-pound-test line, knot strength is critical. So, take the time to learn how to tie knots properly and avoid the frustration of losing a slab crappie because the knot failed. Remember, your line is only as strong as the weakest link—the knot. Many anglers are tying knots that can reduce the breaking strength of a line by more than 50%. It's easy to understand why lots of big fish are lost on light lines.

Before each fishing trip, spool up with fresh, premium line; *don't* use the bargain basement stuff. A strong knot tied with quality monofilament line will hold the biggest crappie that swims. The accompanying illustrations describe a few knots that'll help you catch more crappies.

## TRILENE KNOT

This knot retains up to 90% of the original line strength. Use it for tying hooks and artificial lures to monofilament line.

### Trilene Knot

1. Run end of line through eye of hook or lure and double back through the eye a second time.

2. Loop around standing part of line 5 or 6 times.

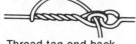

3. Thread tag end back between the eye and the coils as shown.

4. Pull up tight and trim tag end.

## LOOP KNOT

This knot only has 60 to 70 percent of the line strength, but is a good knot to use when you're casting tiny, 1/64- or 1/32-oz. jigs. The loop knot gives small jigs unrestricted action. However, remember to re-tie often.

### Loop Knot

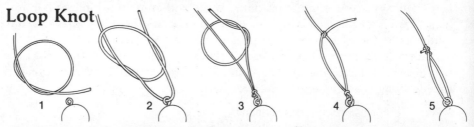

(1) Make an overhand knot. Then (2) pass the free end through the eye of the lure and back through the overhand knot. (3) Snug up the knot by pulling on the free end and standing line. Then tie another overhand knot around the standing line. (4) Snug up the second overhand knot and pull on the standing line to slide the two knots together. (5) Continue pulling until the two knots join. Then trim.

# BOBBER RIGS

Bobber rigs fit the bill for shallow-water, cover-oriented fish, or for fish suspended in or near deep cover. They work equally well with jigs, jig/minnow combos, or the old split-shot/hook/minnow standby.

Long, thin, lightweight, "quill" bobbers are excellent for shallow, calm conditions. They enter the water with a light splash rather than a hard "plop." They're sensitive and betray even the lightest crappie hit. A *slight* twitch will rock the bobber and make your jig dance. Their only weakness is that they're difficult to cast in windy conditions.

Plastic floats like the A-Just-A-Bubble serve several functions. First, you can add water inside them, giving you the weight to cast a light jig in windy conditions. Second, the thread-through, twist grip holds the bobber in place without damaging your line and makes it easy to adjust the depth of your bait. About the only drawback is that its heavier weight makes a splash when it enters the water. Use it under windy conditions, but stick to the quill-type bobber when it's calm.

Slip bobbers work at any depth and are easy to cast even when fishing deep water. It's hard to cast a normal bobber rig that's set deeper than 4 feet. Slip bobbers are simple to use; just slide the bobber stop up or down your line and you can fish from 2 to 20 feet deep—or more!

Bobbers work best with subtle jigs. In fact, since the bobber adds casting weight, you can drop down to tiny 1/16-, 1/32-, or even 1/64-ounce jigs. They are deadly on shallow crappies in brush or reeds. Add a small, lip-hooked, crappie minnow to the jig if the fish are reluctant to hit a plain jig. Give the jig a little dab of a scent-attractor product if it gives you more confidence.

*From left to right: Columns 1 and 2: pencil/quill-type bobbers; Column 3: standard round bobber; A-Just-A-Bubble, slip bobber with stop and bead, #8 hooks and split shot; Column 4: "pinky" jig, Binkelman jighead, Lindy floss-bodied jig, Windels marabou jig.*

# FIXED VS. SLIP BOBBERS

What are the differences between bobbers? Are they important? Yes! While there are many bobbers on the market, they can be divided into two general categories—fixed and slip styles. Fixed floats are clipped, pegged or twisted onto the line, allowing you to fish at a specific depth. Normally, a fixed float is used in shallow water that's 1 to 4 feet deep. This style of float allows the bait to remain at the pre-set depth during a retrieve. A slip bobber, on the other hand, slides on the line until it hits the bobber stop. Therefore, you can fish much deeper without causing any casting problems. A slip bobber also allows you to fish at a controlled depth. However, during a retrieve, the bait has a tendency to rise toward the surface because line is being pulled through the bobber. So, retrieve very slowly to minimize this yo-yo effect.

# RETRIEVES

Crappie presentations should be slow moving most of the time. That calls for the correct tackle combinations. Light, 1/16- to 1/8-ounce leadhead jigs, fished on 4-pound-test line and a lightweight rod, make casting easy and allow

## Three Typical Retrieves

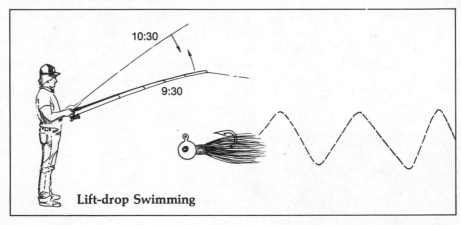

10:30
9:30

**Lift-drop Swimming**

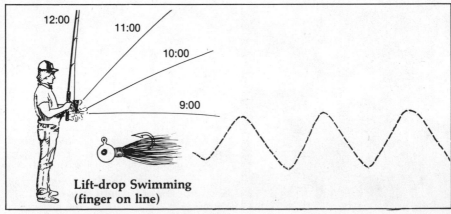

12:00
11:00
10:00
9:00

**Lift-drop Swimming
(finger on line)**

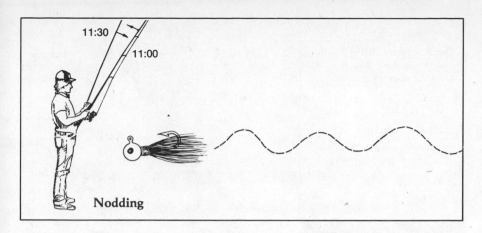

*Two types of lift-drop swimming retrieves are made in different ways but provide the same, basic, jig movement. Try this when it's calm out and you can watch your line for hits. Cast out, raise your rod tip to about 10:30, and count the jig down to the desired depth: "One thousand, two thousand, etc." Let the jig ride down on a tight line for a bit before slowly reeling down to about 9:30, and then lift back to 10:30. The jig will ride, rise and fall in an enticing manner. Expect most hits to occur as the jig falls.*

*When it's windy and you're having trouble watching your line, use your finger to detect hits. Cast out and bring your rod tip to 9:00 as you count the jig down. Engage the reel and place your trigger finger on the line. As the jig falls, it's getting closer to you. Let the jig fall as you hold at 9:00. Bring the rod tip to 10:00 and let the jig fall. Do the same at 11:00 and 12:00. Then quickly reel back to 9:00 and start over.*

*A nodding retrieve is made with the rod tip high. Cast out and count the jig down as you raise the rod tip to 11:00. Your wrist moves the rod tip only from 11:00 to 11:30. Raise the rod tip slowly to 11:30 and then reel back to 11:00.*

the proper drop speed as a jig moves and falls during a retrieve.

Slow and simple is the way to go. Most of the time, either a slow, horizontal, swimming motion or a near-motionless presentation is most effective. That's why vertical fishing is so productive whenever you have crappies "nailed down" in heavy cover. You can set the depth of your lure and then try to hold it there. Of course, this becomes impossible when crappies are "on the move" as they typically are when suspended. Either some type of backtrolling (usually with an electric motor) or a cast and slow, steady, retrieve-type technique works best then.

In general, lures should be fished slowly because crappies seem much more willing to hit presentations moving steadily and horizontally than lures that are moving either erratically or up and down.

## OPEN-WATER ACTION

Drifting, backtrolling or front trolling are efficient ways to search for crappies. Once you've found them, you have several options. If it's windy, the fish are usually deep or scattered, so it may be a good idea to continue to drift or troll. If the fish are pinpointed and deep, you may wish to anchor over them and fish vertically. When fish are found schooled relatively shallow, it's a good idea to mark the fish and pull back off them; then cast to the school.

*Mark the school's location, back off and cast into it using ultralight, spinning gear and small jigs.*

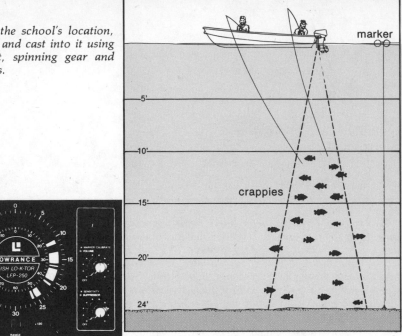

# FLOATING MARKER BUOYS

Floating markers can be used to locate open-water areas. They're perfect for marking a place where you spotted fish on your locator, graph or LCR, or they can be tossed overboard to mark the spot where a crappie was caught. In addition, they are handy for staking out fish attractors, humps, submerged islands, creek channels, submerged timber, weedlines, drop-offs, ledges and other underwater structures.

Markers allow you to target a specific area and enable you to fish more productively. Because your bait will be in potential crappie water a high percent-

age of the time, you'll catch more fish, and that's the name of the game.

There are several different styles, shapes, colors and sizes of marker buoys on the market. Which is best? It depends. Most markers are constructed of polyethylene and are either flat or barbell in shape. They come with 50 to 75 feet of nylon cord that wraps around the marker for storage and a heavy lead weight to securely anchor the marker on the bottom. The best flat and low-profile, barbell markers contain balanced ballast weights inside to prevent them from unwinding in current or wind. These low-profile markers offer good visibility if you're close by, yet are difficult for other anglers to spot from a distance.

An innovative company has designed an illuminated marker buoy for night fishing. The unit is powered by a AA battery and burns up to 10 hours. This unit is perfect for night-fishing addicts.

A new, high-visibility, upright, floating buoy is also available. Unlike the low-profile types, this marker has a 7-inch high, cylindrical top with a one-inch strip of reflective tape for added visibility. Like the other markers, this buoy is self-contained. This vertical-style marker will provide high visibility under most conditions—even at a distance—and the reflective tape makes it easier to find at night.

Most markers are either bright yellow or orange and are easy to spot. White, a favorite color for homemade, styrofoam markers is very difficult to locate under bright conditions. If you plan on using a homemade marker, paint it a fluorescent color, and regulate the length of the cord to match the depth of the water. Typically, these homespun markers unwind easily and may keep you off the fish.

In summary, floating marker buoys are a must. Don't leave the dock without them.

# DRIFT, DABBLE OR DRAG?

Cover and wind determine your best crappie approach. Here are three examples requiring slightly different approaches.

**DRAG:** This approach works well with sparse cover and little or no wind. Simply cast a quill-type, bobber/jig combination past the cover (reed clump, flooded brush, stump, etc.) and slowly reel it up to the cover. Pause. Let it sit for 8 to 10 seconds and then give it a *slight* twitch. Repeat the process. Work your jig along the very edge of the cover.

A quill-type bobber is a key part of this presentation. The quill bobber is heavy enough to cast easily, yet it lands with a soft "plop" that won't spook shallow fish. Because the bobber is set at a fixed position on the line, the bait remains at a specific depth during the retrieve (drag).

**DRIFT:** Drifting works well in sparse cover, although you can rapidly (perhaps too rapidly!) drift a jig and bobber past thick cover, too. Cast slightly upward from the cover and let the bobber drift up the edge. Once it reaches the edge, hold it in place; twitch it, and then let it sit.

No bites? Point your rod tip to the right or left and *steer* the bobber around the edge of the cover. Once it clears the edge, release some line and let it drift by.

This approach works *around* single cover items like a brush pile or *through* sparse areas of cover like thin reed clumps. With repeated casts and a little steering, you can maneuver a bobber rig through a wide area of cover without repositioning the boat.

This type of bobber is perfect for casting in wind. Add water to the float to give you enough weight to cast. In addition, because the bobber is firmly attached to the line, the bait stays at the proper depth during the drift.

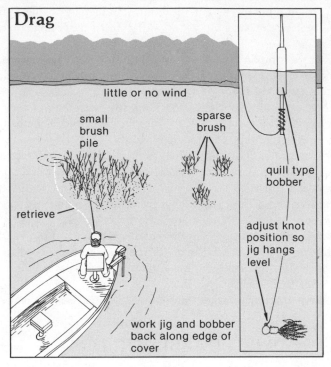

**DABBLE:** Thick cover requires a dabbling approach. Unless the crappies are very active, they won't come out to the edge. A bobber/jig combo that drags or drifts past the edge won't entice them. Roll up your sleeves and go in after 'em.

A simple cane pole or a 10- to 14-foot, telescoping rod works great under these conditions. Position the boat 6 to 10 feet from the cover; reach out with the rod tip and "flip" the tiny jig into the cover. Ever-so-slowly lower it through the cover, pausing occasionally. Give the jig a slight "wiggle," and pause again.

Don't be in too much of a hurry. Tease the fish. When a fish inhales the jig, don't *jerk*. Simply lift up in a steady, sweeping motion. The flex of the long rod will lift the fish up through cover to the surface. Once the fish is up, drag it slightly away from the cover. When it's in the open, *then* fight it. Don't go toe-in-toe *in* cover, or *you'll lose*.

Think you'll spook 'em? When fish first move into the shallows in spring, they'll be very spooky. After they're in the shallows awhile, they become more fearless. Once fish start to display their dark spawning colors, you can usually approach them quite easily.

This approach works best with light wind conditions when you can hold the

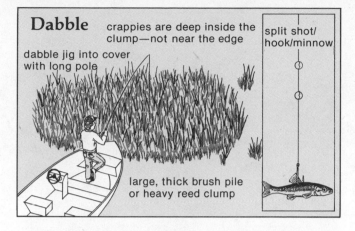

**Dabble** crappies are deep inside the clump—not near the edge

dabble jig into cover with long pole

split shot/ hook/minnow

large, thick brush pile or heavy reed clump

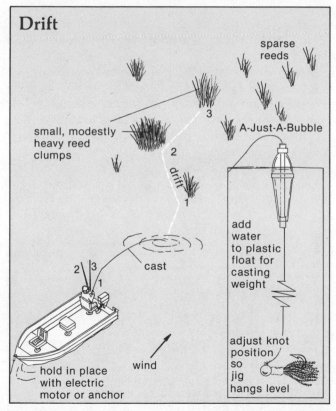

**Drift**

sparse reeds

small, modestly heavy reed clumps

3

2

drift

1

A-Just-A-Bubble

add water to plastic float for casting weight

cast

2  3

1

hold in place with electric motor or anchor

wind

adjust knot position so jig hangs level

*Cast bobber slightly upwind of first reed clump and let it drift to the edge. Steer it left by pointing your rod tip left. Little by little, let out more line. With enough line out and by swinging the rod left to ROD POSITION 2, the bobber will drift to CLUMP 2. Similarly, more line and bringing the rod back to ROD POSITION 3 will drift the bobber to CLUMP 3.*

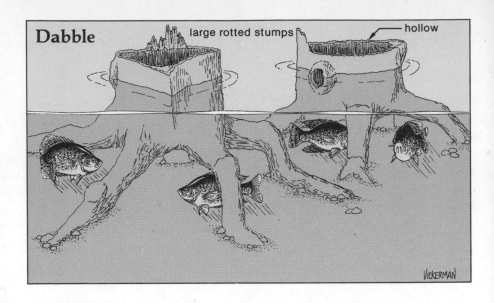

**Dabble**

large rotted stumps

hollow

VICKERMAN

boat in place with an electric motor. It is very difficult to fish heavy cover with a strong wind, however, unless you anchor in exactly the right position on the upwind side of the cover.

In some reservoirs, oxbow lakes and river backwaters, stumps and brush attract crappies. Carefully dabble the bait into the cover, working around a stump's root system. Don't forget to probe for crappies *inside* large, hollow, rotted logs. In some waters, this "stump knocking" technique is deadly.

**LEVERAGE:** If you can, use the end of a branch or a broken reed as a *lever*. Flip your line over the top, near the tip. The lure will drop straight down from there. This is better than casting horizontally *into* heavy cover, because you'll probably snag up if you do. Fish the jig slowly up and down with frequent pauses. When a fish bites, lift it up and over the cover. You can fish light cover like reeds with 6-pound-test line; whereas heavy brush might require 10- to 30-pound test to muscle the fish out.

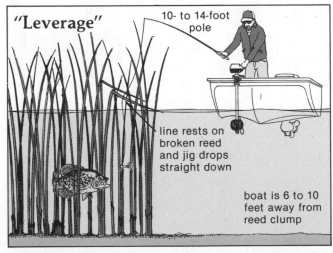

**"Leverage"**

10- to 14-foot pole

line rests on broken reed and jig drops straight down

boat is 6 to 10 feet away from reed clump

# UP AND IN

When fishing in cover (reed clumps or brush), the "up and in" technique is the best method for quickly getting a fish out of cover and into the boat. The long crappie pole gives you the leverage necessary to put pressure on the fish without breaking the line. In addition, it absorbs the shock when a slab crappie makes a mad dash for freedom. Crappies have a fragile, "paper thin" mouth, so don't horse 'em or you'll probably tear the hook out—goodbye fish.

*A jig worked with a fly rod or long, limber crappie pole is an effective and fun way to catch crappies. This outfit provides maximum "feel" and the softest bite can easily be detected.*

When a crappie bites, *don't* rear back and sock-it-to-'em with both hands to set the hook. Usually, all that's necessary is a quick, gentle, upward motion of the pole; the small, sharp hook will easily penetrate the crappie's mouth. In cover, lift the fish up and out of the reeds or brush and swing it gently into the boat. It's much more effective than trying to pull a crappie *through* cover, which often results in a broken line and a lost fish. Remember, "up and in!"

When conditions permit, a fish can also be lifted out of cover, then pulled across the surface on its side to the boat. This technique is great for getting slab crappies up and away from heavy cover bordered by an open area. Also, don't forget a landing net because giant, 2-pound-plus crappies may require a net to get them into the boat. Remember, always carry a net whenever you're on slab-crappie waters; it'll save you the frustration of losing a large crappie at the boat.

## COVER, DEPTH AND BOTTOM CONTENT

Pre-spawn crappies will seek out the best available combination of depth, cover and bottom content. Depth and cover can be fairly obvious and easy to locate. Simply use your eyes in clear water. Polarized sunglasses will help you spot bottom conditions; if it's not too windy, the polarized lenses cut the glare

Heavy, deeper (4-5 feet) reeds are some of the best, big-crappie spawning areas on natural lakes. The prime spots have thick, bent or broken reeds in conjunction with a bottom darker than the surrounding area.

Polarized sunglasses cut glare and enable you to pick out prime, pre-spawn/spawn crappie areas. If the water is fairly clear, you can pick out the best spots and sometimes even see the fish!

*This is what reeds look like when you approach them with the sun in your face. The back, shaded sides of the reeds stand out in vivid contrast, betraying the heaviest clumps. It's much easier to fish clumps from this direction. In general, pre-spawn/spawn, natural-lake crappies—particularly the big slabs—will select the deepest, heaviest reed clumps with the proper bottom content. Heavy clumps in 4 to 5 feet of water are more likely to hold larger fish than those in 2 feet.*

*Always check out areas adjacent to beaver lodges for submerged wood. Many times the slightly deep water and sunken branches will draw early season crappies. This type of cover is ideal crappie habitat.*

and enable you to see bottom. Pick out the darker areas in conjunction with cover at a likely depth (usually 2 to 5 feet). Under ideal conditions (clear water, sunny skies, no wind) you'll often spot the crappies, too! In dark or stained waters, fish will often spawn at the depth of maximum light penetration.

# CRAPPIE RIG

First used in the large lakes of Kentucky and Tennessee, the dingy waters of Lake Barkley and Kentucky Lake gave the crappie rig its fame. Professional guides use it during every season of the year for consistent catches of slab crappies. The crappie rig allows you to present baits at two different depths at the same time. Remember, depth control is crucial in crappie fishing. Deeper-water (12 to 20 feet) anglers favor a vertical, "tightline" technique. This "spreader" rig consists of two hooks with a bell sinker on the bottom.

The crappie rig is designed to be used both with live minnows and with artificial jigs. Shiner minnows are the most common bait, but your favorite marabou or hollow-bodied jig can easily be substituted.

By bouncing bottom with this double-hook rig you can let the sinker be your eyes to the bottom. Any contact with brush, stake beds, etc., is telegraphed to you via the line and pole. Although two fish may be taken at one time, the real purpose of the double hook rig is to present the bait at two different depths. Whether the crappies are holding tight to cover or slightly suspended, you'll have both depths covered.

*These slab black and white crappies were "tightlined" from cover located at the edge of a creek channel. Do you recognize the white crappie on the left?*

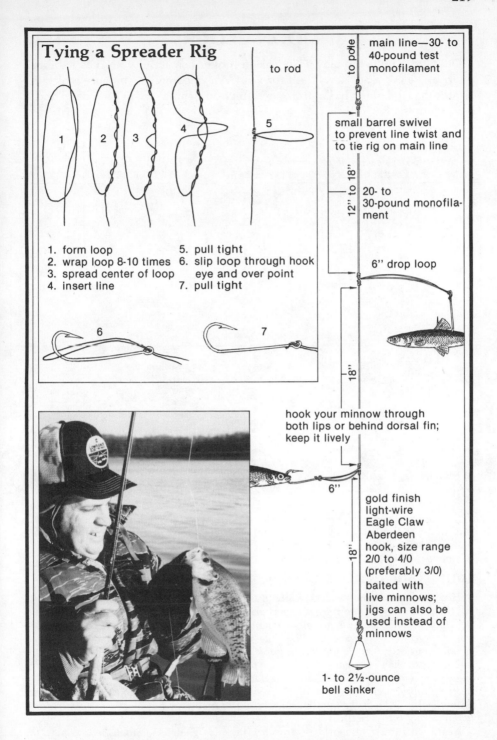

# Tying a Spreader Rig

to rod

1. form loop
2. wrap loop 8-10 times
3. spread center of loop
4. insert line
5. pull tight
6. slip loop through hook eye and over point
7. pull tight

to pole

main line—30- to 40-pound test monofilament

small barrel swivel to prevent line twist and to tie rig on main line

12" to 18"

20- to 30-pound monofila-ment

6" drop loop

18"

hook your minnow through both lips or behind dorsal fin; keep it lively

6"

gold finish light-wire Eagle Claw Aberdeen hook, size range 2/0 to 4/0 (preferably 3/0)

baited with live minnows; jigs can also be used instead of minnows

18"

1- to 2½-ounce bell sinker

*The entire, double-hook rig is tied from one piece of monofilament. The drops are "double loops" where a hook can slide on by putting the line through the hook's eye. Hooks can be changed without cutting the line.*

# MOON CLOCK

Does lunar influence play a key role in lunker fish activity and catchability? Well, we've got a hot news flash for you! We've compiled evidence which indicates that the moon has a profound effect on fishing—both on a daily and a monthly basis!

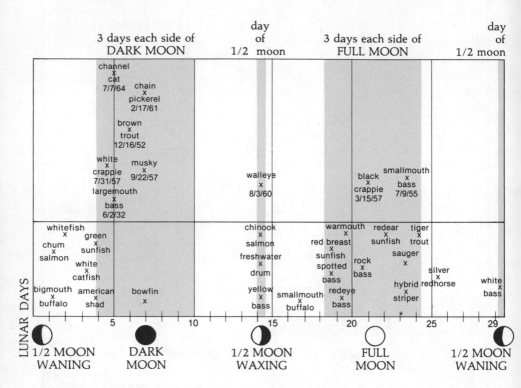

*Selected world-record, gamefish catches.(Note: Since all records are not included in this group, it is intended only to represent individual records and not to show a complete picture.)*

*New world records during 1970-1979.*

## Important Periods During The Lunar Month

*Having reached firm conclusions about the importance of monthly periods surrounding the dark and full moon, we became curious about the success other anglers had during these periods. Because no one apparently kept records as elaborate as Doug Hannon's, we could only go to the 1979 (the year we compiled the information) International Game Fish Association record book and check record fish against the part of the lunar month they were caught. What we found was amazing! The three days on each side of the dark and full moons plus the day of each half-moon, represented about 54% of the month, yet held 73% of the world records caught from 1970-1979! More dramatically, 24% of the month around the full moon held 41% of the world records taken during this period!*

*Next, we turned to world records for popular gamefish established outside the 1970-1979 period. The white and black crappie, channel catfish, chain pickerel, brown trout, musky, smallmouth and largemouth bass records were all caught within a three-day period either side of the dark or full moon. Clearly, these periods are significant for large fish.*

The moon exerts an intense gravitational influence on the earth and this, in turn, seems to affect animal (fish) behavior. Doug Hannon, a true fishing scholar, recognized the significance of the moon's influence. In a manner that anyone can understand, he condensed data and detailed how this information can be related to fishing.

Basically, Hannon identified daily periods of lunar influence—"excellent" and "good" activity periods that coincide with moon-up and moon-down. Major (excellent) periods are triggered by the moon's being directly above or below a particular area of the earth at a given time. Minor (good) periods occur exactly halfway between the major periods.

The real breakthrough, however, is yet to be revealed and may change your fishing habits forever. Are you ready? OK. Fish are also influenced by the moon on a monthly basis. Hannon identified a 3- to 4-day period before and after the new (dark) and full moon, plus the day of the half moon, that has particular significance for trophy fish. An astounding 73% of the world-record fish caught during the years 1970-1979 fell within these time frames.

## VEST POCKET GUIDE TO CRAPPIES

| Season | Fish Location | Presentation |
|---|---|---|
| Spring: March, April, May, June | 3' to 15' Near: Shallow Bays Feeder Creeks Creek Channels Brush Piles, Stumps & Trees Protected Weed Shorelines | Jig & Minnow Bobber Rigs Spinners Live Bait: Leeches, Worms, Mayfly Nymphs |
| Summer: July, August, September | 3' to 20' Near: Pockets in Shallow Weeds and Reeds Brush Piles, Stumps & Trees Weedy Bays Deep Edges of Weeds and Timber Weeds and Timber— Both On and Off Bottom | Jig & Plastic Grub Bobber Rigs Spinners Small Crankbaits Live Bait: Minnows, Leeches, Worms, Crickets, Grasshoppers |
| Fall/Winter: October, November, December, January, February | 8' to 30' Near: Sharp Weedline Drop-Offs Deep Rock Piles Deep Channel Edges Deep Creek Channel Bends Deep Brush Piles and Timber | Jig & Minnow Bobber Rigs Live Bait Rigs Live Bait: Minnows, Leeches Mousies, Meal- worms, Waxworms |

We've researched reams of data and it all boils down to this: Lunar influence will affect your fishing.

Weather and other environmental factors are bound to affect lunar periods.

It's obvious that unstable weather can cancel the positive effects of the moon. On the other hand, if you combine stable weather conditions with lunar influence and intelligent fishing, the results will amaze you. We're talkin' big crappies and lots of 'em!

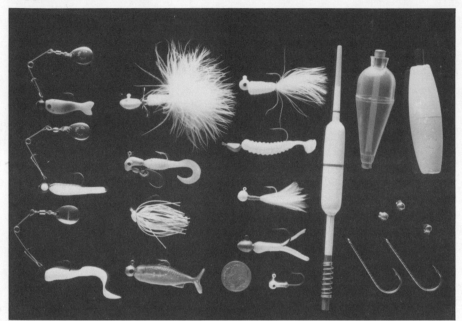

*A simple assortment of crappie tackle will cover nearly any situation, wherever you fish. Just match your choice to the conditions.*

*When crappies are aggressive, use an action jig to complement their positive mood. Spinner/jig combos like (COLUMN 1) Bass Buster's Chumm'n Minnow and Beetle Spin, a Whizker Spin, or (COLUMN 2) Northland Whistler or Blakemore Roadrunner are excellent swimming/fluttering lures.*

*When crappies are less aggressive, you must "subtle-up" your presentation with less flash/vibration, or reduce the jig's movement. Any of the 1/32- to 1/16-ounce jigs shown here will do the trick. Pictured are (COLUMN 2, bottom): a Gopher Mushroom Head Jig, and Earl's Swimming Minnow, (COLUMN 3) shows a Lindy Fuzz-E-Grub, Charlie's Brewer Slider, Windels Crappie Jig, Garland Jig, and a Jack's Jighead (add a minnow).*

*The ultimate in subtlety is a bobber/jig approach. All of the bobbers shown here let you easily adjust the depth your jig hangs at; set it so it suspends just above the top of a brushpile or stake bed.*

*Also pictured are several #3/0 Eagle Claw Aberdeen hooks and a few split shot for making a tightline rig. Yes, the hooks are large, but they won't spook fish as long as the water is stained to dark. A strong pull with 20- to 30-pound-test line will straighten 'em out if they get snagged, and you'll get your rig back.*

The general tendency of crappie behavior is a gradual, shallow-to-deep-water movement as the season progresses. In spring, crappies typically invade the edges of shallower areas for spawning. After spawning the crappies filter out into adjacent flats. During summer, crappies will suspend in confined open water, grazing on zooplankton, insects and minnows. In early fall, crappies may once again invade the shallower flats, but as winter approaches they drop into deep water.

Even though this pattern seems rather simple, it is important to understand that crappie habitat requirements change seasonally and so does crappie location. You won't catch crappies consistently by beating the shoreline all season long.

Keep in mind that water clarity also plays a major role in crappie movement, because it will often influence the depth of the fish. For example, in dark-water lakes, crappies may spawn in 18 inches of water, while in clear-water lakes the fish may spawn 10 or more feet deep. Remember, habitat affects habits.

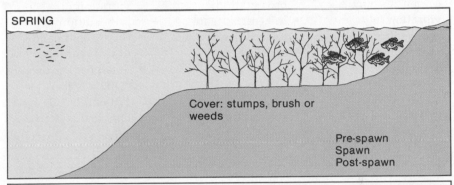

SPRING

Cover: stumps, brush or weeds

Pre-spawn
Spawn
Post-spawn

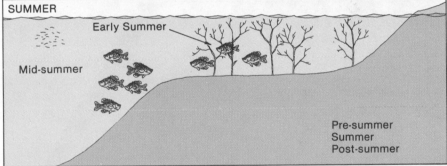

SUMMER

Early Summer

Mid-summer

Pre-summer
Summer
Post-summer

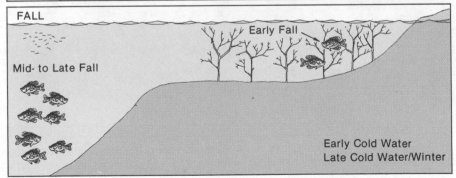

FALL

Early Fall

Mid- to Late Fall

Early Cold Water
Late Cold Water/Winter

# PRESENTATION TIPS

| Clear Water | Stained Water | Dark Water |
|---|---|---|
| • Light line preferred (2-, 4-, 6-lb. test)<br>• Small artificial lures<br>• Subtle colors (white, yellow, black)<br>• Swimming retrieves<br>• Long casts<br>• Minimize sound/vibration in presentation<br>• Low-light conditions favorable<br>• Small jigs best (1/64-, 1/32-, (1/16-oz.)<br>• Live bait very effective | • In-between condition<br>• Fish have mixed reactions based on amount of stain in water<br>• Trial and error is the key to proper presentation<br>• In general, lean toward dark-water approach | • Heavier line acceptable (12-, 17-, 20-lb.-plus test)<br>• Bright fluorescent colors (chartreuse)<br>• Short casts<br>• Maximum sound/vibration in presentation<br>• Bright-light conditions favorable<br>• Small jigs productive (1/32-, 1/16-, 1/8-oz.)<br>• Live bait effective |

*Crappie terminal tackle is simple but important. Normally, an ultralight or light-action spinning rod and open-bail reel combo is preferred. However, a cane pole or a crappie stick is the standby of many crappie anglers. Grab a few jigs, hooks, sinkers and bobbers and you're all set.*

## Chapter 15

# NIGHT-BITE CRAPPIES

"How'd ya do?"

"Got 15 nice crappies; all of 'em are between 1 and 2 pounds."

"Really! When?"

"Last night around midnight."

"What! You've gotta be kiddin'—at night?"

"You betcha! Bit like crazy."

"Huh! Ya know, I got skunked yesterday afternoon. There must be somethin' to that night-fishing business. Maybe I'll try it."

If you want to catch numbers of slab crappies plus beat the scorching summer heat, other anglers, or water skiers, then try nighttime crappie fishing. Fishing for crappies at night is an effective way to deal with clear-water lakes and reservoirs that house spooky, hard-to-catch crappies. Under the cloak of darkness even the wiliest fish become catchable.

While many anglers only fish at night in summer, crappies can be caught during other seasons as well. For example, during early winter many of the largest crappies of the year are caught in southern reservoirs by night anglers. This approach has often proven to be the answer to the real trophy fish. Likewise, anglers in the North ice fish for crappies at night during winter with excellent success.

Several, fisheries research studies support the fact that crappies are diurnal (dusk-to-dawn) feeders on many lakes, rivers and reservoirs. Generally, if the water is clear to slightly stained, adult crappies will usually be more active during low-light periods. Such periods include heavily overcast days plus the twilight hours of dusk and dawn. A creel census in Lake Havasu, CA/AZ (an ultra-clear reservoir) revealed that the night-angler catch was 16 times greater than the daytime harvest. While crappies may feed all day long on some waters, the heaviest feeding usually occurs at dusk and dawn.

In addition, there appears to be a general movement of fish into shallower water during low-light periods. On some waters, crappies may move to the edges of shallow-water cover like weeds, brush or trees. On other waters, suspended fish may simply migrate toward the surface to feed.

During summer, zooplankton, aquatic insects and small minnows may congregate near the surface and provide a real smorgasbord for night-feeding crappies. In fact, on a warm, calm summer night, crappies will be feeding just under the surface. Many times their backs will break the surface, and alert anglers can easily spot this activity. This situation is perfect for a fly fisherman.

In contrast, in many dark-water lakes and reservoirs, crappies may feed all day long. This is a common situation on many southern reeservoirs that contain white crappies. However, even on these waters, slab crappies can be a duck-soup proposition at night. Here's how to get your share of nighttime crappies.

The secret to successful night fishing is *organization*. Keep things simple. If you're fishing from a boat, make sure that it is orderly and bring a minimum amount of tackle. Nothing will spook fish quicker than banging around in a boat.

Here's a tip that'll help you keep quiet and catch more fish: Place a piece of indoor-outdoor carpeting on the floor of the boat (especially in aluminum boats). The carpet will significantly cut down the noise level. Shuffling feet, rattling tackle boxes and banging anchors will all spook the fish. In addition, the carpet will provide a nonslip surface.

Tackle should be simple. A 10' to 16', cane or fiberglass/graphite, crappie pole is best. This presentation is effective because there are no backlashes or line snarls to worry about. No muss, no fuss, just more fishing time.

Of course, you can use spinning tackle, as well. Normally, a 6- to 7-foot, light-action spinning rod and open-bail spinning reel spooled with 6- to 10-pound line is adequate for most situations. However, heavier line will be necessary when fishing around heavy cover. If you have problems tying knots and seeing the line at night, try this trick. Get a portable, ultraviolet (black) light and spool your reels with fluorescent line. When the light is activated the line will literally glow in the dark, so tying knots and removing tangles from line will be much easier.

When night fishing it's normally best to have a couple rods rigged and ready

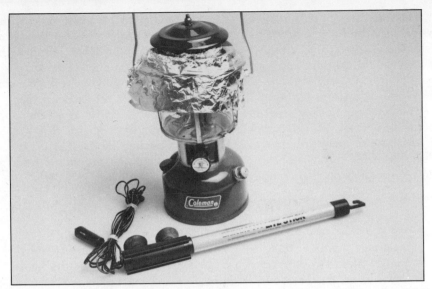

*A gas lantern or battery powered lamp hung over the water will draw baitfish and crappies. Note the reflective shield made from aluminum foil that directs the light down into the water.*

to use. Rig one with a slip-bobber rig and minnow and the other with a crappie jig or small spinner. Start fishing by using the bobber rig and minnow, and when the action gets hot just toss the jig out and haul 'em in.

Nighttime crappies and a food source go hand-in-hand. Here's how to create a crappie, fast-food restaurant that'll bring the fish to you. At night, a strong light will attract light-seeking organisms. Zooplankton, terrestrial and aquatic insects, minnows and small fish are all attracted to the light. Once these critters are swarming around, it's just a matter of time until the crappies stop by for a snack.

*Here's a floating, battery-powered crappie light that's just the ticket for attracting fish. However, make sure that lights are legal for night fishing in your state before using one.*

There are many lights available that you can use to attract crappies. Some anglers simply hang a gas lantern over the water from a pole or tree limb, while others prefer the battery-powered, floating crappie lights that shine into the water. In addition, mercury-vapor lights located on marina docks, parks, boat houses, streets or bridges will also attract fish. Be sure to check your state and local regulations for restrictions on portable lights before using one.

The best crappie bite generally takes place at dusk and may last a couple hours. However, all-night crappie bites are common on many clear waters. Typically, the most productive fishing occurs during the dark of the moon. Pick the three days before and after the dark of the moon for peak action—especially on slab crappies.

## PRIME FISHING SPOTS

- Tip and sides of long, tapering main-lake points or bars
- Sunken islands with cover
- Underwater, hard-bottomed humps
- Drop-off near mouth of bay or cove
- Drop-off area of creek channel
- Tree or brushline
- Flooded timber or brush
- Manmade attractors (mats, marinas, piers, etc.)
- Junction of two creek channels
- Bridges and causeways

Look for fish in the confined open water adjacent to these areas. If you have a flasher or graph, watch carefully for suspended crappies and note their

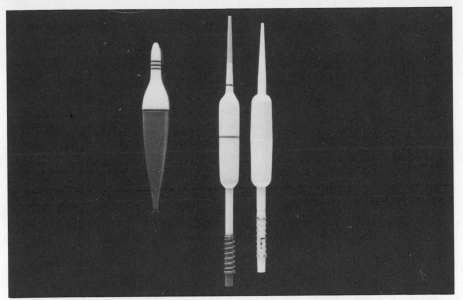

*Lighted bobbers and highly reflective fluorescent bobbers are both top-notch choices for your night fishing bag of tricks.*

depth. When casting, count your lure down so you will know the approximate depth you're fishing. By carefully fishing from top to bottom in this manner, you'll thoroughly cover the water. When fish contact is made you'll know the depth the crappies are at.

When you approach a potential fishing area, cut the big motor and quietly approach with an electric motor, or drift into the spot. Sneaking into an area will allow you to catch fish a lot faster than if you come crashing in. Once you've located a good spot, put your crappie light out and start fishing.

Shore fishing for crappies at night can be a super, family, fishing adventure. Pack up the kids, find a marina, fishing dock or bridge illuminated with a bright light, and you're all set. The light will allow you to keep an eye on the kids, plus it'll draw food for the crappies.

When fishing around piers and bridges, fish as close to the support pilings as possible. Bump the wood and work the lure at different depths to locate fish. If possible, fish around and under the dock or pier. Where it's legal, a crappie attractor (brush pile, etc.) can be placed off the end of the dock—a sure-fire trick. Attractors greatly enhance the areas around floating docks (common on reservoirs) where there is good, overhead cover but few submerged objects to concentrate fish.

In general, bridges and causeways in shallow coves are superb, springtime areas since they form bottlenecks which fish must pass through on their way in and out of spawning areas. Bridges out in the deeper main body of a reservoir tend to attract more fish during summer, fall and winter.

# SAFETY

Keep the fun in fishing by practicing a few, simple guidelines that'll ensure a safe trip. If you're fishing from a boat, make certain that the navigation lights operate properly and that all required safety devices are on board. It's always a good idea to have along a horn or whistle, compass and several extra flares. Know the water where you plan to fish. Don't go exploring at night into unknown areas. A little common sense will keep you from getting lost or running into something.

Always wear a Coast Guard-approved life jacket when fishing at night. In fact, a couple strips of reflective tape on the front and back of the vest and on the boat will make you much easier to see by other boaters.

Since it probably will be cool at night, a light nylon windbreaker and a thermos of your favorite warm beverage are both handy items.

*Crappies and family fishing fun go hand-in-hand. Atta boy!*

## Chapter 16

# U.S. CRAPPIE RECORDS

When it comes to state records, crappies may be the most interesting of all freshwater fish species. Why? Well, even as this book is being written, records are being broken. For example, during 1985, Tennessee established a new black crappie record.

Here's an interesting bit of trivia. Approximately 24 state records for black and white crappies were set between 1980-1985. Four state record crappies were caught in 1984. Apparently, there are lots of trophy crappies swimming around today.

Actually, a 2-pound crappie is a huge fish, and a 3- or 4-pounder is mind-boggling. But fish in the 4- to 5-pound range are trophies in every sense of the word. They rank right up there in stature with other, more publicized game-fish like bass, muskies and walleyes.

Here's a summary of the types of waters which record crappies were pulled from: 8 from rivers, 49 from lakes & reservoirs, and 15 from ponds & pits. Check out the record fish in your state. Then, using the information, tips and techniques in this book, grab a rod and get in on the action.

# U.S. Crappie Records

| STATE | WEIGHT lbs. | oz. | WATERS | YEAR |
|---|---|---|---|---|
| Alabama | | | | |
| Black | 4 | 4 | Paint Creek | 1984 |
| White | 4 | 8 | Guntersville Reservoir | 1974 |
| Alaska | No Record | | | |
| Arizona | | | | |
| Black | 4 | 10 | San Carlos Lake | 1959 |
| White | 3 | 5 | Lake Pleasant | 1982 |
| Arkansas | | | | |
| Black | 4 | 9 | Oladale Lake | 1976 |
| White | 4 | 3 | Reservoir | 1975 |
| California | | | | |
| Black | 4 | 1 | New Hogan Lake | 1975 |
| White | 4 | 8 | Clear Lake | 1971 |
| Colorado | | | | |
| Black | 3 | 0 | CF & I Reservoir #3 | 1980 |
| White | 4 | 3¾ | Northglenn Lake | 1975 |
| Connecticut | | | | |
| Black | 4 | 0 | Pataganset Lake | 1974 |
| Delaware | | | | |
| Black | 4 | 9 | Noxontown Pond | 1976 |
| Florida | | | | |
| Black | 3 | 12 | Newnans Lake | 1964 |
| Georgia | | | | |
| Black | 4 | 4 | Acree's Lake | 1971 |
| White | 5 | 0 | Private Pond | 1984 |
| Hawaii | No Record | | | |
| Idaho | | | | |
| Black | 2 | 8 | Shepherd Lake | 1954 |
| Illinois | | | | |
| Black | 4 | 8 | Rend Lake | 1976 |
| White | 4 | 7 | Farm Pond | 1973 |
| Indiana | | | | |
| Black | 4 | 9 | Big Chapman Lake | 1978 |
| Iowa | | | | |
| Black | 4 | 9 | Green Castle Lake | 1981 |

| | | | | |
|---|---|---|---|---|
| **Kansas** | | | | |
| Black | 4 | 10 | Woodson County State Lake | 1957 |
| White | 4 | ¼ | Farm Pond | 1964 |
| **Kentucky** | | | | |
| Unknown | 4 | 3 | Lake Pewee | 1969 |
| **Louisiana** | | | | |
| Black | 6 | 0 | Seaplane Canal Westwego | 1969 |
| **Maine** | No Record | | | |
| **Maryland** | | | | |
| Black | 3 | 14 | Depot Pond | 1977 |
| White | 2 | 9 | Tuckahoe River | 1979 |
| **Massachusetts** | | | | |
| Black | 4 | 10 | Jakes Pond | 1980 |
| White | 3 | 0 | Quabbin Reservoir | 1977 |
| **Michigan** | | | | |
| Black | 4 | 2 | Lincoln Lake | 1947 |
| White | 2 | 10 | Kent Lake | 1977 |
| **Minnesota** | | | | |
| Black | 5 | 0 | Vermilion River | 1940 |
| White | 2 | 12 | Coon Lake | 1982 |
| **Mississippi** | | | | |
| Black | 2 | 10 | Ross Barnett Reservoir | 1984 |
| White | 5 | 3 | Enid Reservoir | 1957 |
| **Missouri** | | | | |
| Black | 4 | 8 | Farm Pond | 1967 |
| White | 4 | 5 | Missouri River | 1981 |
| **Montana** | | | | |
| Black | 3 | 2 | Tongue River Reservoir | 1973 |
| White | 2 | 2 | Tongue River Reservoir | 1978 |
| **Nebraska** | | | | |
| Black | 4 | 2 | Red Willow Reservoir | 1981 |
| White | 4 | 1 | Red Willow Reservoir | 1980 |
| **Nevada** | | | | |
| Black | 3 | 2 | Lake Mead | 1976 |
| White | 2 | 8 | Lahontan Reservoir | 1968 |
| **New Hampshire** | | | | |
| Black | 2 | 7½ | Balch Pond | 1983 |
| **New Jersey** | | | | |
| Black | 3 | 8 | Farm Pond | 1980 |
| White | 2 | 8 | Woodstown Lake | 1984 |
| **New Mexico** | | | | |
| Black | 4 | 9 | Black River | 1983 |
| **New York** | | | | |
| Black | 3 | 1 | Indian Lake | 1977 |
| **North Carolina** | | | | |
| Black | 4 | 15 | Asheboro City Lake #4 | 1980 |

| | | | | |
|---|---|---|---|---|
| **North Dakota** | | | | |
| Black | 3 | 1 | Nelson Lake | 1981 |
| **Ohio** | | | | |
| Black | 4 | 8 | Private Lake | 1981 |
| White | 3 | 10 | Sandy Lake | 1981 |
| **Oklahoma** | | | | |
| Black | 4 | 10 | Ottawa County Pond | 1974 |
| White | 4 | 13 | Tillman County Pond | 1967 |
| **Oregon** | | | | |
| Black | 4 | 0 | Lost River | 1973 |
| White | 4 | 12 | Gerber Reservoir | 1967 |
| **Pennsylvania** | | | | |
| White | 3 | 6 | Delaware River | 1983 |
| **Rhode Island** | | | | |
| Black | 3 | 0 | Watchaug Pond | 1976 |
| **South Carolina** | | | | |
| Black | 5 | 0 | Lake Moultrie | 1957 |
| White | 5 | 1 | Lake Murray | 1949 |
| **South Dakota** | | | | |
| Black | 3 | 4 | South Buffalo Lake | 1976 |
| White | 3 | 9 | Hughes County Farm Pond | 1974 |
| **Tennessee** | | | | |
| Black | 4 | 4 | Brown's Creek Lake | 1985 |
| White | 5 | 1 | Garner Brown's Pond | 1968 |
| **Texas** | | | | |
| White | 4 | 9 | Navarro Mills Lake | 1968 |
| **Utah** | | | | |
| Black | 2 | 11 | Lake Powell | 1982 |
| **Vermont** | | | | |
| Black | 1 | 13 | Charcoal Creek | 1976 |
| **Virginia** | No Record | | (Records will begin July 1, 1985) | |
| **Washington** | | | | |
| Black | 4 | 8 | Lake Washington | 1956 |
| **West Virginia** | | | | |
| Unknown | 4 | 0 | Meathouse Fork | 1971 |
| **Wisconsin** | | | | |
| Black | 3 | 5 | Lake Wingra | 1981 |
| White | 4 | 8 | Gile Flowage | 1967 |
| **Wyoming** | | | | |
| Black | 2 | 3 | Crook County | 1983 |

## Chapter 17

# CARE AND KEEPING OF THE CATCH

### A Little-Known Art

Care and keeping of the catch is a little-known art that few anglers understand. Take pride in mastering it. But why master keeping-the-catch in this age of catch and release fishing?

There's more to fishing than pre-trip anticipation, on-the-spot fish location and presentation, and catching and releasing fish. For most folks, fishing still means keeping some of the catch. A fishing trip doesn't end until the fish have been cleaned and eaten. Those who enjoy cleaning and cooking their catch, double their fishing fun.

It's a crime what some folks do to the fish they eat. Dragged, tossed, bumped, bruised; left to hang on a stringer in lukewarm water after dying; ground into a soiled, oily, boat floor; filleted with a dirty knife run through festering intestinal tracts; gilled and gutted too late, if at all; improperly cooled, if indeed cooled at all; and then mercifully frozen, but unmercifully frozen improperly.

We have met the enemy and it is us. But we can change. Here's how.

Before you leave home, decide if you're going to keep or release the fish. Being prepared in advance ensures a greater survival rate for released fish and better tasting fish for the table.

Make the decision to keep or release fish when they're caught, and bop the "keepers" on the head (kill them) and put them on ice. This prevents them from jumping around and becoming bruised. Fish flesh is extremely delicate and very perishable—treat it gently with TLC.

Bacterial growth and enzyme action are two primary enemies of fresh fish. In order to keep fish fit for the table, anglers must fight these two enemies from the moment a fish is caught until it is cooked.

It's vital to keep fish as cool (preferably cold) as possible. Fish may be iced whole, but the highest quality fish results when the gills and entrails are removed.

Blood remaining in the flesh produces rancidness in frozen fish and increases their deterioration in cold but not frozen storage. Fish should be bled before they're iced, if they aren't gutted and gilled. With the fish lying flat, cut the blood vessels in the tail with an incision to the bone, or simply clip off the tail with a snippers. Another method is to insert a knife into the chest cavity slightly back of the point where it meets the gills. Move the knife around to ensure cutting blood vessels.

# USING ICE

Crushed ice is best for icing fish because it packs closer and cools them faster than blocks or cubes. Place ice inside the body cavity and around a fish so that blood, slime and digestive juices drain to the bottom of your ice chest. Never let a fish soak in water, even cold water, for long. Fish can generally be kept in crushed ice for about 3 days without significantly affecting table quality.

If you want to cool your fish quickly (the quicker the better) or aren't able to freeze or cook your catch for several days, super-chill them. Super-chilled fish can be held for up to 7 days without losing much eating quality.

# TO SUPER-CHILL

1. Line the bottom of an insulated ice chest with several inches of ice. Leave the bottom drain open.
2. In another container, make a salt/ice mixture, using a 1:20 ratio of coarse, ice cream salt to crushed ice. About one pound of salt to 20 pounds of ice is a good start for most coolers.
3. Arrange the fish in layers in the ice chest, making sure there's plenty of salted ice between each fish.
4. Before chilling fillets or steaks, wrap them in plastic wrap.

When you are ice fishing, there is no shortage of ice to chill fish. The problem is preventing fish from freezing. Freezing and refreezing them greatly reduces their table quality. If fish do freeze, leave them frozen, wrap them, and place them in the freezer. Then dress fish before they're completely thawed.

A stream angler who doesn't have ice should wait until the last several hours of the trip to keep fish. Place them in an aerated creel lined with a layer of wet

# Super Chilly!

*If you're going to keep fish, carry a fish club to dispatch fish with a blow to the back of the head. You need a knife to gut and gill and bleed fish immediately, and a towel is handy to wipe fish with after you've rinsed them. Transfer them to a bed of crushed ice, immediately.*

*Super-chilling lowers the temperature surrounding fish to about 28°F and allows properly cleaned fish to keep for up to 7 days. Add 1 part of rock salt to 20 parts of crushed ice to make a salt/ice mixture. Make a 3-inch bed of salted ice on the bottom of the cooler and add the fish. Open the drain. Wrap fillets with cling wrap to protect them and to leave space between fish. Add salted ice as needed to keep fish cold.*

moss to hold moisture. Evaporation cools the gutted fish.

If fish must be held for more than a few hours, clean, wash and wipe the body cavity dry. Then sprinkle the fish with table salt. Keep them in a cool, slightly moist, shaded container like an aerated creel. Fish will keep up to 24 hours like this. It's a good way to bring fish out of remote areas.

## AT THE CLEANING TABLE

At the cleaning table, or wherever you clean your catch, sanitation is critical. Also be sure to have ice available to keep fish that have already been chilled and to cool fish that are still alive when they reach the cleaning table.

Let's say you will be filleting your catch. At the cleaning table you should have:

1. Cleaning utensils including fillet knives and sharpening tools.
2. A bowl of cold water (add ice cubes) to soak fillets in for a short time to

remove blood and bacteria.

3. Several clean towels for wiping slime from fish and keeping the fillet board clean. Another towel to pat fillets dry with after they have soaked for a bit, if they are to be stored without freezing. (A solution of one teaspoon of vinegar to 3 quarts of water helps to cut fish slime.)

4. Packaging material for freezing fish or keeping them in the refrigerator, until they're eaten.

Let's proceed:

1. If the fish are alive, dispatch them with a sharp blow to the head. Bleed them.

2. Remove the fillets, being careful not to rupture the digestive tract with your knife.

3. Pop the fillet into cold water to help remove blood, bacteria and enzymes. Don't let them soak too long. Rinse them with cold, clean water.

4. Discard the carcass; wipe the board and your knife clean, and start another fish. Replace the water in the bowl when it begins to thicken from fish juices.

## At the Cleaning Table

PHOTO 1

*At the cleaning table you need a cleaning board, a fish dispatcher (club), knives and sharpening tools, clean towels and a bowl of cold water (PHOTO 1). Add ice cubes to the water to chill it. A 1/2 teaspoon of salt (to help neutralize acids and draw out blood) is fine to use with lean fish like walleyes or crappies but may increase rancidity in fatty fish like lake trout or salmon.*

PHOTO 2

*Kill the fish by hitting it behind the head with your fish dispatcher. Bleed the fish (PHOTO 2). As you remove the fillets, be careful not to cut into the intestinal tract. Keep everything including your knife clean (PHOTO 3). Remove bacteria from the fillets by soaking them in cold water for a bit.*

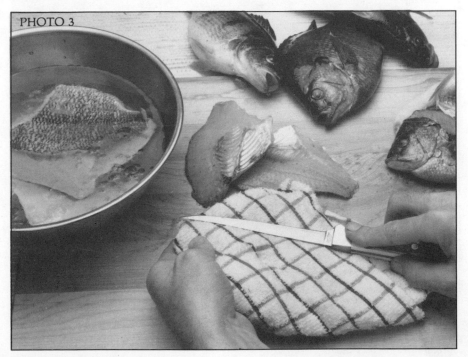

PHOTO 3

# PACKAGING FOR THE REFRIGERATOR

Placing fish in ice keeps them at 32°F rather than 40°F, which is the approximate temperature of most refrigerators. This allows them to be kept in the refrigerator for several days before they are eaten. Periodically drain the melt water.

Another method also maintains fish quality, although at a slightly reduced level. You can store fish for several days in the refrigerator by starting with clean fillets and keeping them slightly moist but absolutely not wet. Throwing fish into a plastic bag and allowing them to lie in fish juices encourages bacterial growth and deterioration. It's one of the fastest ways to reduce fantastic, firm, fresh fish to smelly mush.

Pat the fillets dry after they've soaked and been rinsed in water. Even though you've patted them dry, they will still be slightly moist. Take a clean, dry dish towel and sprinkle drops of water on it so it's barely moist but not wet. Line the bottom of a bowl or pan with the towel and spread your fillets on it. Cover the bowl with a tight-fitting plastic wrap. The towel soaks up any excess moisture from the fish, yet the fillets don't dry out.

Use the same procedure with whole fish (pan dressed) or steaks.

## Packaging for the Refrigerator

PHOTO 1

*Method 1—Fill a bowl half full with ice and place the fish on the ice. Cover the fish with more ice and the bowl with cling wrap. Periodically drain the melt water. Fish stored at almost 32°F keep longer than fish stored at 40°F, the temperature of most refrigerators (PHOTO 1).*

PHOTO 2

*Method 2—Remove the fillets and pat them dry with a towel. Sprinkle water droplets onto a clean, dry towel so it's damp but not wet. Line a bowl with it and place the fillets on the towel (PHOTO 2). Use cling wrap to seal the bowl. The fish will keep for up to 3 days.*

# FREEZING FISH

Freezing, the method most often used for long-term fish storage, can keep fish in quality condition for months. Unfortunately, few anglers freeze fish properly. Mistakes usually fall into one, or all, of three categories: (1) using the wrong type of protective packaging, (2) not considering that some fish species can be frozen for a longer time than others, and (3) keeping fish at the wrong storage temperature.

Most fish deteriorate during freezer storage through either (1) dehydration, or (2) oxidation. Freezer burn is an advanced stage of dehydration caused by using porous packaging material that allows water vapor to be sucked from the fish.

Oxidation also results from improper packaging, either by using porous packaging material or not removing the air from the package. The polyunsaturated fats and oils in fish turn rancid when they are in contact with oxygen for long periods of time.

# PACKAGING MATERIALS

Proper packaging materials must provide effective oxygen and water vapor barriers. The materials should also cling to fish to prevent air pockets that keep fish in contact with oxygen.

Surprise! Polyethylene bags such as bread bags fail on both counts and are not suitable for storing fish. Waxed paper and cellophane are also poor freezer wraps.

Aluminum foil and polyvinylidene chloride wraps, called cling wraps (like Saran Wrap), provide good barriers to both oxygen and water vapor. It also clings to the fillets which prevents air pockets. However, aluminum foil punctures easily. While it is a good initial wrap, it doesn't serve well as an only or final wrap.

Freezer bags made of polyester also provide good barriers to oxygen and water vapor. Polyester bags include most heavy bags marketed as "freezer" bags. To force the air out of these bags before freezing, submerge the bag in water. Seal the bag or even add a small amount of water to the bag to help force the air out.

Freezer wrapping paper is a fair oxygen and water vapor barrier that serves best as an outer wrap over an inner wrap such as cling wrap or aluminum foil. It's easy to mark the type of catch, the freezing date, and other pertinent information on freezer wrap.

## Good Freezing Approaches

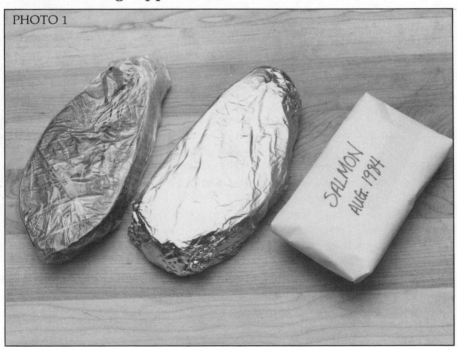

PHOTO 1

*One of the best ways to freeze fish is tightly wrapped in cling wrap or aluminum foil. A secondary wrapping in freezer wrapping puper is advisable (PHOTO 1). Write the contents and the date it was frozen on the package.*

*This is the best method for storing fatty fish like lake trout, whitefish, salmon and trout, but it works for all fish.*

PHOTO 2

*Another method is to put fish into a polyester freezer bag and submerge the bag in a sink full of water to squeeze out the air (PHOTO 2). Seal the bag, or even add a small amount of water to the bag to help force the air out.*

## FREEZING IN WATER

Commercial freezers often glaze fish with a coating of ice. Glazing isn't practical for you because it takes an inordinate amount of time and an extremely low freezer temperature.

There are several good techniques for freezing fish in water, however. Fish can be tightly packed into plastic containers such as Tupperware and covered with water. The fish must be covered, but too much water draws nutrients from them and causes them to freeze slowly. The pressure from too much ice crushes fish and makes it mushy, too. Add a little more water to each container after freezing, to cover any fish portions that protrude from the ice.

## FINAL FREEZING TIPS

- Divide your fish into family-size servings.
- The faster fish freezes, the better. Place packages in the coldest part of your freezer, usually near the bottom. Don't overload your freezer, and keep it at 0°F, if possible.
- Thawing fish at room temperature may let some parts of fish spoil. Thaw them in the refrigerator, and expect it to take 24 hours for a 1-pound

package. For faster thawing, hold the fish in cold water until it's thawed. Be sure to keep it in the vapor-proof wrapping while it's thawing.

- Refrozen fish are safe to eat but usually taste terrible.
- Properly frozen crappies will keep for 8 to 12 months.

# BON APPETIT!

Follow these tips and the fish you keep will taste better than they ever have, whether you eat them immediately or 3 days or 3 months later.

*Another scrappy crappie for the frying pan.*

# CONCLUSION

This is the fifth book in the *IN-FISHERMAN* Masterpiece Series. *CRAPPIE WISDOM: A Handbook of Strategies* takes an indepth look at crappies and how they operate in many waters. Understanding the how's and why's of fish behavior will help you catch more crappies regardless of where you live and fish.

While this book is comprehensive it is not "complete," because as further research is conducted, more nuances of the crappie's personality and lifestyle will be discovered. However, the information contained in this book is an up-to-the-minute compendium of the most productive, crappie fishing methods—they're dynamite.

In addition to this book, we encourage you to read the other books in our *IN-FISHERMAN* Masterpiece Series: *WALLEYE WISDOM: A Handbook of Strategies*; *BASS: A Handbook of Strategies*; *PIKE: A Handbook of Strategies*, and *SMALLMOUTH BASS: A Handbook of Strategies*.

Because of the vast scope of each volume, no one man has enough knowledge to tackle such an undertaking. Instead, we took another avenue; each book is written by a collective group of top anglers. Each of these writer's background, experience and expertise qualifies him as a true expert. And they tell all; they hold nothing back.

If you are truly interested in becoming a top-flight angler, we urge you to subscribe to our *IN-FISHERMAN* Magazine, the foundation of this knowledge. We offer a brochure free of charge which lists the books and magazines we publish. Simply write to *IN-FISHERMAN*, Box 999, Brainerd, MN 56401, and ask for the free brochure.

In closing, the staff wishes you tight lines and good fishing. Remember, catch a lot of fish; keep a few to eat and release the rest.

# the In-Fisherman
# GLOSSARY

**ADAPTATION:** The process of adjusting to or fitting into a particular set of environmental circumstances.

**AGGREGATION:** A group of gamefish or preyfish holding in an area, but not necessarily moving together in a school. See *school*.

**ALGAE:** Simple, one-cell plants usually having the ability to photosynthesize sunlight into energy.

**ALLEY:** Parallel openings between patches of emergent weeds (usually bulrushes), or between emergent weeds and shoreline.

**APPETITE MOODS:** The three basic attitudes of fish toward feeding. See *positive, neutral and negative feeding moods*.

**BACKTROLLING:** A system of boat control involving moving a boat slowly in reverse while using lure or bait presentations (casting or trolling).

**BACKWATERS:** Normally, a shallow-water area off a river.

**BASIC NATURE:** A species' inherent makeup or tendencies which determine its niche or place in an environment.

**BASIC NEEDS:** The three basic survival requirements of any fish species: *reproduction, suitable habitat,* and *food*. A favorable environment fulfills these needs.

**BASIN ZONE:** A lake zone. The area lying below the deep-water zone, beginning where hard bottom ends and soft bottom begins. This zone includes the deepest water areas.

**BIOLOGY:** The study of living things.

**BITING:** The feeding action of a hungry fish. See *striking*.

**BOAT CONTROL:** Boat use to aid bait or lure presentation. See *backtrolling, controlled drifting, front trolling, speedtrolling*.

**BOTTOM-BUMPER:** A lure or rig which strikes the bottom (i.e. jig).

**BOTTOM CONFIGURATION:** A locational factor; the relative make-up (shape, size, depth, humps, etc.) of an area of the bottom.

**BOTTOM CONTENT:** Bottom types in a body of water (rock, sand, gravel, silt, muck, submerged cribs, brush and/or trees, etc.).

**BREAK:** Any variation in otherwise constant portions of the environment.

**BREAKLINE:** That point in a body of water where there is a definite change in depth—either shallower or deeper—or a change in a weedline or brushline; a change in bottom composition; where two layers of water meet and differ in temperature, density, oxygen and/or turbidity; the limit of effective light penetration, etc.

**BREAKLINE, SECONDARY:** A second or auxiliary point of change. For example, a second definite increase in depth after the first drop-off.

**BRUSHLINE:** The inside or outside edge of a line of brush.

**CABBAGE:** Any of the pondweeds (*Potamogeton*) usually attractive to gamefish.

**CALENDAR, *IN-FISHERMAN*:** A calendar based on ten identifiable periods of activity for various species of gamefish. These ten periods constitute a *fish cycle*.

**CALENDAR PERIOD:** Any of the ten periods of fish activity in the *IN-FISHERMAN* Calendar.

**CLEAN BOTTOM:** The bottom (usually hard bottom) of a body of water that is free of debris, etc.

**CLIMATE:** Average weather conditions for a region.

**COLD FRONT:** The line of impact where cold air forces warm air upward. As a cold front moves, cold air beneath piles up as it is slowed down by contact with the ground. This pile of cold air forces warm air up very rapidly, often causing storms. See *post-front*.

**COLD-WATER PERIOD:** A period of the fish cycle which occurs twice—in early spring between the Frozen Water and Pre-spawn Periods and in late fall between the Turnover and Frozen Water Periods. Usually applied to the fall season.

**COMPETITIVE SPECIES:** A *social condition* involving the relationship of species within a body of water, particularly in regard to available food and spawning areas.

**CONFINED OPEN WATER:** An area of open water adjacent to a structural element, as opposed to an expansive area which is far away from it.

**CONTROLLED DRIFT:** A system of *boat control* using an outboard, electric trolling motor or oars to keep a boat drifting along a specific course.

**COSMIC CLOCK:** The sun's effect on water and local weather factors, such as barometric pressure, wind, cloud cover, seasonal change, etc.

**COVE:** A flooded creek arm in a reservoir.

**CRANKBAIT:** A lipped, diving plug.

**CUT:** A small reservoir bay without an active, inflowing creek.

**DEEP-WATER ZONE:** A lake zone. Hard bottom lying below the first major drop-off and below the open-water zone. It ends where soft bottom begins.

**DEPTH CONTROL:** One of two primary factors involved in successful bait or lure presentation. Keeping a lure or bait at a desired depth level.

**DISSOLVED OXYGEN:** Oxygen chemically bound into water by forces such as wind and plants. It is utilized by fish.

**DROP-OFF:** A point of definite increase in depth.

**ECOLOGY:** The study of the relationship between organisms and their environment.

**ECOSYSTEM:** A system formed by the interaction of a community of organisms and their environment.

**ELECTROPHORESIS:** A chemical-testing process that can determine the genetic make-up of fish.

**EPILIMNION:** The wàrmer layer of water above the *thermocline*.

**EROSION:** The process by which the surface of the earth is continually worn away. The elements most responsible for erosion are rivers, streams, wind, waves and glaciers.

**EUTROPHIC:** A *lake classification* or lake type characterized by high levels of nutrients in proportion to total volume of water.

**FANCAST:** A series of systematic casts to cover an area.

**FISH ATTRACTOR:** Manmade brush pile, stake bed, mat or crib designed to provide cover and attract fish.

**FISH CONTACT:** Locating fish, usually by catching them. Includes visual observation.

**FISH CYCLE:** All ten Calendar Periods. See *Calendar, IN FISHERMAN*.

**FISHING PRESSURE:** The number of anglers using a body of water, and/or how sophisticated their approach is.

**FLAT:** An area characterized by little or no change in depth.

**FOOD CHAIN:** A step-by-step feeding relationship in a community. Food chains originate with the sun's energy and each link in the chain represents energy transfer. All of the food chains in a community constitute a food web.

**FOOD-PRODUCING AREA:** Portions of a body of water with the characteristics necessary to stimulate food chain production; usually the littoral or shoreline-connected (shallow) areas, because they receive sunlight which fuels plant photosynthesis which in turn stimulates each successive step in the food chain.

**FRONT TROLLING:** A system of *boat control* with the boat moving forward.

**GEOLOGY:** The science dealing with the earth's physical history.

**HABITAT:** The place where a plant or animal species lives.

**HARD BOTTOM:** Firm-bottom areas (sand, clay, rock, gravel, etc.).

**HIGH-PROTEIN FORAGE:** High-fat-content, soft-rayed, forage species such as ciscoes and whitefish.

**HOLDING STATION:** Any specific position regardless of depth where fish spend much of their time.

**HYPOED LAKE:** A body of water stocked with a species of fish to bolster the natural fishery.

**HYPOLIMNION:** The colder layer of water below the *thermocline*.

**IMPOUNDMENT:** A confined area where water accumulates, usually the result of damming a river. See *reservoir*.

**INFILLING:** The process by which higher surrounding terrain tends to fill in lower terrain.

**INSIDE EDGE (OF WEEDS):** A line of weeds between the shoreline and the weedline, or the shallow edge of a particular weed type. See *outside edge* (of weeds).

**LAKE CLASSIFICATION:** Broad categories of lake types: oligotrophic (infertile), mesotrophic (fertile), eutrophic (very fertile).

**LAKE-MODIFICATION FORCES:** Forces such as ice, wave and wind erosion, etc., which can change the characteristics of a body of water.

**LAKE TYPE:** A group of bodies of water with characteristics similar enough to one another so they can be viewed from an angling standpoint in much the same manner. See *lake classifications*.

**LAKE ZONES:** Four designated *IN-FISHERMAN* water zones: *shallow water, open water, deep water and basin zones*.

**LIMNOLOGY:** The study of the biological, chemical, geographical and physical features of bodies of water.

**LITTORAL ZONE:** Shallow-water zone.

**LOCAL WEATHER FACTORS:** Prevailing weather conditions affecting the day-to-day locational patterns of a fish species.

**LOCATIONAL PATTERN:** Where, why and how a species positions itself to take advantage of its surroundings.

**LOOSE-ACTION PLUG:** A lure with wide, distinct, side-to-side movements.

**MARL:** Deposits of sand, clay and silt with a high concentration of shells (calcium carbonate).

**MESOTROPHIC:** *Lake classification* used to describe fertile bodies of water between late-stage *oligotrophic* and early-stage *eutrophic* classifications.

**MIGRATION:** The movement of fish from one area to another. Migrations generally occur on a seasonal basis, from one set of distinct environmental conditions to another, such as from winter habitat toward spawning areas. They should not be confused with *movements*.

**MORAINE:** A mass of rocks, sand, etc., deposited by a glacier.

**MOVEMENT:** The locational shift of fish from one area to another, generally on a daily or even hourly basis. Also can refer to fish changing from a neutral to a positive feeding mood, with fish shifting only a few feet from a resting to an advantageous feeding position. A *directional* movement is usually made at a fast rate of speed and from one specific area to another. A *random* movement is slow, milling activity within a specific area.

**NEGATIVE FEEDING MOOD:** An *appetite mood* in which the biting attitude of fish is negative. Fish also are said to be inactive.

**NEUTRAL FEEDING MOOD:** An *appetite mood*. An attitude of fish which are not actively feeding but could be tempted by a refined presentation. See *striking*.

**NICHE:** A particular role and physical surroundings which an organism assumes within an ecosystem, based on that species' characteristics and depending on competing species.

**NURSERY AREA:** Areas where fish species are reared to the fingerling stage.

**OLIGOTROPHIC:** *Lake classification* used to describe bodies of water characterized by a low amount of nutrients in proportion to the total volume of water. Infertile.

**OPEN-WATER ZONE:** A lake zone. The upper water layer from the outside edge of the first major drop-off down to the deep-water zone.

**OUTSIDE EDGE (OF WEEDS):** The *weedline*. The outside edge of a line of weeds.

**OXBOW:** A lake formed by a change in the course of a river channel; a section of river channel cut off from the main river by a change in the river's path.

**PATTERN:** Any consistently reoccurring locational/presentational situation.

**PHOTOSYNTHESIS:** The process by which chlorophyll cells in green plants use the sun's energy to manufacture a simple sugar from water and carbon dioxide. Oxygen is a by-product of this process.

**PIT:** Flooded, manmade water that is a by-product of excavation—usually mining.

**POND:** Small artificial or natural body of water. Area, depth, and water quality are factors in the resulting fishery.

**POPULATION DENSITY:** The number of individuals occupying a certain area. For example, the number of bass per acre.

**POSITIVE FEEDING MOOD:** An *appetite mood*. The attitude of actively feeding fish.

**POST-FRONT:** That period after a weather front. Usually used in reference to a cold front when the atmosphere becomes clear and bright, accompanied by strong winds and a significant temperature drop.

**POST-SPAWN PERIOD:** The period immediately following spawning.

**POST-SUMMER PERIOD:** A period of the fish cycle following the Summer Period. It can mean a week or more of terrific fishing.

**PRECAMBRIAN SHIELD:** The Canadian Shield. A geological, rock formation covering much of eastern and central Canada and some of the north central U.S.A.

**PREDATOR/PREY RELATIONSHIP:** An inter-relationship between a species and an accessible and suitable forage.

**PREFERRED FOOD:** Food or forage best suited to a species' basic needs.

**PRE-SPAWN PERIOD:** The period of the fish cycle immediately before spawning when fish position themselves near their spawning grounds.

**PRE-SUMMER PERIOD:** The period of the fish cycle immediately following post-spawn. Fish mood is often positive, but they establish a wide variety of patterns.

**REEDS:** Bulrushes or rushes.

**RESERVOIR:** Impoundment. A place where water is collected and stored.

**RIG:** A fishing boat; the hook, snell and other terminal tackle for live bait fishing; assembling tackle.

**RIVER (OR CREEK) CHANNEL:** The original river or creek bed which was flooded when a reservoir was formed.

**RIVERINE:** Refers to a river-like environment.

**SADDLE:** A site where a structural element narrows before widening again, or deepens before shallowing again.

**SCHOOL (OF FISH):** A number of fish of the same or similar species grouped together and moving as a unit to benefit from the defensive and/or feeding advantages associated with coordinated activity.

**SECONDARY COVE:** A small, shallow cove connected to a larger cove.

**SHALLOW-WATER ZONE:** A *lake zone*. The area out to the first major drop-off.

**SHIELD WATER:** Body of water located on the Precambrian or Canadian Shield. Specifically, a body of water in an area where the nutrient-producing rock and sediment layers in the basin and surrounding terrain were eroded away by glaciers.

**SLICK:** A sand or clay bar, point or drop-off devoid of weeds, brush, rock or boulders, etc. A section of calm, surface water in a river.

**SOFT BOTTOM:** Bottoms (silt, mud, muck, marl, etc.) which are not hard.

**SOCIAL CONDITION:** One of three elements helping to determine a species' locational pattern. It includes population density, food availability, competitive species, and how these interrelate.

**SNAKETROLLING:** A system of *boat control* in which a lure or bait is trolled in a weaving manner to cover a wide area and a range of depth levels.

**SPAWN PERIOD:** A brief period of the fish cycle when a species reproduces. This period is directly linked to seasonal progression and suitable temperatures.

**SPECIES:** Closely related organisms which produce offspring when they mate.

**SPEED CONTROL:** One of the two primary factors in bait or lure presentation. The other is depth.

**SPEEDTROLLING:** A system of *boat control* in which a lure is trolled behind a fast-moving boat.

**SPOOKING:** Frightening or "turning off" one or more fish.

**STRAGGLERS:** Fish lingering apart from others of their species after a movement.

**STRIKING:** An involuntary reflex action prompted by a bait or lure. Fish are made to bite. See *biting*.

**STRUCTURAL CONDITION:** One of three elements which determine a species' locational patterns. Structure includes bottom configuration, bottom content, water characteristics, vegetation types and water exchange rate.

**STRUCTURAL ELEMENT:** Almost any natural or manmade, physical feature in a body of water. See *bottom configuration*.

**SUMMER PERIOD:** A period in the fish cycle when fish generally hold to patterns established during the last part of the Summer Peak Period.

**SUMMER PEAK PERIOD:** A short period in the fish cycle after the Pre-summer Period when fish are grouped in advantageous feeding areas. A prelude to the Summer Period.

**SUSPENDED FISH:** Fish in open water which are hovering considerably above the bottom.

**TAPER:** An area that slopes toward deeper water.

**THERMOCLINE:** The center area of temperature stratification in a body of water. Specifically, the division between the epilimnion and hypolimnion. Temperature changes very quickly.

**TIGHT-ACTION PLUG:** A lure with short, distinct, side-to-side movements.

**TOPWATER PLUG:** A floating lure designed for use on the surface of the water.

**TOTAL ENVIRONMENT:** Both the body of water a species lives in, and any outside stimuli influencing it.

**TRANSITION (BOTTOM):** The point where one type of bottom material changes to another.

**TRIGGER:** Lure or bait characteristics (action, color, size, shape, scent, sound, vibration, texture) designed to stimulate positive responses from fish by appealing to the sensory organs of a species.

**TURNOVER PERIOD:** A very brief period in the fish cycle when some lakes or reservoirs are in turmoil. A mixing or "turning over" of the water takes place as cold water on the surface settles and warmer water from below rises. This turnover reoxygenates and homogenizes lakes that have thermoclined (layered according to water temperature) in summer.

**TVA:** Tennessee Valley Authority.

**TWO-STORY LAKE:** A body of water where warm water species inhabit the upper portion and cold water species inhabit the deeper portion.

**WATER CHARACTERISTICS:** The characteristics of a body of water, usually referred to in terms of mineral content (soft, few minerals; medium, some minerals; hard, many minerals). The mineral content determines fertility.

**WATER COLOR:** The clarity of a body of water. There are three basic degrees of water clarity: clear (6-foot-plus visibility), stained (2- to 6-foot visibility), and dark (less than 2-foot visibility).

**WATER EXCHANGE RATE:** The rate at which water enters or leaves a body of water.

**WINTER PERIOD:** A period of the fish cycle when a body of water is mostly or completely covered by ice. In southern waters which rarely freeze, the sustained period of coldest water.

**WORKING METHOD:** The aspect of presentation consisting of triggers, controls, gear selection and technique.